Practical
Pre-School

Building a Portfolio for

Early Years Care and Education S/NVQ Level 3

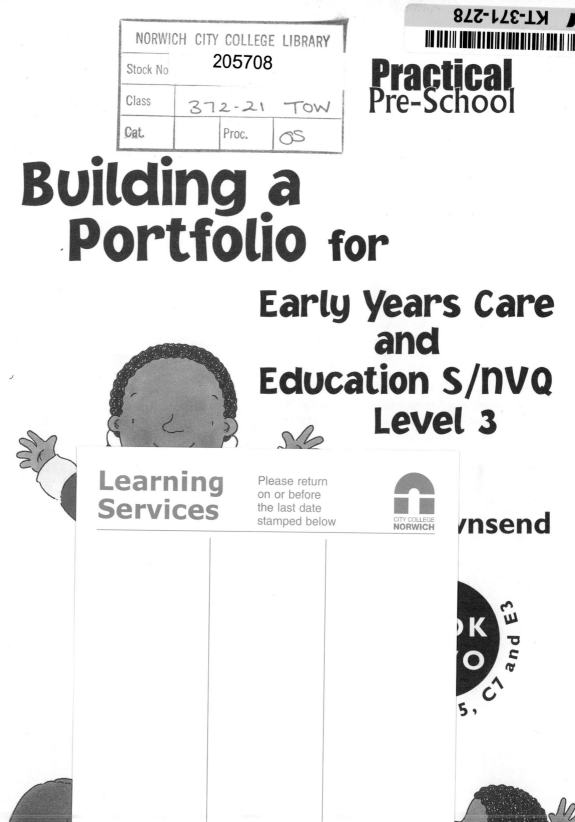

...nsend

Illustrated by Cathy Hughes

About the author

Mary Townsend started her career as a nursery nurse working in day nurseries. While her family were young she worked as a childminder and ran a playgroup for five years. She then trained as an infant teacher and worked in infant schools for 14 years. She went on to lecture in a college of further education and during that time set up an assessment centre and became an NVQ co-ordinator and internal and external verifier.

More recently as an independent consultant, she has carried out projects for the Early Years National Training Organisation and the Qualifications and Curriculum Authority. Her current work includes inspection of training in Early Years Care and Education NVQs for the Adult Learning Inspectorate and policy development in the Early Years and Childcare Unit for the Department for Education and Skills.

She is deeply committed to raising standards in the early years sector and firmly believes that a well delivered and assessed National Vocational Qualification can make a significant contribution to achieving high quality care and education for our children.

While we have made every effort to contact people whose articles are featured in this book, we apologise if any authors have not been notified.

Published by Step Forward Publishing Limited
Coach House, Cross Road, Milverton, Leamington Spa, CV32 5PB   Tel: 01926 420046
© Step Forward Publishing Limited 2001

Building a Portfolio for Early Years Care and Education S/NVQ Level 3, Book 2   ISBN: 1-902438-55 8

Chapter 1

Introduction   6
Gathering evidence   9
Personal skills review   19
Assessment planning   20

Chapter 2: C2 Provide for children's physical needs

About this unit – Values – Getting started   33

Element C2.1 Plan, prepare and provide food and drink for children
Key issues – Which type of evidence?   34

Element C2.2 Contribute to children's personal hygiene
Key issues – Which type of evidence?   34

Element C2.3 Respond to illness in children
Key issues – Which type of evidence?   35

Element C2.4 Plan and provide quiet periods for children
Key issues – Which type of evidence?   35

Related resources:
Providing meals and snacks   37
Food safety   39
Approaches to snack time   40
Personal hygiene and disinfection   41
Children and handwashing   42
Toilet regulations and routines   43
The value of health education   46
Promoting healthy living   48

Chapter 3: E3 Plan and equip environments for children

About this unit – Values – Getting started   51

Element E3.1 Establish and maintain a safe environment for children
Key issues – Which type of evidence?   52

Element E3.2 Establish and carry out safety and emergency procedures
Key issues – Which type of evidence?   52

Element E3.3 Select furniture and equipment for children
Key issues – Which type of evidence?   53

Element E3.4 Organise and maintain the physical environment of children
Key issues – Which type of evidence?   53

Related resources:
Providing a quality environment   55
Creating a quality environment: displays   58
The multicultural classroom   60
Playing safely – accident prevention   61
20 tips for a safer pre-school   63
20 top home safety tips   64
Fire precautions   65
Fire precautions check-list   68
First aid and resuscitation   69

contents

Policies and procedures   71
Handling insurance claims   74
Taking risks – or learning life skills?   76
Organising a road safety walk   78
The Disability Discrimination Act   79
Buying tables and chairs   81
Inspection and maintenance of play equipment   83
Literacy in the outdoor play area   87
Every nursery needs a camera   88
Keeping warm in winter   90
How to save energy   92

Chapter 4: C3 Promote the physical development of children

About this unit – Values – Getting started   94

Element C3.1 Develop children's confidence in movement
Key issues – Which type of evidence?   95

Element C3.2 Develop children's skills of locomotion and balance
Key issues – Which type of evidence?   96

Element C3.3 Develop children's gross motor skills
Key issues – Which type of evidence?   97

Element C3.4 Develop children's fine motor skills
Key issues – Which type of evidence?   97

Related resources:
Physical Development   99
Recognising changes in our bodies   103
Developing spatial awareness   104
Including the child with Down's syndrome   105
Including the child with cerebral palsy   107
Action songs   109
Non-competitive games   110
Balancing activities   111
Improving balancing skills   112
Using wheeled toys   113
Improving ball skills   114
Using hand apparatus   115
Parachute play   117
Developing fine motor skills   118
Good pencil control   119
Using scissors   121
Working with playdough   122

Chapter 5: C5 Promote children's social and emotional development

About this unit – Values – Getting started   123

Element C5.1 Enable children to adjust to the setting
Key issues – Which type of evidence?   124

Element C5.2 Enable children to relate to others
Key issues – Which type of evidence?   124

Element C5.3 Develop children's self-reliance and self-esteem
Key issues – Which type of evidence?   125

Element C5.4 Enable children to recognise and deal with their feelings
Key issues – Which type of evidence?   126

Element C5.5 Enable children to develop a positive self-image and identity
Key issues – Which type of evidence?   127

Element C5.6 Prepare children to move on to new settings
Key issues – Which type of evidence?   128

Related resources:
Personal, Social and Emotional Development   129
Settling-in procedures   131
Forming relationships   133
Learning to say please and thank-you   134
Organising circle time   135
Thinking of others   138
Taking turns and sharing   139
Learning to take turns   140
Talking all about me   141
Getting dressed   142
Developing children's self-esteem   143
Supporting a child who has a disfigurement   145
Special days   147
Puppets and emotional development   149
Expressing feelings and emotions   151
Teaching right from wrong   152
Coping with loss and bereavement   153
Coping with divorce and family breakdown   157
Getting ready for 'big' school   161

Chapter 6: C7 Provide a framework for the management of behaviour

About this unit – Values – Getting started   164

Element C7.1 Negotiate and set goals and boundaries for behaviour
Key issues – Which type of evidence?   165

Element C7.2 Promote positive aspects of behaviour
Key issues – Which type of evidence?   165

Element C7.3 Respond to unwanted behaviour
Key issues – Which type of evidence?   166

Related resources:
Managing children's behaviour   168
Establishing codes of behaviour   170
Establishing better behaviour   171

All articles have been published previously in *Practical Pre-School*, except for 'Settling-in procedures' pages 131-132.

Chapter 1

Introduction

So you're about to start a National Vocational Qualification (NVQ) Level 3 in Early Years Care and Education. That's good, because it means that you will have a nationally recognised qualification which will enable you to get a job anywhere in the United Kingdom, or even further afield. Early years provision is growing rapidly in the UK, and many more qualified early years practitioners are needed.

NVQs are based on the National Occupational Standards which have been agreed by experts working in a range of settings across the early years field. They cover all the competences expected of an early years practitioner. There are three levels - Level 2 for people working under supervision, as an assistant or voluntary worker; Level 3 for people working under their own initiative as supervisors; and Level 4 for people in a managerial role, with responsibility for complex and non-routine tasks, or responsibility for quality control in a number of establishments.

'I didn't really think about why I did things before, but now I think much more about how it is going to help the children.'

NVQ candidate

This qualification will help you to gain a better understanding of children's needs - it will help you to reflect on why you do certain things with and for children. And the great thing about NVQ is that you don't have to give up work to do it, because it's based on the work you do every day. You can also work towards an NVQ as a volunteer, or combine a part-time job with voluntary work in order to gain wider experience. You may not even have to go to college at all - that will depend on how much experience you have, and whether you have done any previous training. We will talk about this in more detail later.

NVQs are not like other qualifications. Instead of doing a course at college, you gather your own evidence that you can do all of the things you need to do to keep children safe and happy, and help them to develop. A lot of your evidence will come from what you are doing with the children every day. You will put all your evidence into a folder, or portfolio.

For Level 3 there are 11 mandatory units which you have to do, and you choose three optional units to suit your own job role and interests. What you choose will depend on which kind of setting you work in, or which area of work you are most interested in. You should by now have been given a copy of your candidate handbook with full details of the units. Don't be put off by your first look through it. It looks complicated, but once you have worked through one unit, the others will seem much more clear. You don't have to start at the beginning and work through the units in a particular order. You can choose which unit you feel most confident about, and start with that.

By now, you may have had an induction at your NVQ assessment centre. The staff will have explained what NVQs are all about, and how the centre operates. Each centre operates differently, although they all use the same Early Years Standards. The centre will allocate an assessor to you, who will work with you throughout your NVQ. You will get to know your assessor really well, and work closely with her or him. She will help you to plan what sort of evidence you will need to provide. She will also visit you in your setting and observe you working with the children.

The aim of this book is to help you to gather your evidence from the things you do every day with the children, rather than having to work through set tasks and assignments which are often not appropriate to your situation. That means it will be individual and meaningful to you, which is what NVQ is all about. We will look at the different ways you can gather the evidence and give you some useful formats to use, as well as resources to help you with your planning. Throughout this book, we will be referring to your candidate handbook. This is the book which contains the Early Years National Occupational Standards, which you will have been given when you registered. You will always need that with you.

You need to bear in mind that your centre may require you to work in a particular way, and in that case you may not have the freedom to gather the evidence in the way we recommend, but you will still find the book very useful.

How do NVQs work?

NVQ Level 3 is made up of 11 mandatory units and three optional units. Each unit describes a particular area of early years work. Each unit is broken down into elements, which identify all the things you need to be able to do, to show you are competent in that area of work. You will find all of the units in your handbook.

Let's take an example - Unit C2. If you work as a childminder or in a full day care setting, this unit might be a good place to start, because it's all about things you do every day with the children. The title of the unit is 'Provide for children's physical needs'.

Find it in your candidate handbook. Read the list of the elements at the beginning of the unit. Don't worry about all the other reading at the beginning of the unit yet. We will go back to that. These are the elements:

C2.1: Plan, prepare and provide food and drink for children

C2.2: Contribute to children's personal hygiene

C2.3: Respond to illness in children

C2.4: Plan and provide quiet periods for children

If you are a childminder or you work in a full day care setting, these things will be part of your daily routine and you will easily be able to provide most of the evidence you will need. If you work in a pre-school, nursery class or school, it may not be quite so easy to gather the evidence - for instance, you do not normally prepare and serve meals. In this case, you may need to plan special activities such as cooking something for snack time, or a picnic, to cover the evidence you need. Have a look at the performance criteria and the range in each element. If you're not sure what some of them mean, look at the 'Notes on this element' on the appropriate page in the handbook.

You will notice that each element has two main parts - performance criteria and range. The *performance criteria* (we will refer to these as PCs) are all the things you need to show you can do for that element - for example, in C2.1, the first PC states: 'Food and drinks planned and provided meet nutritional requirements and the cultural and religious practices of children's families, are safe for consumption and are presented in ways that are attractive and appetising to all of the children'.

The statement covers a lot of important things. Let's break it down and look at each one in turn. The first bit is 'Food and

drinks planned and provided meet nutritional requirements …' That means that you have to both plan and provide nutritious meals. If you are a childminder, you will be doing this all the time. If you work in a day nursery, you may be able to spend some time in the kitchen, where you can help to plan and prepare meals. If you are not involved in preparing and serving meals, you could organise a picnic or party, or plan a cookery session. You also need to show that you have provided a nutritious meal. To do that you need to know what the nutritional requirements are. If you don't know already, you will need to do some reading and research into what kind of foods provide children with the right sources of protein, vitamins and so on.

> *'I understand a lot more now. I can put it into practice straight away because I'm working with the children every day.'*
> NVQ candidate

The next bit says '…and the cultural and religious practices of children's families…' That means that when you're planning meals you need to know what the cultural and religious practices of each child's family are. This information is usually collected when the child starts the nursery, but you need to be aware of it, so that you don't give the children things they shouldn't have.

The next bit says '… are safe for consumption…' That means you need to know the hygiene requirements when storing and preparing food. The best way of doing this is to take a Food Hygiene course. These are easily available through most assessment centres, so check with yours.

And finally, '…and are presented in ways that are attractive and appetising to all of the children'. It goes without saying that children will be more likely to eat food if it looks and tastes good.

This first PC is quite complicated, as you can see, and contains a lot of information. Others, such as PC 7, are much more straightforward. Make sure you provide all the evidence you need for each PC.

Useful tip
Some performance criteria can seem very complicated. If you break them down into bits, as we have shown you, it will help to make them clearer. It will also stop you missing vital bits.

Now look at the *range*. This means all the different situations you may have to work in - for example, you need to cover main meals, snacks and drinks, children with and without special needs and those with special dietary requirements. The range will be different for each element, but by the time you have completed all the units, you will have covered every aspect of child care and development you are likely to come across.

This does not mean that you will necessarily have done all of these things. Sometimes, you will not be able to show that you have actually carried out all of the range, but you will need to show evidence that you could do it should the need arise. Your assessor has to observe at least one aspect of each range category, so she could observe you providing a snack for children with no eating difficulties, which would cover the observation requirement for the range for C2.1.

Your assessor will want to observe as many of the performance criteria and range as possible, and she will plan with you when and how she will do that. She will also plan with you how you will provide the rest of the evidence you need. We will look at the different sorts of evidence you can use later in the chapter. If you need any help with ideas or activities for the element or unit you are working on, you will find some useful articles in each chapter. For example, if you need ideas about providing meals and snacks for children there is an article on pages 37-38.

There are two other important sections in each unit which you need to be aware of. At the front of your candidate handbook you will find a section called the 'Statement of underlying principles'. They include:

◆ the welfare of the child

◆ keeping children safe

◆ working in partnership with parents/families

◆ children's learning and development

◆ equality of opportunity

◆ anti-discrimination

◆ celebrating diversity

◆ confidentiality

◆ working with other professionals

◆ the reflective practitioner

These are the principles which every early years worker must always adhere to if they are to commit themselves to giving

children the best possible care and education in their early years. They have taken into account the United Nations Convention on the Rights of the Child and the Children Act 1989. You may have had them explained to you in your induction, but if not, you need to go back to the front of your candidate handbook to find a full explanation of what each one means. If you can, talk them through with your assessor. It would also be useful to discuss them with your colleagues in your work setting.

When you're gathering your evidence for each unit, you must always be aware of the underlying principles. To help you to do this, there is a grid at the beginning of each unit which shows which underlying principles, or values, you need to show evidence of in each element. (Throughout the book, we will refer to them as values, for short.)

Let's go back to the beginning of Unit C2 and look for the grid entitled 'Values statement' under the heading 'Principles of good practice'. Under each element it shows you which PCs refer to some aspect of the principles, or values. Try using the grid now to find the relevant element and PC, and think about how you might show that you are aware of the values. If you have any difficulty with this, go through it with your assessor.

Here's an example:
Go to the column headed *Element 2*. Look down the grid until you come to numbers 4, 5, 6, 9. This means *performance criteria 4, 5, 6, 9* in Element 2.

Look across to the left to see which value it covers. You will find *working in partnership with parents and families.*

Now go to Element 2 in your handbook (headed C2.2) and look at PC6. It says 'Methods and timing of toilet training are clearly discussed with parents to ensure consistency of care'.

Obviously, it's of paramount importance during toilet training that parents and carers follow the same procedure, and agree on the right time to start, otherwise the child would become very confused, and toilet training would not be achieved successfully.

Finally, we need to look at the *description of knowledge, understanding and skills.* You will find this at the end of each unit, after the last element. This is where you need to provide evidence that you have the knowledge and understanding to show that you know why you do the things you do with the children in your care. This section looks a bit daunting, but don't panic! You will be able to cover a lot of it through the evidence you will be collecting for each element.

This section is divided under four main headings:

- ◆ Development

- ◆ Curriculum practice

- ◆ Equipment, materials, environment

- ◆ Relationships

However, you will find when you start working with them that there is quite a lot of overlap from one section to another, and we will show you how you can cut down on the work by taking several points together. We will do this within the chapter for each unit, so don't worry about it at this stage.

Many assessment centres will provide teaching sessions either in the daytime or evening, or learning packs which you can use at home, and will usually recommend some text books. Your local Early Years Development and Childcare Partnership (EYDCP) will probably also have courses you can attend. Your setting should receive information about these. If not, ring your local education authority and ask what is available. It's especially important that you attend training on first aid and child protection carried out by experts in these fields. Although it's not a requirement for your NVQ to take a recognised course in these areas, all early years practitioners should have a thorough knowledge of both.

You are not required to attend a course to gain your underpinning knowledge for NVQ, unless attendance at college is a requirement in order to gain funding. If you're an experienced practitioner, you may feel that you already have the knowledge you need, or feel confident to fill any gaps through your own reading and research. If you're less experienced, you will gain a great deal from attending the training sessions, and from sharing your ideas with other candidates.

note:
This book does not aim to provide you with all of the underpinning knowledge you will need for your NVQ. It is a resource book and guide, to help you to gather your evidence for each unit.

Gathering evidence

NVQ is different to other qualifications in that, instead of taking an examination, you show that you are competent by collecting evidence of what you do in your day-to-day work with the children. The role of your assessor is to judge whether your evidence is sufficient to prove that you are competent.

Your candidate handbook has an explanation of the different sorts of evidence you can use. You will find this in the section at the beginning entitled 'The assessment process'. You may have already had the methods explained to you at your induction, but we will explain them again here.

There are two main types of evidence:

- ◆ Performance evidence - what you can do

- ◆ Knowledge evidence - what you know

At the beginning of each unit there is a description of the different ways you can collect your evidence. It's not the same for every unit, but it will always be from the following approved methods of evidence collection listed in your candidate handbook:

- ◆ Direct observation by a qualified assessor

- ◆ Questioning

- ◆ Witness testimony

- ◆ Work plans

- ◆ Inspection of the setting by a qualified assessor

- ◆ Reflective accounts

- ◆ Log books, diaries and notes

- ◆ Work products

- ◆ Case studies, assignments or projects

- ◆ Child observations

- ◆ Simulation, role play or skills rehearsals

- ◆ Skills transferable from other performance

- ◆ Past achievements

- ◆ Formal written or oral tests/extended questioning

To make it easier for you to collect the evidence, we will look at some useful formats you can use. Your assessment centre may have their own formats, so you need to check first. Evidence does **not** have to be written. If you feel worried about doing a lot of writing there are other methods you can use. For instance, you can record your evidence onto a tape recorder, or use a word processor. We have already said that your assessor will ask you oral questions. You may be able to make an arrangement with her to do extra questioning.

This will depend on the amount of time she is allowed for assessment because, of course, it will be more time-consuming for her. If you feel that you may be eligible for extra support, talk to your assessor. Many centres are able to access funds to help candidates with additional needs. Some assessment centres have access to a range of specialised equipment available for people with disabilities.

Direct observation

The most important type of evidence is direct observation by a qualified assessor. You will see in the section on performance evidence in your candidate handbook that there are some PCs (performance criteria) which must be observed. Your assessor will also have to observe at least one aspect of each range category. For the rest of the range, PCs and knowledge, you will provide other types of evidence from the list above. Your assessor will write down what she observes on an *observation record* which is provided by the assessment centre. She will give you this to keep in your portfolio. An example of what it may look like is given below.

Date	OBSERVATION RECORD	PCs range	Knowledge evidence
21.7.00	Sarah supervised snack time with the children – fruit and drinks. She let the children pour their own drinks, and they passed the cut-up fruit – a choice of apple, orange and banana – around the table. Sarah talked with the children and was aware of their needs, giving help where necessary. When they had finished she asked them to wash their hands in preparation for the cooking activity they were about to do, and cleaned the table with antibacterial spray.	C2.1.1,5,8 R2,3,4	C2KE2,7,11
		C2.2.11 R2,6	
	She helped the children to put on aprons. It was a large group but other adults were helping. Sarah showed the children the scales, and how to weigh out the ingredients for the pizza base. The children helped with the weighing, and Sarah melted the butter in the microwave. She talked about how it had changed from solid to liquid as she showed the children the difference. She put the ingredients into several bowls and the children took turns in mixing the dough.	C10.3.1,5,6 R2,3,6	C10KE8,11,16,17,21,31
		M7.3.2, 3 4,5 R2,3, 6,7,8,9	M7KE2,8,10,22, 23
		C3.4.1,2,3,4, 6,7 R2,4,6	C3KE11,13,16
	Sarah then gave the children cheese to grate, or vegetables to cut up, and she and the other adults supervised them closely. There was a lot of conversation about colour, shape and so on. Once the vegetables and cheese were ready, every child had a piece of dough, which they rolled out. They really enjoyed this. Sarah placed the vegetables and cheese within easy reach of the children, and they chose what they wanted to put on their pizza. There was a brief squabble between two children, which Sarah dealt with calmly. She gave praise and encouragement throughout the activity.	C11.2.2,4,5, 6,7 R7,9,11	(This observation may not cover the whole of the knowledge evidence for these sections)
		C5.2.1,2,3 R1,4	
		C5.3.3,5, 6,7,8 R2,4,6	

Signed...Anne Other........................(assessor)   Sarah Bright................................(candidate)

Questioning

Your assessor will often ask you questions about what she has observed, to check your understanding. She will write down answers to any oral questions she asks you. She will give you these to keep in your portfolio. The question sheet may be a similar format to the one below:

Date	ORAL QUESTION RECORD	PCs range	Knowledge evidence
1.2.01	1. Can you give examples of where parents have had different expectations about self-reliance and behaviour to those you expect in the nursery?		
	We've had examples of parents doing everything for the child. We would encourage the child to do as much as possible in the nursery, then show the parent what the child can do, and discuss with the parent how they might encourage the child to be more independent.	C5.3R1 C5.3.4, 9	C5 KE6
	One day a mother ignored her child jumping on the table, which is unacceptable in the nursery. I lifted him down and said 'We don't do that at nursery, do we?' The parent made no comment.	C7.1.5 C7.2R2 C7.2.5 C7.3.1	
	2. How do you promote positive attitudes to children and adults of different cultural groups and people with disabilities?		
	Through posters, pictures and books and through activities such as cooking. We cooked noodles at Chinese New Year. The children went to a multicultural event at the library where the librarian read Caribbean stories, and they ate Caribbean food.	C5.5.2, 3, 4, 5	C5 KE24, 34
	We had a visit from a guide dog for the blind and its trainer recently.		

Signed........A. N. Other...(assessor) ......Dalvinder Kaur...(candidate)

Witness testimony

For things which your assessor is not able to observe easily, or to cover areas of the range, you can ask other people you work with to write a witness testimony. If you are a childminder you can ask parents and other professionals who visit you to write a witness testimony. You may need to explain the National Occupational Standards to them, so that what they write is relevant. You will need to have a list of people who have supplied witness testimonies in your portfolio, with a note of their job role or status. An example is given below.

Date	WITNESS TESTIMONY	PCs range	Knowledge evidence
6.11.00	The nursery has an open door policy so parents feel welcome to come to the nursery at any time. Sarah is very relaxed with the parents and encourages them to talk to her about their child's development, and any worries and concerns they may have.	C11.1.1 P2.1.1,4,5 R1,2,3 P2.3.2 C5.1.9	C11KE8 P2KE4,6
	She also shows the parents the activities the children have been doing that day when they come to collect them, and encourages the children to talk about what they have done. Often parents just like to chat, and Sarah is always willing to listen. She upholds the nursery's policy on confidentiality at all times.	P2.3.5, 6,7,8 R1,4 C5.3.10, R3,6	C11KE12 P2KE10 C5KE32 C11KE31 P2KE8
	Sarah was concerned about a Chinese boy who was not speaking much at nursery. She talked to his mum, who said his English is good and he chatted away at home, and she was surprised he didn't at the nursery. Since then Sarah has encouraged him to join in with group activities and he is gradually starting to talk more.	P2.1.8,10 C11.1.5 R2,4 C11.5.6 P2.1.9 C5.1.8,10 R3	

Signed...... V Goode ....witness .... Sarah Bright ....(candidate)

Status of witness........... Nursery Manager ....

Work plans

If you are involved in planning the routine and curriculum in your setting, you can use your plans as evidence. If you do this, you will need to write a brief explanation of how you were involved in the planning. It would be useful extra evidence to say how the plans were put into practice, and to evaluate their effectiveness - what the children gained from them, whether you would change them next time and so on.

If you are not involved in the planning, you will need to produce some evidence that you are able to plan. The activity plan on pages 28-29 will help you to do this. If you answer the questions thoroughly, this activity plan will cover much of the knowledge evidence you will need. (An example of a completed activity plan is also provided, on pages 14-15, to give you an idea of what is expected.)

Inspection of the setting

For some units, such as E3 which covers health and safety, and planning the environment, your assessor will need to inspect your setting. She will ask you questions about how far you are responsible for these areas of work, and whether you understand the reasons for things being the way they are. She will usually record this on the direct observation and oral question records.

Reflective accounts

These are a really useful way of writing (or talking) about things you have done which your assessor was not able to observe. There is no special format, you can write on ordinary A4 paper; an example is given below. (Alternatively, you can put your reflective account onto audio tape.)

Perhaps something unexpected happened in the nursery, or you dealt with an accident, or a query from a parent. It could cover areas of the range. It's useful to try and identify which elements or units it will be relevant for, then you can make sure you cover the relevant details. When you write your account, try to reflect on why you dealt with it the way you did and what you learned from it. Don't forget to refer to the knowledge evidence section, and cover any relevant points.

Reflective account of how I provide rest/quiet periods for the children

Before lunch time the children always have story time, when the group sit together and an adult reads a story. It is important to have quiet times during the day to allow the children to recoup their energy. Also at different times during the week the children listen to relaxing music and are encouraged to lie down and relax.

After lunch occasionally a child, especially one of the younger children aged two and a half, gets tired and needs a sleep. I take them to the toilet, and settle them on the sofa with their comforter (blanket, teddy or dummy). Some children prefer it if you stay with them and chat for a while, or I might read them a story before they go to sleep.

All children are different in their sleep habits and some do not need as much sleep as others do. I believe in children having a sleep if they need it. My own children always had a sleep in the afternoon when they were nursery school age.

If a child is having a sleep in the afternoon the other children are encouraged to choose quiet activities such as drawing or jigsaws so that they don't disturb the resting child. When the child wakes up, they shouldn't be hurried or rushed, and given time to wake up slowly.

Evidence covered

C2 KE6, 9, 25 C2.4.1, 5, 6, 7, 8, 9, 10, R1, 2, 3, 4, 5

Signed...A N Other...............(assessor) . Dalvinder Kaur...............(candidate)

A significant feature of the NVQ is that it aims to make early years workers into reflective practitioners who are constantly reviewing the way they do things, so that they can improve their practice. None of us ever stop learning, no matter how experienced we are.

Log books, diaries and notes
These can be used to record your day-to-day work with the children. You may if you wish keep a daily diary, but they can become repetitive. It's useful to have a sample of your routine, but once you have written that for perhaps a week, be more discerning about what you write.

You may find it helpful to carry a notebook around with you to record things which happen during the day. You can then write anything relevant in more detail in quiet times during the day, or when you get home. Aim to pick out significant events rather than list all the routine things you do day after day. To record these events you can use the free description format of a reflective account, or you may find the format shown on page 16 helpful because it's a bit more structured.

Work products
You can use things like:
◆ policies and procedures of your setting - you must write a short note to show either how you have been involved in preparing them or how you use them in your daily work.

◆ curriculum plans - write a note to say how you were involved in planning and carrying out the activities. Evaluate how successful they were and what the children gained from them.

◆ examples of activities you have done with the children - only if you feel they are needed to support the evidence. Don't include a lot of children's work.

◆ menus, charts, details of outings and special events - explain how you were involved in preparing these.

◆ letters to parents, children's records, child observations and anything else you feel is a relevant piece of evidence - you must get permission from your supervisor or employer, and always remove names and check that the child or adult will not be recognised from anything in the piece of evidence, in order to maintain confidentiality.

◆ photographs of yourself working with the children, with a caption saying what the activity is, and how you are involved.

Remember!
Whatever evidence you use from your workplace, do check with your employer that you can use it first.

ACTIVITY PLAN

NAME: Isaac Harding **DATE:** 13.5.01 **ACTIVITY:** Music and movement **AGE OF CHILDREN:** 3 - 4yrs

Before the activity:
Describe the activity you are planning. Describe how it fulfils the values statements for the element or unit you are working on.
A movement session where the children are encouraged to move in different ways to music from 'Jungle Book' and 'Pocahontas'

Why have you chosen this activity? What do you think the children will gain from it? *(Think about areas of development.)*
I have chosen this activity because the music will help the children to move rhythmically and expressively, and develop their confidence in movement. Also the language I will use will label the parts of the body and different types of movements, and develop their understanding. One piece of music is very lively, the other is more soft and flowing.

Which children will be involved? Why? *(Will it be free choice? Have you targeted children who need particular help with, for instance, colour recognition?)*
A group of 6 to 8 children will do the activity.

ACTIVITY PLAN continued

What equipment/resources/preparation do you need?

I have prepared a tape of music and I will also give the children silk scarves for the Pocahontas music.

What will you do during the activity? *(Language you will use, help you will give, etc.)*

During the session I will encourage the children to join in, and use descriptive words such as 'stretch your hands high up to the sky'. I will show the children as well as telling them what to do. I will use language for parts of the body - arms, legs, feet, hands - and also position and descriptive words - up, down, side, under, over, heavy, light, running, jumping, stamping, fast, slow.

After the activity:

Did the activity go well? Why? If not, why not?

The activity went really well. The children joined in and responded well to the different types of music, adjusting their movements appropriately.

Would you change it next time? If so, how and why?

I wouldn't change anything next time.

How would you adapt the activity for older/younger children? For children with additional needs or disabilities?

Children with limited mobility might need physical help to enable them to join in, like holding their hands. A child in a wheelchair could join in, especially with waving the scarf. A child who lacked confidence would need lots of encouragement.

What did the children gain from the activity? Was it what you thought they would?

It helped the children develop an awareness of their own bodies and how they can move in different ways. It developed their gross motor skills, co-ordination and awareness of space. It helped them to learn new words.

What did you learn from it?

I was surprised and pleased to discover how well the children responded to the music.

Signed ......Isaac Harding...... (candidate)

Evidence covered: C3.1 R3, 4   C10 KE13, C11KE32
                     C3.2 R1, 2, 3, 4   C10.3 R4
                     C3.3.1, 2, 3, 4, 5, 6, 7, 8   C3 KE9, 10

If anyone observed you ask them to sign that this a true record, and to comment if possible.

Signed ...A N Other...... **Role:** ...Assessor............

Comment: The music and movement session was lovely. The children gained a lot from it.

CANDIDATE DIARY

NAME: Dalvinder Kaur **DATE:** 10.1.01 **INCIDENT:** Disruptive behaviour

What happened? Who was involved? *(Don't use names - number of staff/children/parents)*
At register time, everyone was sitting quietly. Jane took her shoes off and banged them on the floor. She hit a child sitting close by. The adult taking register told her to stop because it was unkind. She looked very angry and went over to the window and started hitting that.

How did you react? What did you do?
I took Jane out of the room to calm down, and had a chat with her to find out what was wrong. She couldn't tell me because she was crying. I explained that she was hurting the other child, and that it was dangerous to hit glass windows because they might break. I gave her a hug, and after a few minutes we were able to rejoin the group.

Why did you do it this way?
I took Jane out of the room because she was upsetting and disrupting the rest of the group. I gave her an explanation as to why she couldn't behave as she had, so that she understood the reasons why. I gave her a hug because she was upset.

Did it work? If not, why not?
Yes, Jane calmed down and we rejoined the group after a few minutes.

What have you learned from it? What would you do differently next time?
(Think about the values statements)
That it's best to be calm and remove the child from the situation if necessary. I wouldn't change anything next time, except that it obviously depends on the situation and the child.

Which PCs/range/knowledge does this relate to?
C6.4 R7, C6.4.5, C6 KE7, 9, 17, 30
C7.2.3, C7.3 R3,5, C7.3.1, 2, 3, C7 KE9, 10, 18, 19

If anyone observed you, ask them to sign that this is an accurate record and to make a comment.

Witness..........V. Goode...

Status..........Nursery Manager...

Witness comment (if applicable)
Dalvinder dealt with the situation calmly and effectively, and continued to give extra attention to Jane after the event, to reassure her.

Case studies, assignments or projects

This covers a range of other evidence, such as:

◆ assignments and projects set by your centre:
  - your centre may ask you at the beginning of the NVQ programme to carry out a project to cover all aspects of child development, because several of the units ask you to show your knowledge of this, and it's easier to cover it all together.

  - your centre may ask you to do an assignment for Unit C15, Child Protection, because there is very little which can be directly observed.

◆ written work to cover areas of the underpinning knowledge and range which you have not covered with other, work-based evidence, perhaps because it is outside your experience or you needed to do some reading or research.

◆ a case study of a particular child, carried out over a period of time.

Child observations

There is a whole unit dedicated to child observation, but don't wait till you get to C16 to start carrying out observations of children. You need to get into the habit of observing children, because it is an important skill. Observations help you learn a lot about child development, and individual children's needs, and they help you to plan appropriate activities for your children. They are also useful evidence for most of the units. You need to gain permission from the parents before you include observations in your portfolio. Some employers ask for parents' permission for this when their child joins the setting, so check what the position is in your setting. If you are not confident about child observation, read the chapter on C16. A helpful format for you to use when you record your observations is provided on page 18.

Simulation, role play, skills rehearsal

If you are not able to demonstrate a particular competence in your workplace - for instance, if you don't have the opportunity to bath babies or make feeds - you could be observed doing these things in a classroom situation. Or if you wanted to demonstrate your ability to handle a difficult situation with a parent which it would be inappropriate to observe, you could be observed in a role play. These are only used in exceptional circumstances.

Skills transferable from other performance

This can be used when it would be inappropriate to carry out direct observation, such as in the case of a child's disclosure of abuse. Some of the skills you would need in this situation may be observed in other work situations, such as how you support a distressed child, how you communicate or how you handle difficult situations.

Past achievements

You may have a great deal of past experience as well as other relevant qualifications when you embark on your NVQ. You will be able to draw on this as evidence for your portfolio. Your centre will normally be able to advise you on this, and may take you through a process called accreditation of prior learning (APL) or accreditation of prior achievement (APA). In order to include any evidence from the past, you will need to prove that it is your own work, and that the information is not out of date - for instance, the work needs to show an awareness of equal opportunities and anti-discriminatory practice; information related to child safety and protection must take account of the Children Act; and curriculum practice must take account of the Early Learning Goals or the National Curriculum. Evidence from the past cannot take the place of direct observation, but it can be used to cover parts of the range and knowledge evidence.

Formal written or oral tests/extended questioning

It is not usual to use tests as evidence for NVQ, because it is a qualification based on assessment of your competence in the workplace. However, there is a possibility that it may be used in the future for some aspects of assessment.

> **Remember!**
> It is absolutely vital that you keep all of your evidence together in your portfolio, with your assessment plans and feedback records, and keep it in a safe place.

How do I reference and record the evidence?

Your centre will usually show you how they want the portfolio organised. It's usually best to divide the evidence unit by unit, but not essential. If you're working with several units at once, it might be better not to separate it into units, because you need to number it as you go along, so that you can record it onto the unit assessment records. Have a look at your candidate handbook with the standards in it. The format for recording your evidence varies slightly from one awarding body to another, but you will often find that for every PC, range and knowledge evidence statement you have to say what sort of evidence you have used, and what page number it's on, so that your assessor and internal verifier can check it. You need to number every piece of evidence as you do it. This is not easy to get to grips with at first, so ask your assessor to explain how she wants you to do it.

CHILD OBSERVATION

Observation record I	Date 28.06.01

Title of observation:

Settling in

Type of observation: (eg target child, free description, developmental check-list)

Time sample

Aim of observation: (Which aspect of child development/behaviour are you aiming to observe?)

To observe how a Child Copes with settling in to nursery

First name of child: (or fictitious name)   Sandeep   **Age:** (yrs & mths)   2yrs 9mths

Description of setting: (where observation is taking place, number of staff, children, equipment available, etc)

Nursery playroom, 3 staff, 15 Children. Morning session - registration time, play and structured activities, drinks time.

The observation: Write this on a separate piece of paper, or other format you have chosen. Write what you actually observed in detail, using present tense.

Evaluation: Comment on what you learned from the observation - link this to your aims. Evaluate what the child's needs are, and make recommendations for future planning.

Signatures: Sign your observation and ask someone who witnessed the observation to sign it if possible.

Signed...S. Bright...............(candidate)   Signed........Anne Other.........(witness)

Observation

9.00 Sandeep is cuddling her mum and looking anxious. She is watching the other children playing but doesn't join in.

9.30 Sandeep's mum says goodbye and a member of staff sits with Sandeep. She cries for about a minute and then goes to sit with the rest of the children for register time, with the members of staff.

10.00 Sandeep is sitting at the painting table with an apron on. She is absorbed in sponge painting. She finishes her picture and gets up from the table. She watches another child washing his hands. She looks anxious again.

10.30 Snack time. Sandeep sits at the table with the other children but doesn't speak. She is offered a piece of toast but shakes her head. She drinks her orange juice.

11.00 Sandeep is playing with the play people on the carpet. She looks at another child also playing there but doesn't speak.

11.30 Sandeep's mum returns to collect her. She is sitting with the other children listening to the story but as soon as she sees her mum she runs to her smiling.

Evaluation

Sandeep was obviously quite anxious about her mum leaving her but she only cried for a very short time. She spent a lot of time watching other children but didn't speak to anyone, child or adult. She did enjoy painting and later in the morning started playing alongside another child. She will need a lot of reassurance over the next few days. Staff need to gently encourage her to join in with things, but not be too insistent. She will join in when she's ready.

Personal skills review

In the introduction, we suggested that Unit C2, 'Provide for children's physical needs', might be a good unit to start with, but that depends on your setting, your experience, the age of the children you work with and which areas you feel most confident about.

The personal skills review provided will help you to identify the areas of your work you are confident about, and areas where you need to take some action to improve your competence. Read through the summary of units and elements and use Sections 1 to 4 in the skills review first of all to help you to decide which unit to start with. You can photocopy and use the blank review sheet on page 21 (Personal skills profile). You will need your candidate handbook to help you.

When you have chosen a unit, do another personal skills review, this time based on the unit. You may find it easier to do this element by element at first.

◆ Go through the PCs and range for the element you are working on and fill in the appropriate boxes 1 - 5 on the review sheet.

◆ Go to the knowledge evidence section at the end of the unit and pick out the statements which are relevant to the element you are working on. Note which you need some help with in section 6 on the review sheet.

◆ Decide which activities you can arrange for your assessor to observe (box 7), and what other types of evidence you can use.

Note: As you become more confident, use this format to look at the whole unit rather than just one element.

The personal skills review will help you to be prepared for when you and your assessor plan your assessment. If you have done other units already and you feel confident to go straight into planning, you can leave this section out.

Action you may need to take
If you have identified areas you may have difficulty with you will need to discuss with your assessor what you are going to do to put these right. For instance:

Section 2 You may simply need to practise an activity until you feel more confident. Ask your assessor or colleagues for guidance if necessary. If you need ideas for activities you will find the resources in this book helpful.

Section 3 You may need to ask your employer to give you the opportunity to move to a different age group, or to allow you to do things not normally within your role. If there are serious gaps, you may need to spend some time in another setting - for instance, if you work in a creche where you never have the same children for more than an hour, or you only have children under two years old, you do need to consider getting wider experience.

Section 4 If you want to use something from the past as evidence, your assessor will have to make sure that it is sufficient, takes account of current legislation, local regulations and best practice, and that it is authentic and reliable - that is, that it's your own work. Past experience cannot take the place of direct observation.

Section 6 When you fill in this section, remember to check the knowledge evidence. We have identified the relevant knowledge evidence for each element in each of the chapters. You may need to attend some training, ask for support, or do some reading and research to improve your understanding. Your centre may offer training sessions, or learning materials and supported study.

Assessment planning
At this stage you may want to arrange a meeting with your assessor so that you can start planning your assessment. If this is your first unit, we would recommend that you plan together, but once you are confident, you can plan on your own if you wish. You will find a chapter on each of the mandatory units, either in this book or in the other two books in the series, to help you with your planning. Your centre will have an assessment plan format, but an example of what it might look like is given on page 32 (completed version, page 22).

◆ There are two ways of planning your assessment:
   You can take each element separately and plan an activity which your assessor will observe and other evidence you need for that element, **or**:

◆ Plan a whole session which will cover a range of activities and provide evidence for more than one element or unit - we sometimes call this **holistic assessment**. We recommend this method because it is a more effective use of your own and the assessor's time. We will explain this more fully in the section on cross referencing below.

Start by choosing an activity for your assessor to observe which will cover as many of the PCs and the range as possible. Remember to check which PCs must be observed, and remember too that at least one aspect of each area of the range must be observed. It's a good idea to plan the activity using the activity plan format we suggested earlier in the chapter, so that you can make sure that you are well prepared, and also to show your assessor that you have a good knowledge and understanding of the element or unit.

Decide how you will provide the other evidence you need. You will find suggestions about the most appropriate types of evidence at the beginning of the unit. Don't forget to include any work plans from your normal work practice, with a note to say how you were involved in preparing and carrying them out.

Cross referencing
The NVQ process encourages working across elements and units - we call this **holistic assessment**. This means that you can use one piece of evidence in several units. Because every page of evidence is numbered, you simply cross reference to the relevant page, regardless of which unit it is in. For instance, your assessor may have observed you playing a colour matching game with a group of children, which you planned for Element 3 in C10 (we usually write this as C10.3). She will probably have noted how you encouraged children to relate to each other and take turns (C5.2) and how you encouraged and praised children (C5.3). You were probably encouraging concentration (C10.1) and developing language skills (C11.2,5). If your assessor planned to spend some extra time observing tidying up and getting ready for dinner, she would also see evidence for C5.3 - encouraging self-reliance; for E3.1 - maintaining a safe environment; and for C2.2 - contributing to children's personal hygiene. In the same way you can cross reference for areas of the range. You can also do this for any of your written evidence. Some candidates are unable to cope with this at first, and you may need to grow into it. As you become more familiar with your handbook, you will find it easier to cross reference.

You will probably find it easier to concentrate on one unit at a time, but to be aware of when evidence can be cross referenced to other units. To help you to do this, we have given you a simple format (see page 23). Put a copy at the beginning of each unit, and as you find evidence which you think will fit, list it on the sheet, with the page reference. At this stage, you don't need to worry about exactly which PCs,

PERSONAL SKILLS PROFILE

1. Things I feel confident I can do
2. Things I don't feel confident about doing
3. Things I don't have the opportunity to do
4. Things I have done in the past
5. Areas of the range my assessor can observe
6. Things I don't understand (check knowledge evidence)
7. Possible activities my assessor could observe
8. Other types of evidence I could provide

ASSESSMENT PLAN

Description of evidence/activity	To cover PCs/ range	To cover knowledge evidence	Date due
Observation of Circle time - exploring feelings and self-image - things that make them happy and sad, things they like doing at home and in nursery.	C5.4 C5.5		
Write a reflective account of the way goals and boundaries for behaviour are set in the nursery.		C7 KE 4, 5, 9, 11, 14, 15, 16, 18, 19 C7	
Read up on behaviour modification.			
Carry out a child observation on child displaying difficult behaviour - use event sample technique.	C7.1 C7.3	C7 KE2	

Signed.........Dalvinder Kaur..............................(candidate) ....A. N. Other..............................(assessor)

Date.........11.01.01....................................... Date.................11.01.01.......................

CROSS REFERENCING SHEET

Unit	
Description of evidence	**Unit/page reference**

range or knowledge evidence it fits, as long as you know where to find it. When you start working on that unit, you can go back to the evidence and cross reference it into the appropriate place.

Knowledge evidence

Try to incorporate as much knowledge evidence as you can into your activity plan, candidate diary, reflective account, child observation or other work-based evidence. If there are still gaps in your evidence, you can write paragraphs on each relevant point. You should aim to make this short, clear and to the point, and wherever possible, use examples from your own work practice. Don't copy chunks from books, nor include photocopied pages.

Alternatively, if you feel confident that you can give an oral account of your knowledge and understanding, arrange this with your assessor, or include an audio-tape of your answers as evidence.

You may find it easier to pick out the relevant bits of knowledge evidence for each element, to ensure that you have covered all of the evidence but not repeated anything unnecessarily. You will notice in your candidate handbook that alongside each statement in the knowledge evidence there is a reference to the element it is linked to. To help you to identify it, we have included the reference numbers of the relevant statements in each of the elements in the chapters.

The resources in this book will help you with your underpinning knowledge. There are some good practical ideas, and some thought-provoking articles which will help you to reflect on your own practice and improve it. We have placed each article in the unit it is most relevant for but you will notice that many of the articles are relevant for more than one unit.

You will probably need to do further reading from study materials and recommended text books, or make arrangements to attend training sessions. Your centre will be able to advise you on this. A list of books you may find useful is given right.

Suggested reading list

Children with Special Educational Needs by M Alcott (Hodder & Stoughton) 0 340 70152 8.

Child Care and Education by T Bruce and C Meggitt (Hodder & Stoughton) 0 340 64328 5.

Babies and Young Children by Beaver, Brewster *et al* (Stanley Thornes) Book 1 (2nd edition) 0 7487 3974 2; Book 2 0 7847 3975 0.

A Practical Guide to Work with Babies (2nd edition) by Dare and O'Donovan (Stanley Thornes) 0 7487 3635 2.

A Practical Guide to Child Nutrition by Dare and O'Donovan (Stanley Thornes) 0 7487 2375 7.

A Practical Guide to Caring for Children with Special Needs by Dare and O'Donovan (Stanley Thornes) 0 7487 2871 6.

A Practical Guide to Child Observation (2nd edition) by Hobart and Frankel (Stanley Thornes) 0 7487 4500 9.

Good Practice in Child Protection by Hobart and Frankel (Stanley Thornes) 0 7487 3094.

Child Protection and Early Years Work by J Lindon (Hodder & Stoughton) 0 340 70558 2.

Equal Opportunities in Practice by J Lindon (Hodder & Stoughton) 0 340 70559 0.

A Practical Guide to Equal Opportunities by H Malik (Stanley Thornes) 0 7487 3652 2.

Early Years Care and Education by Tassoni, Bulman et al (Heinemann) 435 40160 2.

A-Z of Child Health by Dr N Shabde (Step Forward Publishing) 1 902438 09 4.

Personal, Social and Emotional Development by Sara Stocks in the *What Learning Looks Like* series (Step Forward Publishing) 1 902438 28 0.

Date	OBSERVATION RECORD	PCs range	Knowledge evidence

Signed...(assessor)   ....(candidate)

Date	ORAL QUESTION RECORD	PCs range	Knowledge evidence

Signed..(assessor)   ....(candidate)

Date	WITNESS TESTIMONY	PCs range	Knowledge evidence

Signed..witness ....(candidate)

Status of witness...

ACTIVITY PLAN

NAME: **DATE:**   **ACTIVITY:**   **AGE OF CHILDREN:**

Before the activity:
Describe the activity you are planning. Describe how it fulfils the values statements for the element or unit you are working on.

Why have you chosen this activity? What do you think the children will gain from it?*(Think about areas of development.)*

Which children will be involved? Why? *(Will it be free choice? Have you targeted children who need particular help with, for instance, colour recognition?)*

What equipment/resources/preparation do you need?

What will you do during the activity? *(Language you will use, help you will give, etc.)*

After the activity:
Did the activity go well? Why? If not, why not?

Would you change it next time? If so, how and why?

How would you adapt the activity for older/younger children? For children with additional needs or disabilities?

What did the children gain from the activity? Was it what you thought they would?

What did you learn from it?

Signed .... (candidate) If anyone observed you ask them to sign that this is a true record, and to comment if possible.

Signed .... Role: ....

Comment:

CANDIDATE DIARY

NAME: **DATE:**   **INCIDENT:**

What happened? Who was involved? *(Don't use names - number of staff/children/parents)*

How did you react? What did you do?

Why did you do it this way?

Did it work? If not, why not?

What have you learned from it? What would you do differently next time?
(Think about the values statements)

Which PC's/range/knowledge does this relate to?

If anyone observed you ask them to sign that this is an accurate record and to make a comment.

Witness...   **Status** ....

Witness comment (if applicable)

CHILD OBSERVATION

Candidate's name	**Date**

Title of observation:

Type of observation: (eg target child, free description, developmental check-list)

Aim of observation: (Which aspect of child development/behaviour are you aiming to observe?)

First name of child: (or fictitious name)   **Age:** (yrs & mths)

Description of setting: (where observation is taking place, number of staff, children, equipment available, etc.)

The observation: Write this on a separate piece of paper, or other format you have chosen. Write what you actually observed in detail, using present tense.

Evaluation: Comment on what you learned from the observation - link this to your aims. Evaluate what the child's needs are, and make recommendations for future planning.

Signatures: Sign your observation and ask someone who witnessed the observation to sign it if possible.

Signed......................................(candidate)   **Signed**......................................(witness)

ASSESSMENT PLAN

Description of evidence/activity	To cover PCs/ range	To cover knowledge evidence	Date due

Signed..(assessor) ....(candidate)

Date.. Date..

Chapter 2

Unit C2: Provide for children's physical needs

About this unit

This unit is all about caring for the physical needs of children from birth to eight years, which will include providing food and drink, personal hygiene routines, opportunity for rest and sleep, and dealing with children's illness. You will need to show how you meet the individual needs of every child and how you ensure that the care in the setting is consistent with that in the child's family. There are many links between this unit and E3 'Plan and equip environments for children', so it's a good idea to do the two together, or one after the other, and cross reference the relevant evidence. Have a look through the standards for E3 when you are planning how to gather your evidence for this unit. You will find the guidance and resources on E3 in the next chapter.

> **note:**
> If your setting has children of different ages, it will be beneficial for you to gain experience of working with each age group. If you work with a limited age range, try to get experience in another setting if you can.

Values

The important aspects of the values throughout this unit are the welfare of the child and keeping children safe; also being a reflective practitioner and working in partnership with parents. Equality of opportunity, anti-discrimination and celebrating diversity are important, too. Make sure that you take account of the children's needs and the parents' preferences and beliefs when you are caring for the children. For instance, when providing food and drink, make sure that you take account of parental beliefs, dietary requirements and possible food allergies. It's also important to promote a positive attitude among the children towards differences in cultural practices. Two ways you can do this is by trying foods from different cultures, and having different types of cooking utensils and play food in the home corner.

In Element 2 you must ensure that you comply with family and cultural practices when you are caring for children's skin and hair. In Element 3 you need to show that you are able to pass on accurate and relevant information to other professionals

and that you maintain confidentiality when you are dealing with sick children.

Getting started

In this unit you will need to show that you can:

- ◆ Plan, prepare and provide food and drink for children
- ◆ Contribute to children's personal hygiene
- ◆ Respond to illness in children
- ◆ Plan and provide quiet periods for children

Have a look through the elements and use the personal skills profile, which you will find in Chapter 1, to identify which areas you feel confident about and which you need to gain further experience or training in. If you have any evidence from past experience, make sure it is up to date and can be authenticated as your own work.

> **Remember!**
> To check your cross-referencing sheet to see whether you have relevant evidence from other units. If you think some of the evidence for this unit will fit another unit, write it on the appropriate sheet.

If you need further training, find out what is available in your assessment centre or Early Years Development and Childcare Partnership, or do your own reading and research. When you're ready for assessment, plan with your assessor how you want to gather your evidence. If you're a childminder or work in a full day care setting, one observation by your assessor could cover the whole dinnertime routine. You can supervise the children going to the toilet and washing hands, organise their dinnertime and then plan and provide a quiet time after the meal when some children may have a sleep while others have quiet activities. If you work in a setting where you are not involved in preparing meals, it may be more difficult to organise. Your observation may have to be based on snack times, cookery sessions, a party or picnic.

Element C2.1 Plan, prepare and provide food and drink for children

Key issues

This element requires a good understanding of nutritional requirements for healthy eating. You need to know the dietary requirements of children who have allergies or medical conditions, and of those who have particular beliefs and values. You need to provide eating aids appropriate for the age and stage of development of the child, and know about special equipment for children with disabilities which make eating difficult. In addition, you have to be scrupulous about food hygiene, and health and safety requirements. We strongly recommend that you gain a recognised food hygiene certificate. Most early years training providers give you the opportunity to take this course as part of your NVQ.

Which type of evidence?

Your assessor has to *observe* all of the PCs and one aspect of each range category for this element. If you are not directly involved in preparing and serving meals, your assessor will be able to observe snack time and a cookery session, but this may not provide all the evidence you will need. You could try to arrange to spend some time in the kitchen if your setting has one, or think about other situations where you have prepared meals - perhaps you have organised a picnic or a party for children. Write a *candidate diary* or *reflective account* of events like these. Think about how you would cater for children of different ages when you are writing your account. You can use *work products* such as records of children's dietary requirements and menus, but don't just put in your setting's menu if you had no part in preparing it. Ask if you can help to prepare a menu if your setting provides meals. If not, write a menu yourself, showing your awareness of nutritional values. Include your food hygiene *certificate* to supplement your evidence, and any other *evidence from past experience.* If you have no experience of working with children with additional needs or special dietary requirements, you will need to do some research and write an *assignment* on how you would fulfil their needs. Check the knowledge requirements so that you include all that you need in one piece of work.

> ### Remember!
> You don't need *all* of this evidence. Choose the most suitable ones for your situation, but you must have direct observation where the standards require it. You will find the formats for the different types of evidence in Chapter 1.

The *knowledge evidence* statements for this element are 1, 2, 3, 4, 5, 7, 8, 11, 12, 13, 16. The articles at the end of the chapter will give you useful information about healthy eating, special diets and food safety, and you can also read books such as *A Practical Guide to Child Nutrition* by Dare and O'Donovan (Stanley Thornes).

Element C2.2 Contribute to children's personal hygiene

Key issues

The key issue in this element is that you need to be meticulous in your personal hygiene, and in the routines you carry out with children. You also need to communicate to the children the importance of good personal hygiene. There is a useful article on the value of health education, and how to put it into practice, in this chapter. Make sure that you know what the legal requirements and the setting's health and safety policies are, and that you are aware of the issues relating to HIV and AIDS. If you take these measures you will minimise the risk of infection being passed from one child to another. It will be worthwhile to have some training in these areas, so find out what is on offer locally.

You need to be aware of the needs of children from different minority ethnic groups in relation to hygiene, and skin and hair care. Families from some religious backgrounds have strict rules about personal hygiene. Black skin usually needs moisturising to keep it in good condition, so check with parents whether you need to use anything while the child is in your care. Make sure African Caribbean children have their hair covered when playing in the sand, because it's difficult to remove, especially if the child has braids or plaits.

Which type of evidence?

Your assessor only needs to observe the first three and last two PCs in this element. This is because it is important to respect the privacy of children during toileting and hygiene routines. If you work with very young children, this may not be an issue, and your assessor may be able to observe more. Otherwise, she may ask you oral questions about how you meet the children's needs, and she may inspect the setting. She will report on her inspection on an observation record and note your answers to her questions on an oral question record. If she is satisfied that you have covered all of the evidence for the PCs and range, you will not need to write any more. If you have previous examples of when you have cared for children who were infectious or had other additional needs, either tell your assessor or write a *reflective account* or *candidate diary* describing how you dealt with it.

If you don't have a knowledge of how to deal with infectious children, or the methods and timing of toilet training, you will need to do some further training or research, using the suggested book list or other materials. You will find an article on toilet training later in the chapter. Write a short *assignment* to cover the areas in which you don't have direct experience. Some of the PCs and range are closely linked to the knowledge evidence, so check through it and cover both together as far as you can. The *knowledge evidence* statements relating to this element are 1, 14, 15, 16, 17, 23.

Element C2.3 Respond to illness in children

Key issues

Children will become ill from time to time while in your care and you need to be able to identify signs and symptoms of common ailments and infectious diseases, or recognise signs of more serious conditions which need urgent medical attention, especially when children are too young to tell you why they feel ill. Remember that children will feel miserable when they are ill, and you will need to comfort and reassure them until their parents arrive. If possible, lie them down in a quiet place, away from the other children, but don't leave them on their own. You need to keep an accurate record of the child's symptoms. Always refer children on to a senior colleague or other professional if you have any doubts. If you are responsible for contacting the parents, don't alarm them unnecessarily, but do give them the facts as clearly as possible.

The setting will have collected information from parents about any chronic conditions their children have, and what the procedures are for dealing with them. Make sure you know the relevant details of the children in your care, and what action you need to take. Many children suffer from asthma, and it's important that you know how to deal with an attack quickly when it occurs.

Your setting will have strict policies about the storing and administering of medicine. It is imperative that you know what they are, and adhere to them strictly.

Unit E3 deals with unconsciousness, and if you have already completed that unit you will be able to cross reference the evidence. We would strongly recommend that you gain a recognised qualification in first aid, so that you can deal confidently with any accident.

Which type of evidence?

Your assessor is only required to carry out *inspection* for two PCs in this unit - to check that medication is stored appropriately and accurately labelled and that your records of any illness are satisfactory. It is unlikely that she will be present when illness occurs, and in any case, the main priority will be the care of the child, not your assessment. However, if you have a work-based assessor she may be in a position to observe you in such a situation, or a colleague could write a *witness testimony.*

Make a note of any children who have become ill in the course of your work, and write a *candidate diary* or *reflective account* of how you cared for them, how you informed the parents and so on. Look through the PCs and the range when you are writing it to make sure that you cover the relevant points. *Work products* can include copies of your setting's policies on dealing with illness and administering medication, and examples of records of children's illness which you have kept (with names removed). Write a brief explanation of how you have used the policies in your work.

The *knowledge evidence* statements related to this element are 1, 14, 16, 18, 19, 20, 21, 24. You will already have much of the evidence you need if you have collected the information we have suggested. For number 18 you will ideally need to have done a basic first aid course, which is also a requirement for E3 number 9.

If there are any gaps in your knowledge, write a short *assignment* to cover them. You may need to do some further reading on some aspects such as symptoms of common illnesses and medical conditions. Step Forward Publishing's *A-Z of Child Health* is a useful reference – see book list on page 24.

Don't forget!
Check that you have evidence which covers all of the range statements and knowledge.

Element C2.4 Plan and provide quiet periods for children

Key issues

Many children don't sleep during the day from the age of three or even younger, and parents sometimes express a wish that their child doesn't have a sleep during the day because it stops them sleeping at night. You may need to come to a compromise with parents about this, if you find that the child really needs a sleep.

It's important that all children, of whatever age, have quiet periods during the day. Where you have some children sleeping and some not, you need to balance the needs of both. You can give the children who stay awake the opportunity to have quiet activities such as reading, small construction, drawing and so on, to give them a chance to relax and unwind. Try to sit and relax with them, rather than using the time to rush around getting jobs done. This will help them to see the value of quiet times and also minimise the amount of disturbance for the sleeping children.

At sleep times for younger children, you need to take account of particular settling routines some children prefer. It's important that you have consulted parents about whether their children need a comfort object or blanket, or whether they like to be cuddled, rocked or massaged as they fall asleep. This will reassure the children and give continuity of care between home and setting routines.

Which type of evidence?

Your assessor will need to **observe** all but two of the PCs and one aspect of each range category. She may have fitted this in with an observation of the dinnertime routine, especially if you work with younger children who usually sleep after dinner, or at least have a quiet time. She may have already observed a quiet time for some of the other activities you have carried out - perhaps at a story time or snack time. Your assessor may ask you **oral questions** about some PCs to ensure that you understand the need for things like adequate ventilation, or being relaxed and unhurried with waking children. If you haven't covered all of the range, write a **candidate diary** or **reflective account** of times when a child has needed to rest or sleep and how you dealt with that, or about how your routine allows for quiet times.

The knowledge evidence statements for this element are 1, 4, 9, 10, 16, 22, 25. Try to cover them in your other evidence. If there are any gaps, write a short **assignment** to provide the evidence, but remember, it doesn't have to be an essay!

In the following pages, you will find some useful articles which cover some of the knowledge you will need for this unit.

The pre-school years are the ideal time to influence children's eating habits. If your setting provides meals or even just snacks, can you be sure that your influence is a good one? Ruth Breese offers some advice on healthy eating and planning a balanced diet

Providing meals and snacks

Eating patterns in childhood often continue into adult life. Whether you offer meals or a simple snack you have the chance to affect the long-term health of children in your care. Eating is also a social and educational occasion and should be enjoyable. You can show this through the meals, snacks and drinks you provide, as well as through what you teach and by example.

Even if you have a Reception class in a school you can introduce children to different healthy foods and give guidance to parents on what their children might bring in for snacks at break-time or in their lunch boxes.

The key to healthy eating

From six months of age, children can be given most family foods, with the aim of slowly moving them on to a healthy adult diet by the age of five. Healthy eating guidelines for adults are not appropriate for the under twos, but between the age of two and five you can gradually start reducing the amount of fat eaten (for example, swapping full cream milk for semi-skimmed) and increasing portions of bread, other cereals and potatoes.

A balanced diet is achieved by eating a variety of foods from each of five food groups:

■ Bread, other cereals and potato (including breakfast cereal, rice, pasta, noodles)

■ Fruit and vegetables (all types, fresh or frozen; fruit tinned in juice is also suitable)

■ Meat, fish and alternatives (eggs, beans, lentils, nuts*)

■ Milk and dairy foods (cheese, yoghurt or fromage frais)

■ Foods containing fat and foods containing sugar (in moderate quantities**)

* Many nurseries no longer use any nuts because of the risk of an allergic reaction. Whole nuts should never be given to children under the age of five because of the risk of choking.

** Teeth are more prone to decay if sugar is consumed frequently during the day and/or for a long time (for example, chewing sweets, sucking at a bottle for half an hour). For this reason sugar-free between-meal snacks are recommended (raw carrot, slices of apple, savoury biscuits), as are sugar free drinks such as milk and water. It is also good practice to encourage children to take drinks from a cup rather than sucking them from a bottle.

Most children need three meals a day with nutritious snacks between meals. This balanced diet should be followed by all children regardless of any food restriction due to religion or illness.

What about special diets?

If a special diet is required, the child should have seen a State Registered Dietician. Always ask parents for a copy of their child's diet sheet. Contact their State Registered Dietician if you have any concerns. For most special diets, only a few foods have to be omitted, so most of the food given to other children can be used. Substitute a food from the same food group if possible (for example, swap meat for lentils or rice for bread). If a whole food group has to be removed (for example, dairy products due to milk intolerance), a substitute is usually available - check what the parents use. If you use ready prepared foods, check labels carefully to make sure that they do not contain the foods children should avoid.

Remember to think about the child on a special diet when you plan a food-related activity and try to use foods that they can eat. For example if a child has diabetes, a session making cakes may worry the child unless you include a low sugar cake. Let the child know before the session that the food being prepared is suitable for them.

Catering for vegetarians

There are many different types of vegetarian, so check exactly what every child is allowed to eat.

Lacto-vegetarians avoid all meat and fish, but will eat dairy products.

Lacto-ovo-vegetarians eat as above, but also include eggs.

Many people call themselves vegetarian but just avoid red meat while eating poultry and fish.

Vegans eat no animal products at all. Instead they eat vegetables, pulses, fruit, cereals, nuts and seeds.

Most Hindus, Muslims, Sikhs and Rastafarians will not eat meat; many also avoid fish, eggs and cheese.

Use beans and lentils instead of meat and fish. If the family eats eggs, these are also a good substitute for meat. If a child does not eat dairy products, you will need to check which soya milk (fortified with calcium), they use at home. Many manufactured foods, such as biscuits or food in breadcrumbs, contain animal products so it is best to check labels and buy vegetarian varieties of these foods as they are suitable for all. There are many vegetarian cookbooks which will give you some good ideas for meals.

Some nurseries find that it is easier to provide meat-free meals for all the children when a high percentage are vegetarian. If this is easiest for you, advertise it in your prospectus.

So what can you give children?

Children's appetites vary enormously, so it is impossible to give you a meal plan that will suit all of them. You should aim to use as wide a variety of foods as possible. It might be a good idea to give parents a taste of some of the meals you offer at open evenings.

Main meals

Lasagne with chopped salad vegetables followed by fromage frais

Bean casserole with rice followed by yoghurt

Macaroni cheese with peas followed by sliced fruit

Shepherds' pie with carrots followed by rice pudding

Lentil curry with chappati and yoghurt followed by tinned fruit

Roast meat with mashed potatoes and vegetables followed by milk jelly

Grilled fish fingers with chips and ratatouille

Snack meals

Baked beans or scrambled egg on toast

Smooth peanut butter* or ham sandwiches

Hummus, mashed egg or grated cheese with mayonnaise on toast, pitta bread or sliced chappati

Small baked potato with grated cheese or tuna fish followed by fruit, yoghurt or a small cake

*check for allergies

What if they refuse to eat?

The pre-school years are a common time for asserting independence, especially around food. This is best tackled before it becomes a problem, so you and the parents need to agree your approach to food. For example:

■ the routine of meals and snacks for the child;

■ being consistent in the approach to food and meal times;

■ not allowing the child to fill up on sugary drinks and sugary/fatty snacks to the detriment of meals or more nutritious snacks;

■ identifying foods genuinely disliked.

If an approach does not work, discuss it with the parents before making any changes. It helps if staff eat their meals with the children. This will show that food is enjoyable as well as teaching some of the social aspects of eating.

> Think about the messages any reward system gives the children. Giving a child a gold star is just as rewarding as giving a sweet, but lasts longer, is kinder to their teeth and does not reinforce the idea that sweets are a reward.

Learning about food

The pre-school years are an ideal time to permanently influence the eating habits of children. Food tasting and cooking sessions are popular and can introduce children to new tastes and experiences. Many nurseries have food tasting at least once a week. Trying a different fruit is very popular. Your local supermarket may be able to provide the fruit for you, or even organise a session.

A wide range of books and teaching packs are available on food related issues. Contact your local library or Health Promotion Department for advice.

Information for parents

It helps if you let parents know your policies on food and drink, both at meal times and during sessions.

Some nurseries include a statement about this in their prospectus. For example: 'This nursery has a healthy eating policy so a balanced meal is provided daily containing meat or an alternative, potato or rice and a vegetable. A fruit based pudding follows' or 'While we do not provide meals, there is a break in each session when the children are given a drink and a snack. This nursery has a healthy eating policy so we offer milk or water to drink and toast, fruit or a savoury biscuit to eat.'

Make sure that the information you give parents is accurate. You might want to consider training on infant feeding issues. It is worth contacting your local Dietetic Department or College of Further Education to see what courses are available.

Further information on feeding children can be obtained from health visitors or State Registered Dietitians. You can get resources such as leaflets, posters and teaching packs from your local Health Promotion Departments.

Ruth Breese, community dietician

Whether you provide hot meals for the children in your care or just a drink and a biscuit, there are certain regulations which by law you must keep to. Rob Chapleo, an environmental health officer, offers a quick guide and lists common hygiene hazards

Food safety

Young children are vulnerable to food poisoning and other infectious intestinal diseases, but many cases can be prevented by employing simple hygienic practices.

Safe food
Most cases of food poisoning are caused by poor temperature control or by unintentional contamination. These cases can be avoided by training food handlers in hygiene techniques, identifying where food may be exposed to conditions favourable to the growth of bacteria or to contamination, and using the techniques to ensure safe food.

Training
It is vital that all food handlers receive proper training. Suitable courses include the

Registration as food premises
Local authorities have a duty to register premises where any food and drink, even a milk and biscuit, is dispensed. Proprietors of registered nurseries who care for more than six children, not including those for whom they have parental responsibilities, are also required to register as a food business if they provide any food or drink. If your nursery or pre-school is run from a church or village hall or community centre, the premises may already be registered. This is something you should check.

Inspections
All nursery proprietors who dispense food are required to comply with the food hygiene regulations and will have their premises inspected by the local council's environmental health officer. However, compliance is usually not as onerous as some people think. Inspectors will look for evidence that the nursery or pre-school is generally in good repair and clean and that the factors outlined in the rest of this page are being addressed.

Basic Food Hygiene Certificate of the Chartered Institute of Environmental Health. Your local council environmental health department will be able to give details of a convenient course.

Relevant legislation
- The Food Premises (Registration) Regulations 1991
- The Food Safety Act 1990
- The Food Safety (General Food Hygiene) Regulations 1995
- The Food Safety (Temperature Control) Regulations 1995

Temperature control
Food left out at room temperature allows bacteria to grow. Many people assume that cold food is safer than a hot meal. This is not so; it must be kept in a clean refrigerator which is large enough to hold all cold egg, meat, fish and dairy products, pies, salads, and so on, until they are served. Sandwiches are a risky commodity and packed lunches should be kept in the refrigerator. Milk should also be kept chilled. Hot food must be quickly cooled or kept really hot.

Personal cleanliness
It is human nature to take short cuts. Careful observation of working kitchens proves that many food handlers, rushing to provide food, would rather wipe their hands on their apron or cloth, for example, than use a wash basin which is out of reach. It is imperative not only that basins are conveniently accessible but that food handlers are trained to use them regularly. The skin is a haven for food poisoning bacteria, especially after hands have been used for inherently dirty activities.

Hazard spotting
Nursery and pre-school kitchens are potential minefields for risks of contamination.
Points to watch out for include:
- unauthorised entry by cats, dogs and flies
- uncontrolled dirty laundry
- unwashed children

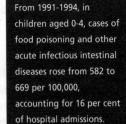
From 1991-1994, in children aged 0-4, cases of food poisoning and other acute infectious intestinal diseases rose from 582 to 669 per 100,000, accounting for 16 per cent of hospital admissions.

- use of the kitchen as a potting shed, chemical laboratory and boot wash area!

Catering arrangements are all different. Nursery managers must look at what food and drink is provided and how it is prepared and served in their particular business. You must:
• Identify the hazards ie the points at which things can go wrong, including:
- growth of bacteria
- survival of bacteria
- opportunities for contamination
• Decide which points are critical and which, if not controlled, may lead to food safety problems. For example, if food is undercooked then it may allow poisoning bacteria to survive.

• Ensure effective controls and monitoring. For example, a control is the thorough cooking of meat. The monitoring would be the measuring, from time to time, of the temperature of the meat to ensure that the time given in the oven is enough to ensure thorough cooking. This is especially important in the case of microwave cooking where the power of an oven deteriorates over time.

• Review the system. From time to time look again at what food service is being provided, whether any changes have been made, hazards introduced, and whether different controls need to be implemented.

For more detailed guidance on any of the areas covered here your first point of contact should be your local environmental health department.

Rob Chapleo, environmental health officer

Different settings have developed their own approaches to snack time as a way of promoting children's learning. Here are three tried and tested good ideas

Approaches to snack time

Learning independence

There are always a few surprised faces when I inform parents (and teachers, I should add!) that we do not have a set time for our drinks, but instead allow the children to decide WHEN to have their drink, WHAT to have and WHO to sit with.

We have a drinks table seating three children, to be used throughout the session, encouraging the children to be independent in another activity in the classroom. It does take a while to 'train' the children to select a cup, pour themselves a drink and put their empty cup in the bucket (and they do need occasional reminders!) but probably no longer than it takes to train them to wear an apron during water play and replace it after tidying up. We do have spills, though very rarely (honestly!) and there is a cloth for the children to clear up after themselves. We aim not to interrupt their free-flowing play and incorporate the drinks table as yet another learning activity within the classroom which encourages each child's independence.

Julie Taylor, Poringland Primary School, Norfolk.

Time out

A four-hour period between breakfast and dinner is a long haul for a young child. We have found that setting a little time aside for milk and a biscuit provides not just sustenance but a relaxed and reassuring 'bridge' between nursery/playgroup and school. It is a time when even the most fidgety child will happily sit in a circle absorbing the conventions of courtesy and patience, recognising the social importance of this shared experience, passing cups, pouring, accepting and quietly eating a biscuit. It is 'time out' for the children when few demands are made but much incidental learning takes place through talk, games and counting.

We organise milk time ten minutes before playtime, when the Reception children accompany the classroom assistant to the hall. In a mixed classroom this confers another advantage, as I am able to spend this time on more challenging blends and number bonds with a blissfully quiet Year 1 group.

Claire Jordan, Carleton Rode Primary School, Norfolk.

Fruit platters

We decided on a healthy snack time when our nursery first opened. I based snack time on the Australian idea of 'sharing fruit with our friends'.

Each child brings in a piece of fruit, cheese, carrot sticks, raisins or even bread sticks. The children then help to prepare the fruit platters and pour the drinks (we take it in turns).

The fruit platters are sometimes a good discussion point - occasionally we deliberately omit a type of fruit and ask 'What is missing today?' Or we add a different fruit, such as pineapple, and discuss the smell/flavour.

The children have cups of water to drink - most children do drink water, although some parents say they don't!

During snack time the adults sit with the children, and fruit time becomes an informal circle time for chatting. We pass the fruit platter around the table, deciding and discussing what we will choose to eat next.

Occasionally, we have a different healthy food day - we tried various breads one day, and different cheeses another day.

The aims for our fruit time are to:
- ❑ promote healthy eating and drinking
- ❑ share with our friends
- ❑ make choices and perhaps try new food
- ❑ enjoy our snack (it doesn't matter if we forget to bring a snack sometimes - there is always enough to go round)
- ❑ sit with our friends and socialise at snack time
- ❑ encourage independence in helping to prepare the fruit and drinks
- ❑ use fruit time as another learning experience
- ❑ encourage politeness - 'please', 'thank you', sharing.

Snack time is a healthy, educational, happy part of our new nursery routine.

Heather Kirby, Hillside Avenue Nursery, Norfolk.

The contributions on this page all appeared first in Norfolk County Council's Early Years Newsletter (March 1998) and are reproduced with their kind permission.

Rob Chapleo lists some basic hygiene precautions which are neither complicated nor expensive. Following them will help to maintain the health, safety and welfare of both your young customers and yourselves

Personal hygiene and disinfection

Hand hygiene

• The single most important measure in reducing cross-infection is hand washing, but studies have shown that it is rarely carried out properly. The areas of the hands which are often missed are the wrist creases, thumbs, finger tips and under finger nails. Jewellery should, for this reason, be kept to an absolute minimum by carers (wedding band only) and removed while washing.

• **When?**
Hands should be washed:
  - after handling contaminated articles
  - after using the toilet, blowing the nose, covering a sneeze
  - whenever hands become visibly dirty
  - before eating, drinking or handling food, and before and after smoking.

• **How?**
  - wet the wrists and hands before applying soap
  - apply the soap all over, rub vigorously and lather well
  - rinse under running water
  - dry thoroughly, especially between the fingers

• **What with?**
  - liquid soap is preferable to bar soap which can harbour bacteria
  - a bactericidal detergent is best

• **Where?**
  - in a separate wash basin rather than the kitchen sink
  - wash basins must be located close to toilets and it is good practice to have one by the entrance to kitchens
  - hot and cold water must be supplied or water mixed to about 45 degrees centigrade
  - any towel on which the same part can be used more than once is not recommended. Paper towels are best.

• All cuts, abrasions and moist skin conditions should be covered with a waterproof dressing, preferably coloured so that if it falls off it can be more easily retrieved.

Toilet regulations

The 1989 Children Act says that there must be a minimum of one toilet to every 10 children regardless of the age of the children, the premises or the type of care. There is no stipulation about separate boys' and girls' toilets. If possible, urinals and toilet pedestals should be of a size to suit small children.

There should be one wash-hand basin with warm water for every ten children. Supervise and insist on the hand-washing routine.

In sessions that are open for more than four hours there must be a separate staff toilet. Different authorities may have different standards but inspectors will check annually that these regulations are being met.

Excreta, blood and body fluids

Excreta, blood and body fluids are potentially infectious and precautions are necessary to prevent exposure. Bleach, disposable gloves, towels and plastic bags are essential items for dealing with emergencies and accidents and they should be stored together as an emergency kit.

• A disposable apron and gloves should always be worn.

• When attending to children with diarrhoea, special care must be taken with clothing and other contaminated articles. They should be sponged and then hot washed. The sponge should be thrown away.

• Spillages should be cleaned up as quickly as possible and other children must be kept away.

• Liquid bleach should be used to clean and disinfect after all spillages except for urine, which should be cleared up with paper towels before washing the area with detergent solution.

• If possible, diluted bleach should be poured directly over a blood spill, covered with paper towels and mopped up after two minutes with more disposable towels which are then plastic-bagged and disposed of. The site of the spillage should then be disinfected again after the gross spillage has been cleared.

Disinfection

The routine use of disinfectants for general cleaning is unnecessary. Thorough regular use of detergent and hot water is sufficient for routine purposes, except for items which are contaminated with body fluids.

All disinfectants are potentially hazardous and must be used with caution and in accordance with the manufacturers' instructions. An assessment of the products should form part of the assessment of risk required by the Control of Substances Hazardous to Health Regulations 1994 (COSHH). Your local environmental health officer can give advice on this.

Babies' bottles, teats

• Use pre-sterilised or terminally heat-treated feeds.
• Use pre-sterilised teats and bottles.
• Wash thoroughly, then immerse in hypochlorite solution (125 ppm available chlorine), such as Babysafe or Milton, for a minimum of 30 minutes.

Baby scales

Wipe with detergent and water. Rinse and dry using paper towels.

Crockery, cutlery, feeding cups

Machine wash with rinse temperature above 80 degrees centigrade and dry in air. Or, hand wash with detergent and hot water. Hot rinse and air dry.

Cleaning toilets

Brush the pan using lavatory cleaner. Wash toilet seats with detergent and dry. After use by child with diarrhoea, or if grossly contaminated, clean both sides with hypochlorite (bleach solution) or other chlorine-based disinfectant. Rinse and dry.

Toys

Most toys can either be laundered or washed with detergent and water. If heavily contaminated, they should be disposed of.

How many children know why they should wash their hands and how to wash their hands properly? From my experience of washing more than 2,000 pairs of little hands recently the answer would have to be 'not many', says Marie Ashford

Children and handwashing

Hands are one of the main ways in which bacteria is transferred to food, causing illness in the form of food poisoning. Hands are also responsible for spreading viruses amongst children. Bacteria transmitted to towels are transferred to other hands using that towel.

Many infections are passed to children from animals, especially pets. A large number of dogs and cats carry the salmonella bacteria in their gut and because of their cleaning habits these bacteria are also present in their mouths. That is why children should be discouraged from allowing animals to lick them and to make sure they wash their hands after stroking or handling pets.

The problem children have with handwashing is that bacteria and viruses cannot be seen with the naked eye. They believe that if their hands look clean then they are clean.

When to wash hands
❏ after going to the toilet
❏ before touching and eating food
❏ if they look or feel dirty
❏ after playing with pets
❏ after coughing, sneezing or blowing your nose
❏ during and after farm visits

How to wash
❏ use soap and warm water
❏ rub the soap over both sides of your hands
❏ between every finger and around nails
❏ rinse off with clean warm water
❏ dry hands properly - with a clean towel, paper towels or hot air dryer

So how can we help children to understand about germs, when they should wash their hands and how to wash them properly?

Understanding about germs
Explain that germs:
❏ are all around us
❏ most are good, only some are bad and can make us ill
❏ that you can't see them with your eyes
❏ that washing hands gets rid of the germs

What conditions do germs like? You can carry out an experiment to show this. Take some slices of bread and ask the children to touch half with dirty hands. (Their hands do not have to be obviously dirty - maybe they have not washed their hands after playing outside.) Next, place a clean and a dirty piece of bread in different conditions - dry/moist, warm/cold, dark/light. Leave the bread for a few days to encourage good mould growth.

Talk about how the 'cleaner' bread in dry/cold conditions has less mould growth than the dirty bread in moist/warm conditions, remembering that bacteria need food, moisture, warmth and time to grow.

The yes/no game
This should be carried out after some group discussion on germs and handwashing. Have all the children sitting on the mat. Ask simple questions such as:

❏ Can you see germs with your eyes?
❏ Should you wash your hands after going to the toilet?
❏ Should you wash your hands before eating your lunch?
❏ Does your cat's coat have germs on it?
❏ If your hands look clean might they have germs on them?

The children should reply yes or no to every question. This game can also be played by raising hands for yes or by standing up for yes, staying sitting for no.

Painting hands
This can be carried out at a wash basin or by using bowls of warm water on a stand or table, preferably on a one-to-one basis.

❏ Each child puts on a protective shirt or apron.
❏ Put washable paint on their hands which they rub in, especially between the fingers and around the thumbs and wrists.
❏ The child washes their own hands with warm water and soap (running water is preferable) to remove the paint.
❏ After washing talk about how well they washed their hands and whether any paint is left. Discuss the importance of rubbing the soap well into the whole of the hand - front and back and of rinsing properly.
❏ The hands are dried well with paper towels or a clean hand towel.

Marie Ashford, health promotion officer

Managing personal hygiene is a basic life skill which all children need to learn. It even figures in the list of Early Learning Goals. Whatever your setting, it has implications for the facilities you provide as well as the care you offer

Toilet regulations and routines

Accommodation requirements for maintained nursery schools and classes are specified in the Education (School Premises) Regulations 1998. The Children Act 1989 makes specific recommendations about certain facilities for providers who are registered with the local authority, including day care settings. However, there is little standard guidance relating to children's lavatories. What there is tends to be fairly basic.

Each local authority has its own regulations - or interpretation of the Children Act - which tend to focus on good hygiene practice and issues such as number of toilets.

The D*f*EE (Architects and Building Branch) publishes a useful booklet, called *Designing for Three- to Four-Year-Olds*, which briefly covers the main points for consideration. These include:

❑ There should be at least one toilet - of a suitable size/height - for every ten children in your setting (this applies to schools as well as the voluntary and private sector) with at least the same number of washbasins.
❑ Lavatories should be accessible and easily supervised from the playroom. It is an advantage if they can be reached from the main entrance and outdoor play areas.
❑ The design should allow privacy for the children and space for adults to give assistance yet permit adequate supervision, for example half-height partitions and doors. (Some purpose-built settings now have vision panels in outer doors to enable staff to see in if they need to while still affording children some privacy.) Children should be able to close the cubicle door. If it is bolted on the inside the latch should be so situated that an adult can reach

over to open the door if necessary.
❑ Consideration should be given to making at least one cubicle big enough for children (or visitors) with physical disabilities. There should be wheelchair access.

Good hygiene practice

Children use adults as role models - if they see people caring for themselves and promoting good hygiene practices, they will pick up the good habits themselves.

It is your responsibility to keep toilet areas clean, store cleaning materials safely, and maintain hygiene standards to ensure that the risk of infection is minimised. Each setting should have policies and procedures in place for dealing with bodily fluids, and the arrangements for disposal. You should have guidance on HIV and AIDS for the protection of everyone in the setting.

The overall cleanliness of the toilet area is important - that involves wall and floor surfaces as well as changing mats. Wall and floor surfaces should be washable and durable so that everything can be wiped down easily. Staff should be aware that it is their responsibility to clean up any mess or

Designing for Three- to Four-Year-Olds (ISBN 0 85522 986 1) is available from DfEE Publications; tel 0845 6022260. Quote ref D34YO

spillages that they notice. Make sure that helpers, too, understand the importance of cleaning up bodily fluids.

Staff should be aware of using gloves at all times for their own protection, whether cleaning up, wiping bottoms or changing nappies, and washing their hands and changing gloves after dealing with each child. Many settings now have separate bags for everyday rubbish and clinical waste/soiled articles.

Cleaning cloths can be washed or boiled. Flannels should be used once and then washed.

Lidded bins need to be at child height so if you're asking children to wipe their hands on paper towels they can dispose of them themselves. Most settings use paper towels as some hot air dryers can blow out very hot air. Use disposable paper towels in preference to cloth towels.

Children who are potty training should have named individual potties.

Dealing with accidents

It must be accepted that accidents will happen and you need to expect them and know what to do when they happen. Staff should be understanding and deal with them promptly and quietly without a fuss, with respect for the child's feelings.

They should reassure the child and tell them not to worry, then take them to the toilet to wash them and change their clothes. There could be a puddle or mess on the floor so it might even take two members of staff - one to make sure the area is cleaned up properly and the other to take the child to the toilet.

'Parents and carers need to realise that children may be capable of going to the toilet but that accidents are still likely to happen, often simply because the child is so engrossed in their play that they forget to ask.'

Parents and carers need to realise that children may be capable of going to the toilet but that accidents are still likely to happen, often simply because the child is so engrossed in their play that they forget to ask. Accidents are just that, accidents - they are seldom a deliberate action.

However, if they happen more regularly it can sometimes indicate an underlying emotional difficulty or physical problem and obviously this is something you should discuss with parents.

Most settings ask for parents to supply a spare set of clothing and some build up their own store. Soiled clothes may be rinsed out and sent home with the child at the end of the session or day. If clothes are washed out, follow the correct procedures, in other words, wear gloves and disinfect the areas used for washing.

Staff must always be vigilant in their observations of children in their care. Some parents may expect to toilet train too soon, or think that wetting and soiling is a sign of

disobedience. The parents could be advised to wait until their child is ready to be toilet trained, and to be understanding about accidents. If you notice bruises or marks around the bottom and genital areas of a child, you may feel that there could be a possible problem of abuse of that child.

Allowing time

In pre-school settings, whether within a home or group, children need to gradually become more independent when using the toilet, overseen by the adult, until such time as the child can competently use the toilet and wash hands properly. The time that this takes will depend on each child individually, and the adult must not underestimate the importance of allowing time for the child to become independent in this way.

Allowing time for children to learn how to deal with, for example, fastenings on their clothes, will take time. Patience on the part of the adult and offering praise, will give the child confidence. Rushing the child will cause delay in the long term.

Toilet training would be expected to be completed by the time a child enters the Reception class, although it is accepted that accidents will occasionally happen. With the exception of children with special needs, children would be expected to be able to go to the toilet unaided. It is up to individual teachers to decide how they want to manage procedures - whether they allow children to go freely or all together at set times. The current thinking

Always check that there is soap, especially in school toilets where teachers are less likely to accompany children. Children won't ask!

is that children should be allowed to go whenever they need to go at whatever age. All staff members need to be aware that they should not expect young children to wait too long as it can be harmful and uncomfortable.

The unknown
■ Segregated toilets
A lot of day nurseries have shared toilet facilities. When they start school, children need to learn that there are separate toilets for boys and girls. This can be a big adjustment for some children at a time when there are so many other new things to take on board. Reception teachers can help by making time to introduce children to the different areas of the school which may be unfamiliar, perhaps pointing out the symbols on the doors or the words 'girls' and 'boys'.

■ Urinals
Boys who have not seen a urinal before may spend some time in the school toilets investigating this new discovery! This could be overcome by parents or carers taking male children to public toilets, where urinals are found, and familiarising the child.

■ 'Big toilets'
In some schools, children may only be able to use adult-sized toilets, which can prove difficult for the child who has only ever used a small toilet or had a child seat placed over the adult seat. Children who are wheelchair users should be provided with accessible facilities. Privacy is especially important for a child with special needs who may need more assistance.

■ Routines
In the Reception class, the child should be able to ask to go to the toilet at any time. You will know from experience which child has a genuine reason for asking to be excused. As children get older, they accept that break and meal times are the opportunity to use the toilet. Remember that, even for adults at times, a call of nature cannot be ignored.

Liz Wilcock

Liz Wilcock provides some background information to help you understand the stages in a child's development prior to them joining your pre-school group - and, remember, allowances will need to be made because children develop at different rates

Stages in toilet training

For most adults, cleanliness is important and personal hygiene is a part of everyday routine. Babies, on the other hand, do not understand about being clean. They feel no disgust at emptying their bowels into a nappy. They have no control of their bowels and bladders, and the use of them is an automatic, reflex action. The timing of toilet training should not be determined by the adult at whim, but should only begin when the child is ready. Success is likely if the training is relaxed and unhurried.

There is no point in attempting to start toilet training until there is a sign that the child is ready, and there is a wide variation in the age range at which this will happen.

At 12 months
At about one year of age, the baby's brain is not developed enough to interpret messages from the bladder or bowel that they need emptying. As the brain is responsible for the way the body works, babies need practice at learning skills, such as toilet training, to let their brain receive messages that the skill is being developed.

A potty can be introduced to the baby at this age as a plaything. Some parents may be heard to boast with pride that their baby was potty trained by six to nine months of age - the reality is that the timing was probably luck. A child should never be placed on a potty before they can sit comfortably on it. A fear of overbalancing would take a considerable time to overcome. The child's feet should reach the floor, and the child should be able to sit up alone.

At 15 months
At about 15 months, the child will have the sensation of the bowel and bladder emptying, and may show this by indicating in some way to the parent or carer. Usually, the

child will recognise the sensation of a full bowel before a full bladder.

Most children empty their bowels at a regular time each day. If the parent or carer encourages the use of the potty at this time, the child will possibly use it. Praise is important to children as they develop. The child should be praised if the potty is used - disapproval must not be shown if the potty is not used. This will cause unnecessary upset for the child. The adult should encourage good hygiene practice from the start, always washing the child's hands after the potty has been used. All children of this age will need help in matters of personal hygiene, especially children with special needs, who may need help for a longer time.

At 18 months
At about 18 months of age, a child should be sitting on the potty at regular times of the day. It will help if the child has seen other children using the potty or toilet, so that they can gain an understanding of the process used, and the hygiene arrangements in place. Some children feel insecure about not wearing a nappy. The child should not be hurried into not wearing a nappy until he/she is happy about this. Talking to children about what is happening helps the learning process, and the child will come to understand that everyone uses the toilet, washes their hands, and keeps the area clean.

At 21 months
At about 21 months, the child will have a good awareness of bladder and bowel sensations. Potty training will be well underway, possibly even completed with some children. The potty will be used regularly, and the child may well be using 'the big toilet'. Some children are unsure of

the adult-sized toilet, and the flushing sounds of the water. A toddler-sized seat can be placed over the adult seat, and a step placed so that the child can sit with their feet on a firm surface.

Age two
The independent two-year-old will love the praise given to them when the potty is used. The child will show determination in pulling pants up and in washing hands.

Even if the child is out of nappies during the day, one may still be needed at night time, and during the day time nap.

Age three
Most three-year-olds have full bladder and bowel control during the day, and many will be trained at night as well. The child is able to retain the contents of the bowel and bladder for up to five hours.

Liz Wilcock

Important issues relating to healthy living are approached in a number of different ways and it is sometimes difficult to decide which is the most effective for young children. Jean Evans explores the options and advocates an integrated approach through both planned and routine activities

The value of health education

Health education is about much more than keeping clean and eating well. Young children need to be aware of how their bodies work. They need to know about changes that take place when they are active or when they are ill, and to understand the reasons why they should keep themselves clean, eat well and have regular exercise. If they feel confident with these things and comfortable with their bodies, then they will grow in self-esteem and feel good about themselves as individuals. Children who are developing this inner confidence of mind and body at a young age will be more capable of coping with the changes associated with growing up and, later, dealing with some of the adverse influences of society, such as smoking, alcohol and drugs.

Different approaches

Many settings invite appropriate visitors, such as a dentist or nurse, to talk to the children. This approach, although providing valuable occasional experiences, does not ensure that important messages are reinforced on a regular basis.

Others plan a specific weekly time for health education, incorporating planned activities and appropriate resources. This ensures more regular experiences but treats health education as a separate subject rather than seeing it as part of the child's whole development.

The topic approach favoured by many settings overcomes this to some extent as health issues are introduced across all six areas of

learning. However, the danger with this is that messages may have less emphasis as activities are planned to fit the learning area and topic subject.

A completely integrated approach to health education, one that is flexible and is integrated into planning, routines and regular activities, is the best way to reinforce messages consistently. This approach should also involve the children's families and local community and take account of the children's views and needs.

Teamwork

The best way to begin is by getting together as a staff team to make a list of what you would expect to find in an environment promoting healthy living, for example detailed policies, a consistent approach to the presentation of food, regular opportunities for exercise and the constant involvement of parents. You can then make more detailed plans of how you will cover the points raised and who will be

responsible. There may be some issues important to your setting, such as shortcomings in meeting the dietary needs of the children at home. If this is the case, you may be able to provide training to inform and support parents and carers or perhaps consider providing nutritious meals in your setting.

Children's views and skills

Your starting point must be with what the children already know, so ask them what the word 'healthy' means. Prompt them with appropriate questions to encourage them to express their ideas. Give clear explanations to extend their understanding. Once you have established what the children know about keeping healthy, ask them what it feels like to be healthy. Do they know who helps them to keep healthy and what they can do themselves? How do their own actions and the actions of others make them feel? Having this knowledge of the children's understanding will help during this early planning stage.

It is also useful to have a list of skills you think the children will need, for example, to be self-confident and independent in matters of personal hygiene. You might include the need to make choices, communicate effectively, respect others and have high self-esteem. This list will vary considerably between settings and should take into account each child's home background and family influences.

The Foundation Stage

Foremost in the minds of all practitioners is the need to meet the statutory requirements of the Foundation Stage. Look carefully as a team at the principles for good practice laid down in the *Curriculum Guidance*. Consider them in your planning discussions at all stages. For example, 'practitioners should ensure that all children feel included, secure and valued'. This raises important considerations about your relationships with parents. How can they be developed effectively so that the individual needs of each child can be met? The principle that 'no child should be excluded or disadvantaged' will need to take into account ethnicity, culture or religion, home language, family background, special educational needs, disability, gender and ability.

The Early Learning Goals

Use the *Curriculum Guidance* to help you plan your health education programme by considering each area of learning in turn. For example, one of the significant ways of promoting children's personal, social and emotional well-being is by 'providing opportunities for each child to become a valued member of the group or community so that a strong self-image and self-esteem can be promoted'. An important way to support children's physical development is to 'increase children's understanding of how their bodies work and what they need to be healthy and safe'. Healthy living is clearly linked to these specific aspects of the Foundation Stage.

Next, examine the Early Learning Goals associated with these two statements and think of possible activities to promote them. Links can also be found in other areas, for example the importance of confident use of language to communicate cannot be underestimated and the need to express feelings and ideas through creative media is essential when discovering a sense of self.

Activities and routines

A fully integrated approach to healthy living can be achieved through both planned activities and everyday routines. Base planned activities on the Early Learning Goals. Consider the appropriate learning opportunities created in regular activities such as role play and working with construction equipment and then decide how these opportunities can be varied by rotating resources.

❑ Are the resources easily accessible and do you give the children plenty of choices?

❑ Can they manage in these areas independently, for example putting on aprons, returning equipment to a designated place and washing hands?

Daily routines present many opportunities for children to understand the need for simple rules, personal hygiene and the development of relationships. Analyse how you organise routines such as circle time, meals and snacks, dressing for outdoors, and small and large group activities.

❑ Are you giving consistent messages about health and safety?

❑ Do you encourage parents to continue these messages at home?

❑ If there is a gap between home and group expectancies how can you overcome this or at least narrow the gap by educating families involved in a relaxed, friendly way?

❑ Do parents feel comfortable about spending time in the group?

This is one way of sharing your expectations for good practice.

The next steps

Having looked carefully at the QCA guidance and made a list of appropriate Early Learning Goals you should then be able to incorporate your original ideas for promoting healthy living, your notes on the children's understanding of 'being healthy' and the goals you wish to cover into a curriculum plan for health education. Divide the plan into three sections.

❑ **Daily organisation**

Explain how you will ensure that the indoor and outdoor environment is stimulating, clean, safe and healthy. Include any policies, for example health and safety. Describe how you will plan daily routines to ensure that consistent messages are given. Outline how resources will be organised and rotated in regular activities to give children maximum choice and access.

❑ **Planned activities**

Explain how appropriate activities will be planned and implemented to meet the needs of all members of the group. This will include fitting relevant Early Learning Goals into your overall long-, medium- and short-term planning system. It will list any topics to be undertaken and ensure that there is progression across the Foundation Stage by building in stepping stones for the chosen learning goals.

❑ **Consistent messages**

Explain how all those involved - children, staff, parents, volunteers and students - will be supported so that consistent messages are carried. Do not underestimate the importance of staff as role models. Include equal opportunities and special educational needs policies and the part played by outside professionals. Any necessary training for staff and parents should be included in this section as well as lists of useful contacts. The importance of reaching out into the community should be stressed, for example visits the children could make and how the programme will be linked to the children's home environment.

Make sure that your curriculum plan is reviewed regularly and updated to meet current requirements. Identify weak areas in your practice and modify your plans to overcome these weaknesses.

Make sure that new staff and parents are made aware of your policies and that they follow your good example consistently. Encourage children, too, by giving praise and encouragement for appropriate actions. Spend time with new children ensuring that they feel secure in their new surroundings and understand any simple rules and routines.

By following these step-by-step suggestions it should be easy to create a happy, stimulating environment in which both children and adults demonstrate a positive approach to healthy living.

Jean Evans

To plan an appropriate curriculum for health education you need to know what your children understand about how their bodies work. Jean Evans highlights some key areas and then suggests some headings to use as a framework for your planning

Promoting **healthy** living

Children learn by experience and, until they have had toothache, a sore throat or suffered the irritation of a rash, they will be unaware of the type of discomfort they will be likely to suffer. How can you help children to become familiar with these bodily changes or prepare them beforehand so that they can tell an adult about how they are feeling?

Sharing experiences

Children can be frightened by the unknown. I remember when a friend's three-year-old child came running into the house, distressed, saying that he had 'spilt his teeth all over the garden'. My friend rushed out, unsure what she would find, to discover that he had been sick. He had never been sick before and had been shocked by what was happening to his body and that it was out of his control.

One of the best ways of learning about the symptoms of illness without actually being ill is to share experiences. Children are fascinated by bodily events. We have all experienced the interested group of children gathering round when someone has been sick! Use such an opportunity to take the group away to a quiet area whilst mopping up takes place and ask them to recall when they have been sick and how they felt. Remember to be positive by asking whether they felt better afterwards and explaining why we are sometimes sick. Emphasise that, although being sick is unpleasant, it is usually over quickly.

Injuries

Children can also be frightened by the sight of blood or the pain felt after an injury. Often they will hide or refuse treatment because of this fear of the unknown. Again, share past experiences and introduce role play to act out imaginary scenarios. Look at and handle the items needed to dress wounds and treat injuries on dolls. Invite members of the medical profession to talk

about how they treat people who are hurt. Help children to understand that pain will pass more quickly if it is treated properly.

Aches and pains

It is important to be able to distinguish between children's everyday aches and pains and pain warning of a more serious illness. Children find it difficult to explain where they have a pain and you may not be able to understand their attempts to tell you about it. Topics such as 'All about me', and rhymes, such as 'Head, shoulders, knees and toes', provide useful ways of introducing children to the names of their different body parts. Again, spend time talking about past experiences of aches and pains and the treatment given.

Tiredness and exhaustion

Young children are often unable to tell the difference between tiredness after exercise and the weariness associated with oncoming illness. A young child in my nursery group had suffered considerable illness in his short life, with many hospital visits. He was able to inform staff whether he could manage the planned physical activities or whether he should sit and watch. This knowledge can only come from experience. It is, therefore, important to encourage children to recognise the changes in their bodies after exercise so that they become familiar with normal tiredness, which disappears rapidly after rest, and are then able to tell you when they feel unusually exhausted.

Temperature changes

Children often feel hot after running about but how many will know when they are hot because they are ill? Help them to understand how their bodies heat up normally during exercise. The best way to explain this is by talking about the warm-up exercise at the start of a physical activity session and to finish with a cool-down time. Ask each child in turn to say whether they

are hot, warm, cool or cold so that their awareness of temperature is heightened.

Allergies

Many children suffer from allergies and need to be aware of these so that they can alert adults to avoid certain foods or situations. Discussing allergies with adults, parents and children in the group and talking about the physical effects prevents possible dangers arising. For example, a child with many allergies started at a nursery and her mother compiled a list of the most common ones. However, when the nursery prepared vegetable soup the child suffered a severe reaction. When the mother was telephoned, she knew immediately that it was potato. She had not mentioned it to staff because she did not think nursery children would handle potatoes!

Extending knowledge

Children's understanding of how their bodies work can therefore be increased not only by their own experiences but also by sharing the experiences of others. They can be encouraged to explore these experiences through role play, puppets and small world equipment and also by listening to appropriate stories.

Children should discover more about themselves from several different perspectives. Use these headings as pointers when planning regular activities and as reminders of ideas to promote in your daily routines. They can also be used as a framework for an 'All about me' topic.

❑ How can I keep my body healthy?
❑ How can I keep my body safe?
❑ How am I growing and changing?
❑ Finding out about my feelings and relationships.
❑ Discovering more about my place in the community and environment I live in.

Keeping my body healthy
Inside
Emphasise the importance of eating healthy foods, for example by exploring a selection of fresh vegetables and making soup or having a tasting session with a variety of different fruits. Avoid talking about 'bad' and 'good' foods. Instead stress the importance of eating a balanced diet.

Look at magazines and cut out pictures of different foods. Sort them into piles, such as dairy products, fresh fruit and vegetables, meat and fish, bread and cereals. Make collage pictures of the different categories. Let the children make up a meal of favourite foods by sticking pictures to a paper plate. Display the meals on a board with appropriate captions.

Talk about the importance of drinking regularly. Try making milk shakes using different flavourings.

Talk about how medicine makes us well when we are ill and that it is important to take it, but only in certain amounts and only when given by a known adult. Emphasise that children should never take medicine or tablets themselves.

Talk about how germs are spread and how they enter our bodies. Make a collection of objects that could spread germs, such as a handkerchief, toothbrush and cup, and mix these with some of the children's toys. Ask them to divide them into two groups, things that we share and things that we keep for ourselves. Talk about the reasons for the choices.

Practise using a tissue for sneezes. Fill a spray bottle with water and spray it in the air in front of a child. Ask the child to catch the water with a tissue. Explain that germs are spread by coughs and sneezes and that is why tissues should 'catch them'.

Outside
Make a collection of things we use to keep clean, such as shampoo, soap and bubble bath. Using a large sack as a feely bag, put all the objects inside. Take turns to pull out an object and talk about how we use it.

Invite a parent to come and bath a baby and talk about the items used. Follow up the activity by bathing some dolls.

Make a daily routines chart including washing, bathing and cleaning teeth. Talk about the importance of hygiene routines when visiting the toilet. Hang up some pictorial signs reminding children to wash their hands after a toilet visit.

What happens when we cut our skin? Discuss the importance of washing the wound and look at some of the things, such as plasters and cream, which can be applied. Wash and dress a 'wound' on a doll.

How do we protect ourselves from the weather? Make a display of sunhats, sunglasses, parasols and creams. Make a book about protective clothing and footwear for rain by cutting appropriate pictures from catalogues.

Talk about the pleasurable ways special people show they care, such as kisses and cuddles.

What can we wear to help us to see and hear? Look at a selection of spectacles and hearing aids and talk about how they work.

Keeping my body safe
At home
What do the children think are the dangers in the home? How can they be careful on the stairs? Make a book of electrical appliances using catalogue pictures and look at some examples of electrical appliances. Talk about how they work and emphasise that only adults should handle them. Discuss

the dangers of knives and other sharp utensils. Demonstrate how to hold scissors correctly.

Outdoors
Invite your local road safety or crossing patrol officer to come and talk about appropriate behaviour in traffic. Go for a walk with a small group of children along a busy pavement. If possible, find a pedestrian crossing and show them how to use the controls.

Look at pictures of the sea, rivers and canals. Talk about the dangers of playing near water.

Arrange for a fire engine and crew to visit to emphasise the dangers of fire. Talk about the dangers of playing with matches and appropriate behaviour on Bonfire Night.

Invite a community police officer to talk to the children about speaking to strangers. Discuss when the children can say 'no' and who to turn to when they need help. Encourage them to learn their address and talk about what to do if they get lost.

Real or pretend?
It is important for children to realise the difference between real and fantasy worlds. Make two lists of real and pretend people, animals and places in the children's lives. Encourage them to talk about their fears, for example about monsters. Discuss television programmes they watch. Can they say whether the things they see are real or pretend?

Ask the children if they know what a secret is. When is it good to keep a secret? Are there secrets that we should not keep? Who should we tell?

Growing and changing
Begin by talking about how the body changes as we grow before discussing what is needed to ensure healthy growth. Make a height chart and monitor changes in the children's heights.

Use mirrors and paint self-portraits; discuss differences in features in a positive way.

Make 'All about me' books and include

drawings, photographs, hand and foot prints, favourite foods, toys and places they visit.

Compare photographs of babies, children and adults. Ask parents for two photographs of their child, one as a baby and a recent one. Make a 'lift the flap' display with the baby photograph on top of the recent photograph. Guess who the babies are.

Talk about physical achievements. What can the children do now? What new skills do they expect to develop as they grow older?

How do we manage growing hair and nails? Set up a role-play hair salon and talk about the importance of keeping hair clean. Why should we cut our nails?

Explain how milk teeth fall out and are replaced by stronger adult teeth. How can we prevent teeth from decaying? Put some new toothbrushes and empty toothpaste cartons in the home area and pretend to clean the teeth of nursery dolls. Note: Some nurseries clean teeth as part of the daily routine. However, this must be organised carefully and well supervised as brushes can transmit infection.

Discuss the importance of sleep to restore our bodies after an active day. Talk about bedtime routines. Do the children have favourite bedtime stories or music?

Explain the importance of exercise. What happens during exercise? Ask the children to run or jump until they hear a given signal and then to stand still. How do they feel? Can they feel their hearts beating? Do they feel warmer? What happens to their heart beat if they sit quietly for a while?

Plan some form of lively physical activity for each session. Consider the needs of every child in the group and make sure that some aspects of the course are manageable to everyone.

My feelings and relationships
Encourage the children to express their feelings in different ways. Make sure that the emotional needs of all children in the group are considered and give time for one-to-one work if necessary.

Feelings
Explore a range of music. Lie still and listen to relaxing, soothing music. How does it make the children feel? Dance to music with a strong beat. Can you find music that makes the children feel sad, angry or excited?

Read stories about situations the children may feel worried about. Talk about the characters in the story and encourage the children to relate the events to those in their own lives.

Cut out pictures of faces from magazines, expressing different emotions. Mount them on card and use them to prompt discussions, for example look at an angry or worried face and talk about what might have caused the emotion portrayed.

Relationships
It is important to deal with activities about relationships sensitively and to be aware of the different family circumstances of the children in your group. Ask the children to draw paintings of their families or special people in their lives. Label these and display them.

Talk about the people who love and care for the children. How do they show this love? What do the children do to help the people they live with?

Discuss relationships with siblings. Do the children have to share their toys? Do they have quarrels? How does this make them feel?

What is meant by a friend? Ask the children to choose someone who is a friend and to describe what they like about the person. Sensitively try to ensure that all children are included, perhaps by choosing a child yourself.

Discuss actions that children dislike, such as snatching a toy or pushing. Make a simple list of rules for appropriate behaviour.

What actions do the children consider to be kind? At the end of a session write down one kind action each child feels they have made on a slip of paper. Hang the 'kindness slips' on a small branch as a 'kindness tree'.

My community and the environment I live in
Make a list of the people in your community who help the children to keep healthy. Invite some of these people to visit to talk about their jobs and to emphasise aspects of caring for the body.

Consider the people in the community who help to keep us safe. If possible, organise visits to the places and follow up these visits with appropriate role-play opportunities for the children.

Where are the dangerous places in the locality? Are there rivers or railways? Do the children know the dangers of these places?

Where can the children go for exercise? Do they visit the local swimming pool, gym or parks? Do any of them have dancing lessons? Make a display using children's photographs and paintings and leaflets from the places mentioned.

Where do the children go for family outings? Talk about what they enjoy most. Make a pictorial graph of favourite leisure pursuits.

Display a map and mark on it where the children live with small named flags.

Jean Evans

Chapter 3

Unit E3: Plan and equip environments for children

About this unit

In this unit you will look at the essential aspects of providing and maintaining a safe and secure environment for children. You will think about the sort of furniture and equipment you need to provide, how you organise the physical environment so that the children get the maximum benefit of the space available, and how you ensure that the environment and equipment is kept free from hazards. You will also need to think about how you respond to accidents and emergencies. There are many links between this unit and C2: 'Provide for children's physical needs', so you could do the two units alongside each other, or one after the other, and cross reference as much evidence as possible.

Values

The main emphasis in this unit is on the welfare of the child and keeping children safe. It also requires you, as a reflective practitioner, to think about why you arrange the environment and equipment in a particular way, and whether you could change them to make them better. Sometimes, we arrange furniture and equipment in a particular way because 'that's the way we've always done it', but it may not be the best way, so try experimenting! You also need to think about different types of settings, and the issues related, for example, to childminders working in their own home, or to pre-schools which have to share their accommodation with other organisations.

In Element 2: 'Establish and carry out safety and emergency procedures', you need to ensure that parents are aware of the procedures you will use in the case of accidents and emergencies, and make sure that you have the relevant contact information. You also need to know which other professionals you may need to contact, such as the family doctor. All of this information is collected when the child first starts in the setting. If you work in a group setting, you will need to be aware of the limits of your responsibility, and when to refer a situation on to a more senior member of staff.

In Element 3: 'Select furniture and equipment for children', and Element 4: 'Organise and maintain the physical environment', you need to take account of parental wishes. For instance, if you work with babies, their parents may have a preference

about where their child sleeps during the day (in a cot/pushchair/outside in the fresh air) or what sort of feeding equipment you use. You need to ensure that you know how to adapt furniture and equipment to enable children with disabilities to participate in activities. (Of course, this will vary for each individual.) You also need to reflect cultural diversity and equal opportunities in the equipment you choose. Educational catalogues and book companies have a range of books, toys and equipment which reflect different ethnic groups, non-stereotypical gender roles and people with disabilities.

Getting started

In this unit you will need to show that you can:

- ◆ Establish and maintain a safe environment for children

- ◆ Establish and carry out safety and emergency procedures

- ◆ Select furniture and equipment for children

- ◆ Organise and maintain the physical environment for children

Go through each element and if you need to, use the personal skills profile (page 21) to identify which areas you feel confident about, and where you need to gain further knowledge or experience. Plan how you will gain any necessary experience or knowledge. If you have already done C2, or have other relevant previous experience, have a look at the evidence you have, and cross reference it where possible. When you're ready for assessment, plan either on your own or with your assessor what evidence you will provide, and arrange a date with your assessor for observation and inspection of your setting.

Element E3.1 Establish and maintain a safe environment for children

Key issues

It's crucial that the children's environment is safe and secure, so make sure you know the health and safety legislation requirements for early years settings. Your premises will have been checked by a health and safety officer, who will probably have provided guidelines on the requirements, so that's a good place to start. Be aware of what the staff ratios should be for each age group, and make sure you stick to them. You need to be constantly on the look-out for potential dangers, and never leave children alone, even for a second. Remove and repair, or throw away, any faulty equipment immediately.

Use the articles and check-lists on safety later in the chapter to help you to check how safe your environment is.

Which type of evidence?

You will see that your assessor needs to **observe** you and **inspect the setting** for all of the performance criteria except two. She will probably want to ask you **oral questions** on how much responsibility you have had for organising and maintaining the environment, how well you understand the legal health and safety requirements and how they are reflected in the policies and procedures of the setting.

You can include **policies and procedures** of the setting, but you need to say whether you were involved in putting them in place, or how you use them in your daily work. It would be useful to include a **list** of contents of the first aid box and why certain items are included or not. You could also write a **reflective account** or **diary** to describe how you ensure that the children have a safe environment or how you dealt with particular hazards. Make sure that you cover the full range - your supervisor or a colleague may be able to write a **witness testimony** to cover areas your assessor has not observed.

Don't forget to check the knowledge requirements before you start collecting your evidence. The **knowledge evidence** statements related to this element are 1, 4, 5, 6, 13, 17. You should have covered some of the requirements in the evidence you have provided for the PCs and range. The Royal Society for the Prevention of Accidents has some booklets available on safety (RoSPA, Edgbaston Park, 353 Bristol Road, Birmingham B5 7ST; tel: 0121 248 2000). There are also some useful articles in this chapter.

Don't forget!
Cross reference evidence from other units, especially C2, rather than writing evidence again.

Element E3.2 Establish and carry out safety and emergency procedures

Key issues

This element deals specifically with emergency procedures including fire drills and other emergency evacuations, and first aid in the case of an accident to a child or adult. We very strongly recommend that you take an approved first aid course as part of your NVQ. It's not a requirement, but it means that you can be sure that you are competent in carrying out first aid. There must always be at least one member of staff on site who is a qualified first aider. Always report accidents to the senior member of staff on site, no matter how insignificant. There must also be a record book to record in detail any accidents that occur. This information must be passed on to parents when they come to collect their child, if it has not been serious enough to notify them immediately.

Your setting must have a procedure for fire drill, which is practised regularly, so make sure you know what it is, and try to be involved in carrying out a fire drill as soon as possible if you haven't already done so. If you're a childminder, make sure you have a plan of action in the event of a fire, and practise it regularly. You need to have a list of contact names that you can pick up and take outside quickly and easily. In a group setting, you will also need to take out the register, to ensure that you have all of the children safely outside. Each member of staff should have a particular responsibility, such as checking certain areas as you gather the children together, closing doors as you go, and picking up the contact names and register. Young children are likely to be frightened by the sound of a loud alarm bell, so you need to explain to them beforehand what is going to happen and why you need to practise. Always remain calm and reassuring.

Which type of evidence?

Your assessor needs to **observe** you carrying out an emergency procedure if at all possible, so try to arrange a convenient time with your colleagues and assessor. Only one PC need not be observed. It is unlikely for your assessor to be able to observe you dealing with an accident, unless she happens to be in the setting when it occurs. If it is not possible for her to do any observation, ask a senior colleague to write a **witness testimony**, and write a **reflective account** or **diary** of times when you have dealt with an accident and carried out an emergency procedure. Include a copy of your **emergency procedures** as evidence, and say how you use them, and an example of your **accident record** book. Include a copy of your **first aid certificate** if you have one.

The *knowledge evidence* statements for this element are 3, 7, 8, 9, 10, 18, 19. Try to cover them in your other evidence. If there are any gaps, write a short assignment. You will find a useful article on policies and procedures for accidents and emergencies later in the chapter.

with disabilities and other additional needs. You will find educational catalogues a good source of ideas.

The *knowledge evidence* statements relating to this element are 1, 4, 11, 12, 13. As always, try to cover them in your other evidence, and fill the gaps with a short written assignment if necessary. Check the knowledge statements for E3.4 and write about the two sets together, as they are closely linked. There are some useful articles at the end of this chapter on providing a quality environment for children.

Element E3.3 Select furniture and equipment for children

Key issues
The way you gather evidence for this element will depend a great deal on the setting you work in. If you work in your own home as a childminder, you may not have much space available, and you will need to think about keeping children of all ages safe when they are playing together. For instance, a mobile baby or toddler will be likely to swallow Lego bricks that the four-year-old is playing with. How do you ensure that this doesn't happen?

If you're in a group setting you may not be in a position to make decisions about furniture and equipment. Try to be involved the next time new resources and equipment are being chosen or find out why particular items of equipment have been chosen. Failing that, you could carry out a project on planning an imaginary nursery.

Which sort of evidence?
Your assessor needs to *observe* and *inspect the setting* for three out of the six PCs, and she will also be able to observe what she needs to for E3.4 at the same time. She will want to establish how much involvement you have had in choosing and setting up equipment, by asking you *oral questions*. If you have been responsible for choosing your own equipment, oral questions and inspection by the assessor will probably be all the evidence needed. If not, *plan* your own nursery, as we have already suggested. Think about indoors and out, the children's different areas and levels of development, and what aged children will be grouped together. Choose all the equipment and plan where you will put everything. Read the article later in the chapter on the Disability Discrimination Act and think of ways of improving access for children and parents with disabilities. Look back at what we said about the values and celebrating diversity, and don't forget to think about all aspects of safety, bearing in mind the different ages.

For the range, you need to show how you would equip both an everyday living area such as a house, and an area specifically intended for children's play, so incorporate both into your plan. This will also provide evidence for the next element. Remember to think about how you would adapt the environment for children of different ages and for children

Element E3.4 Organise and maintain the physical environment of children

Key issues
This element is closely linked to the previous one - in E3.3 you were choosing equipment, in E3.4 you are planning where to put it, and how to maximise the use of both indoor and outdoor areas. It is important to use outdoors for a variety of activities, not just for physical play. If you have permanent outdoor sand pits and water play, you need to ensure that they are always covered when not in use, to prevent them from being fouled by animals or vandalised. Indoors, try to have an area where the floor covering is suitable for sand, water and other messy activities, so that the children have the opportunity to use these valuable materials all year round. Use floor protection if necessary, and always have a mop and bucket handy. You also need to plan how to ensure a regular supply of consumables, so that you don't run out of things like red paint and glitter two weeks before Christmas!

You need to think about how the layout will affect the type of activities you want to encourage. If you have large open spaces the children are more likely to charge about and get boisterous rather than settle to activities. If you divide off the room into small areas, the children will be more likely to concentrate on one activity, and work together in small, co-operative groups. If you want the best of both worlds, have moveable cupboards and screens, so that you can adapt the room to suit the activity. Many settings such as pre-schools have to share their space with other organisations and put everything away every day. This makes it harder to create a child-friendly, attractive environment, but with imagination, it can be achieved. If you work in a home setting, you will have particular concerns to address where the children will be playing in everyday living areas. For instance, if you don't have a large space for physical play, how will you make provision for this? What safety measures will you need to take with the kitchen and stairs?

In this element you need to consider how you will ensure that lighting, heating, and ventilation are adequate - again not always easy to achieve if you are not in a purpose-built setting. You need to show how you maintain standards of cleanliness. If you have done C2 you will already have evidence for this, so check and cross reference where possible.

You may find that you don't have responsibility for most of these things. If this is the case, ask if you can take charge of organising the environment for a short time, say a week, so that you can gather suitable evidence.

Which type of evidence?

Your assessor will need to **observe** and **inspect the setting** for all but two PCs, and again, will want to ask you **oral questions** on the extent of your responsibility for the environment in your setting. If you are not directly responsible, you will need to show in your answers to her questions that you understand the reasons for things being organised in a particular way. You may like to write a **reflective account** of times when you have changed the layout of the room for different activities, or checked the consumable stock, or adapted the environment and equipment for a child with an additional need or disability. Add some **photographs** of the layout for different types of activities, and a short explanation.

Remember!
You may not need all these types of evidence. Choose the most appropriate evidence for you.

The **knowledge evidence** statements for this element are 2, 4, 14, 15, 16. You have probably already covered these with E3.3, or as part of your other evidence for this element. The articles on the following pages will help you with your knowledge evidence. Also refer to the recommended book list (see page 24).

Some early years staff work in accommodation that is far from ideal, but it is still possible to enhance and improve the environment for young children, says Ruth Baldwin

Providing a quality environment

A good quality environment allows children to feel confident and secure. It gives parents faith in the competence of the carers and educators. It can even influence people's perceptions of the quality of their own work. Are you happy that you are making the most of your setting?

Always bear in mind some of the key principles of good early years practice:

- Children learn most effectively by doing rather than by being told;
- Children learn most effectively when they are actively involved and interested;
- Children need time and space to produce work of quality and depth; and
- Playing and talking are the main ways through which young children learn about themselves and the world around them.

The way in which the physical environment is organised can help you to uphold principles or it can create a barrier to them being fulfilled.

When you review your learning environment you should consider:

1 Are children and parents valued? displays - photographs - ownership

2 Can children freely access and select resources and materials? storage - use of furniture - labelling

3 Can children move between the different curriculum areas? use of space - designated areas - indoor/outdoor provision

Show that children and parents are valued

Your setting should be inviting and welcoming to all children and adults. Photographs of children and adults working together are a good way of showing the range of curriculum activities which you provide. Notices for parents should be carefully printed and mounted and be written in positive language rather than as instructions. Dual language notices and signs help to welcome all races and religions, and some are available commercially.

Involve the children in helping you decide how to organise the rooms. They can have particularly strong views about which areas work best. Parents should be encouraged to enter the setting with their child to help them start work and you need to think carefully about how this can best be organised.

Displays of children's work help to develop self-esteem and self-worth and offer a stimulus. The work needs to be carefully mounted and labelled to reflect its value and, where possible, the displays should be at children's height.

Everyone needs a safe place to store their personal belongings.

Children need a place for their coat, shoes/ boots and bag. (Bags are now the bane of early years workers' lives but are needed to transport lunches, spare clothing and comfort toys.) This storage space has to be easily reached by the children and be within their sight to give them confidence that their possessions are safe. Adults - whether it be fellow staff or parents who come in to help - need these facilities as well.

The environment for young children often reflects the home in that there are curtains, carpets, plants, photographs and easy chairs. This is important because it allows children to make that move from home to an early years setting more easily. However, the setting must reflect the variety of cultures and backgrounds that children come from. It is usual to mix fabrics, furniture, pictures, and artefacts so that all cultures are represented regardless of the area the setting serves.

The environment should be maintained to a high standard for health and safety reasons. With young children this task is demanding but essential. The mandatory requirements of the Children Act must be met.

Making it easy for children to choose and reach resources

Storing resources and materials properly is the key to ensuring that children can reach and choose for themselves. Young children cannot manage large, floppy board boxes; they need rigid containers, preferably plastic. Because they are small, they also need furniture of the correct size in which to store their resources.

Word and picture labels help young children who cannot read to determine what is inside the boxes. This is made easier if the containers don't have lids. You may be able to stick one of the objects onto the outside of the boxes along with the label. You can also use photographs or pictures cut from commercial resource catalogues.

You can buy plastic containers at competitive prices in most supermarkets, DIY stores and garages. They come in a variety of sizes and colours. Another helpful strategy to help young children choose resources and put them back in the right place is to use silhouettes of the shapes of objects. This is particularly useful for large objects, for example equipment in the sand area.

When storing bricks and construction materials then it is better to store different items separately. For example, when children are working with Mobilo they want to be able to find a connecting joint or a pair of wheels quickly rather than rummaging in the bottom of the box. The speed of access allows the children to create and construct without interruptions. It also teaches them about how things work because they can see the component parts clearly.

Help children use the different curriculum areas freely

Your furniture should be arranged to let children use the resources in the space provided or to carry them in their play to another area. It is important that all the resources and materials needed for a particular activity are stored within the same area or nearby. Other resources may have to be carried by children in their activities, for example role-play clothes. Continuity and consistency in the storage of resources is vital to let children know exactly where to find things.

It is particularly important to provide materials for literacy and numeracy development. Writing materials and books are required in every single area of play to support children's learning. You can do this by providing a clip-board and pencil, for example, in the construction area, along

Temporary displays

Some settings are not allowed to put up permanent displays but many playgroups cleverly overcome these restrictions. Here are some of their ideas:

i) Buy rolls of corrugated card (approximately four feet in height and six feet in length) to pin work on. These rolls are usually best propped around adult upright chairs, and can be re-used time and time again (see diagram).

ii) Buy pieces of pinboard (size 1m x 2m) to use around the room propped up behind low cupboards for displays.

iii) Display children's work three-dimensionally by sticking it onto cardboard and zig-zagging this on cupboard tops or on the floor.

iv) Pin work onto curtains if available (using nappy pins for safety).

v) Use the reverse of low furniture to display work.

vi) Buy perspex clip frames for children's work which may be more acceptable to the other users of rented premises.

with some simple plans and relevant books. To support children's literacy and numeracy you will need to consider the quality and amount of relevant print and numeracy in the environment at children's level. This print will provide children with a stimulus and a starting point for their own reading and writing.

Try to organise the furniture so that the available spaces can be divided up into areas of work. This will help staff to fit out areas for particular curriculum activities and create secure spaces for children to work in. However, the furniture should not stop children from making connections between other areas. For example, children playing in the home area may not have realised that there is a role-play shop at the other end of the room. This may restrict their play and language use. Through their interactions and participation with children adults will be encouraging them to make full use of all the available spaces and resources by modelling and role playing themselves.

As a general rule the furniture should be away from the wall and placed at angles to create distinct areas. Before starting to arrange the furniture you should first consider which areas you want to provide. These should include the following:

- **reading and listening centre**
- **writing centre**
- **construction areas**
- **role-play areas**
- **floor-play area, eg train set**
- **sand and water area**
- **creative area, eg paint, collage**
- **mathematics centre**
- **music area**
- **snack area/food preparation**
- **interest displays of artefacts for investigation**

In addition, staff should also consider where the computer can go (if you have one), and what will be provided outside.

The amount of space available is often regarded by staff as being limited. Often, the space is only limited by the large number of tables and chairs, which are not all necessary and restrict the room available.

You should name the areas which staff create, with the children's help. This naming is important to give children a sense of belonging, to help them understand what adults are referring to and to distinguish between the different spaces. Very occasionally in early years settings one particular area becomes a place where harassment or bullying can occur. Be vigilant about this. Talking to children about the environment will highlight potential problems. In some settings areas are labelled for reinforcement and to help parents, helpers and students. The names given to areas will reflect the resources and activities within them.

The design and location of the areas should take account of the needs of the children. These needs include opportunities for being quiet or resting; lying down to play; splashing or spilling materials like sand and water; being physically active; talking and singing; working in groups, in pairs or alone; and leaving and returning to unfinished activities. After successfully considering all of these needs the result should be an environment which is truly child-centred.

Finally, a good quality environment for young children is dynamic, challenging, inviting and interesting. To ensure that this is true for all settings, staff need to monitor and review their organisation and accommodation regularly.

Ruth M Baldwin

If you want to give the children in your care the best quality educational start, using display wisely is one way to enrich their environment and achieve your aim, argues Rhona Whiteford

Creating a quality environment: displays

Have a single picture spot and change the picture every few days

The learning environment that we provide for children needs to stimulate and motivate them, extend their knowledge, develop their aesthetic awareness, reinforce things they've learned, show an example to follow and reward them by improving their self-esteem.

Who are displays for?

Displays are for everyone's benefit - for the children, their parents and for ourselves. For the children, we can show off their greatest efforts and help them develop a sense of pride in their achievements. We can give them a sense of ownership by putting their name on their work. In this way, they begin to see themselves and the other children as individuals and can be taught to value themselves and others. We can develop a sense of community if all the children contribute to a display, something 'we all did together.'

We're all bothered about the conditions in which we live and work because it affects the way we feel and our effectiveness. We're all concerned about the wider environment and maintaining it for our children's future. So, this is one area where we can be most effective and teach the children in our care to value their environment. Involve the children in making choices about their environment by discussing together at carpet

time where to put a display, what to include, which colours look best. By drawing their attention to changes in their environment for better or worse we can develop their observational skills and also make them more discriminating: 'I like this colour/these things/this play corner because...' Of course, they may need help to voice their feelings but then that's part of their ongoing language development, too.

Messages to parents

For the parents we are sending out several messages when we display things. We are showing them that we value their children. There are few more important messages to send to a parent! To this end it is vital that each child has some quality work displayed for everyone to see, preferably not just one piece to last the year or an insignificant part of a larger picture with no individual name. (One of my children regularly showed me, 'The part of the camel's leg I did when Father Christmas came'. . . It was the only thing with his name on, apart from his coat peg!)

If you can change displays of children's own work regularly, making sure that everyone is fairly represented, then the message to parents is that you are caring and professional and that their child is part of something alive and exciting.

More than pretty pictures

For you to create the kind of quality environment that values individuals you will have to constantly appraise what you are doing, plan new work, consult with parents, children and colleagues. It's almost as if looking at the environment you have developed helps you to see what you have done and where to go next.

The layout and appearance of the physical environment is important for the smooth running and management of pre-schools. The quiet corner needs to be away from the water and paints! Safety is vital and things need to be down at the viewing level of young children. Once the learning areas and the management areas (adult facilities, toilets, washing, coats) are clearly defined and organised you can get down to enhancing the whole with thoughtful display.

When do you do it?

Display is a vital tool in quality education. It helps to make things happen the way you planned. Set aside a planning time after the children have gone home when you and any others can look at your set-up critically. Think in terms of three areas: management, resources and curriculum.

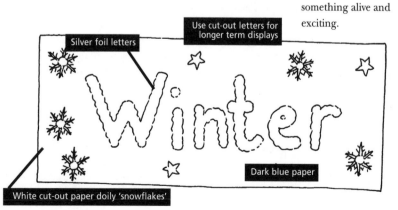

Use cut-out letters for longer term displays

Silver foil letters

Dark blue paper

White cut-out paper doily 'snowflakes'

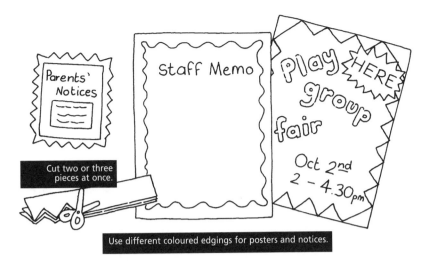

Parents' Notices

Staff Memo

PLAY HERE group fair
Oct 2nd
2 - 4.30pm

Cut two or three pieces at once.

Use different coloured edgings for posters and notices.

For the actual work of displaying, make yourself a weekly appointment, after the children leave, to review the displays and put up something new. With careful planning it should only take you a short while. Keep a display kit ready, with sticky tape, stapler and staples, Blu-tack, drawing pins, scissors and so on. Enlist the help of anyone with a particular artistic bent to mount work and/or display it. Be flexible.

Signs and notices

By management we mean looking at ways in which display can help the general organisation and daily movement in your setting, for example, notices to parents: 'This way in', 'Please bring 20p baking money tomorrow', 'Toilets/baby changing', 'Pram park'. If you have children and parents whose first language is not English, have notices in their home languages. Creating a cordoned-off space for a pram park or providing chairs for visiting parents with a small box of toys for toddlers can help parents to feel noticed and comfortable instead of hanging around in the main learning areas or chasing the toddler. A 'Staff only' area can be a safety asset with a high work surface and high hooks or shelving to store dangerous items like

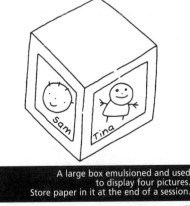

A large box emulsioned and used to display four pictures. Store paper in it at the end of a session.

staplers and scissors. You can also put staff information here, like the lists of children's

groups, staff/leader's responsibilities, fire and accident procedures, vital phone numbers and so on.

Lists and labelling

Organising storage of equipment needs to be logical and well labelled so that people can have access to it quickly and easily.

You need to plan where to store equipment that children can use so that it is in an accessible place and near to the area where it is to be used. For example, dustpans and brushes that the children can use to sweep up sand need to be near the sand tray, large bricks need to be near the carpet area where they are used.

Even lists can have clear titles and be displayed in a sensible place. It's a good idea to label all storage boxes with clear print for those children who are beginning to read. Cut out a catalogue picture to match the label so that reading is helped along.

Labelling adult resources is vital if they are to be found quickly and stored tidily. Good housekeeping is just good management.

Supporting the curriculum

When you are planning the curriculum, give serious thought to display as a major visual aid. Look at your accommodation, whether it be purpose-built nursery area, church hall or spare classroom, look at the wall space, temporary display boards and flat surfaces like window sills or cupboards.

Plan what general resources you will need, like number lines, alphabet friezes, seasonal posters, nursery rhyme pictures, informational pictures, labels and directions and decide where to put these at the start of term. Ensure that the pictures you choose show positive images of different ethnic

groups, people with disablities and non-stereotypical gender roles. Leave a large wall space and a small table ready for use in the first week to display children's first efforts and then move on, on a weekly basis, to change the work displays and informational pictures as the need arises. A building picture can go near the bricks, food pictures in the cooking area. Build up a collection of seasonal posters so that you can have a different picture up for a couple of weeks at a time.

How do you do it?

But where do you get new ideas? How do you begin to enhance the worth of a child's picture or model? How do you make a notice eye-catching? What can you do about those awkward spaces and corners? How do you go about putting up displays when you're in shared, daily accommodation?

Anyone can learn to be more artistic and using display really is simply a case of using your common sense and being prepared to be adaptable. Don't worry about a display being artistic - colour and form are always a matter of opinion and yours is as valid as the next person's. The main point is that you have been neat and careful in your presentation and have drawn attention to the item displayed.

Rhona Whiteford

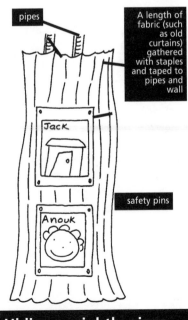

pipes

A length of fabric (such as old curtains) gathered with staples and taped to pipes and wall

Jack

safety pins

Anouk

Hiding unsightly pipes

If you know that multicultural education is something you need to work on, but aren't sure where to begin, here are some ideas to get you started

The multicultural classroom

It may sound obvious, but to be able to provide a multicultural learning environment, you need yourself to have some awareness of different cultures. What are the races, cultures and religions of the world? Start finding out about them together. Ask children to bring in anything they find - postcards from families who have been abroad on holidays or pictures from magazines. In this way, you'll start building up your own resource bank - it doesn't matter if it's only pictures at first. Cut out articles from newspapers for your colleagues. Travel agents are wonderful sources of colourful pictures of other countries. Use them to make displays.

Write to the various embassies or tourist offices explaining that you are keen to promote their country and cultures. Can they help in any way? Some museums specialise in artefacts from around the world. See if there is one near you that you can visit. Most local authorities have a multicultural centre — find out where your nearest centre is and how they might be able to help you. Some have loan services.

And remember, European countries have different cultures, too. Find out about France, Italy, Sweden and Germany as well as India, Pakistan and the West Indies.

People often laugh at different cultures because they are nervous about not understanding. You need to create an environment where children recognise that difference isn't silly and that the key is to ask questions. Why do people in some countries have different hairstyles/paint their bodies/wear different clothes/live in different houses? If children know why people do these things differently they are less likely to find them funny.

One step at a time
If you're starting from scratch, don't feel you have to take on board all the cultures of the world at the same time. Take a systematic and structured approach, one culture at a time. If you do have children or staff from a different country, or even someone in your local community who has lived abroad, start with them.

For example, if you pick the West Indian culture, approach the appropriate embassy and your local multicultural centre to see how they can help. Collect some holiday brochures. Perhaps ask some parents to make some West Indian rag dolls for the home corner or some child-size clothing for role play - one girl's dress and a boy's outfit. Cook some typical West Indian meals and find out if there are any special kitchen utensils you could get. Arrange a trip to your local shops or supermarket to see what fruit or vegetables you need for your recipe. If you know of anyone who can come in to talk to the children about the West Indies, all the better. Find out as much as you can about the people from that country - what they eat, how they speak, what they wear, what jobs they do, where they go to pray, and what festivals they celebrate.

The right resources
Books play an important part in introducing children to different cultures, but they are not the only resources.

The home corner: Are there any special kitchen utensils you could bring in? What about a wok, chopsticks or balti dishes? Have some cookery books with recipes which use ingredients from, say, Italy or Mexico, or some packets or tins of food from different countries. Could you make some rag dolls which represent different races, such as Chinese or Indian?

Dressing-up clothes: Too often these are nothing more than left-over jumble. It is important if you have clothes or costumes from other cultures so that children value

them and look after them. It helps if they are clean, the right size and hung on a rail at child height. It is not enough to have a piece of sari fabric in a box. Would your children know how to wear it correctly? Would you? Invite someone from your local community — or your nearest multicultural centre — to show you how to put a sari on. You and your staff could then all wear one when you celebrate the appropriate festival.

Construction play: Make sure children have the chance to see different architectural styles — what are houses like in Japan, in Switzerland or Australia? Let them use different materials.

Jigsaws: Scenes from different countries will spark off discussions about their similarities and differences.

Posters/wall displays: Find pictures of different countries which show people in everyday situations - at home, at school, at work, at play. Posters are available which illustrate the word 'hello' in different languages.

Songs: Sing songs or play tapes of songs in different languages. You are not *teaching* children French, you are giving them the chance to hear a language other than their own in an environment which says this might be different but it is not silly.

Every setting should have its own procedures which outline the safety standards expected and are produced jointly by everyone concerned. Helen Richardson from the Child Accident Prevention Trust offers some guidelines

Playing safely - accident prevention

Children's accidents result in 502 deaths, thousands of hospital admissions and more than two million attendances at accident and emergency departments every year. That's one child in five - that are recorded. The figure is higher because there are others who go to their local clinic or doctor and these are not included. Accidents are the single biggest killer of children in the UK. Many children are permanently disabled or disfigured every year. Most of these accidents happen in the home and on the road.

Most accidents in day care and early years settings are minor and often involve falls and collisions. They tend to result in bruises and cuts to the head, arms and legs. However, there have been a number of serious injuries and some deaths to children in these settings.

With any provision for children, it is important that safety is seen as an integral part of the whole service and therefore important to workers, managers, parents, advisers, inspectors, funders and to the children themselves.

Each child is an individual. Children from different social and cultural groups and those with special needs may play in different ways and this could affect the safety strategies you use. By working together with children and their families, you can offer all children safe and secure opportunities for development.

Creating a safe environment

There should not be such an emphasis on accident prevention that the availability of day care and play services in an area is inhibited. Day care and play provision can make a

major contribution to child accident prevention by offering a safe environment for children within their own community.

Safety has to be balanced with children's other needs. Children should have a safe environment which gives as much freedom as possible and the opportunity to learn and develop.

Creating a safe environment involves choosing and putting into practice many different measures which remove or reduce accident risks. It does not mean removing all the equipment that involves risk taking, nor writing a large number of rules. This will just confuse and restrict children and workers. It means creating an environment for children that is challenging yet safe, a place in which all kinds of activities, domestic, care, play and administrative, can be carried out safely by workers and children.

Safety inspections need to be carried out so that workers can:

- identify an unsafe condition
- decide what is the corrective action required
- determine who is responsible for correcting it
- follow up to ensure that it was corrected properly.

The following inspection schedules are recommended. Even people working alone in their home will find it useful to follow this pattern through adapting and incorporating these procedures into normal domestic routines.

A safe setting does not only involve safe premises and equipment. It also involves safe behaviour and activities and safe procedures and practice. Each setting should have its own procedures which outline the safety standards expected and are produced jointly by everyone concerned.

1 Each day that a session is run - visual inspection

Every day the setting is used a visual inspection should be carried out before the children arrive. Record

---

Safety inspection schedules

every day or every session	visual inspection
every week or every 10 sessions	'walk over and use' inspection
every 3 months or every term	recorded 'prod and probe' inspection
every year	an independent inspection

that the inspection has taken place. You should look for and correct any problem which might, depending on the nature of the setting, result from:

- ❑ breakages, weather damage or vandalism
- ❑ rubbish or animal faeces
- ❑ inadequate cleaning
- ❑ blocked access to emergency exits or along walkways
- ❑ instability of large equipment, fences or barriers
- ❑ dirty water in pools or water play areas
- ❑ non-functioning of door or gate locks

Routine maintenance such as raking soft surfaces in outside play areas, cleaning sand-pits and trays and ensuring that safety equipment is present, correctly installed and working should also be carried out. In addition, make sure that storage areas are locked and emergency exits are unlocked.

Any equipment or toys that the children will use should be visually inspected beforehand. It is good practice to involve the children in clearing up activities, especially putting toys away. However, this removes an opportunity for workers to inspect the condition of toys. It is therefore recommended that equipment and toys are visually inspected before children use them.

During a session, deal with breakages and spillage immediately and set up systems for supervising and maintaining toilet and bathroom areas.

2 Every week/every ten days - 'walk over and use' inspection

Walk around the entire setting and use all equipment, such as outdoor play equipment and heating and water fittings. By physically using these items and going to every corner of the setting, workers should find anything that has stopped working or is becoming unsafe. In addition, make sure that all moving parts on equipment are appropriately oiled or greased. Record that the inspection has taken place and identify the large pieces of equipment that were involved.

3 Three monthly/termly - recorded 'prod and probe' inspection

This should be recorded in detail. Develop a check-list appropriate to your setting which identifies specific areas and equipment where wear and tear problems are likely to be found. For example, in the outside play area, you should check the depth, fixing and edging of a safety surface, look for signs of corrosion on equipment and inspect the state of the paint work. It can help to have a colleague from outside the setting to help you do this inspection.

Alongside this inspection all workers should have the opportunity to voice specific concerns they may have about the procedures used at the setting. This discussion should take place within a workers' meeting when ideas can be shared and considered. It is important to give enough time to this discussion. (People working alone can discuss their procedures with others doing similar jobs, for example by going to local childminders' groups.)

4 Annual inspection

All settings should have a major independent inspection every year. You will have to pay a small fee for this, so you will need to allocate resources for it in the budget. Local authority officers will carry out an inspection of all registered settings each year. Settings may also have the opportunity to have an independent inspection of the outside play area. If a setting does not have to be registered, workers should find an independent person to do it for them. Get advice from your local authority Social Services department or the National Playing Fields Association on what an annual inspection should involve and who could do it.

Helen Richardson, Training Officer, Child Accident Prevention Trust

The National Playing Fields Association can be contacted at: Stanley House, St Chad's Place, London WC1X 9HH
Telephone: 020 78335360

For more detailed guidance you can contact the Child Accident Prevention Trust at 4th floor, Clerks Court, 18-20 Farringdon Lane, London EC1R 3HA. Tel: 0207 608 3828

When your workplace is your home

Childminders face the challenge of adapting their homes to make them safe places for a number of children to be, while not losing sight of the needs of the other people who live there to have comfort and privacy and to feel that they matter too. Childminders have to consider their own need to be able to relax at the end of the day, to 'go home' from work. It can be difficult to make that mental switch from thinking of your home as a home to thinking of it as a workplace, and back again.

They also need to be constantly on the lookout for possible hazards. A teenager could leave a flex trailing, a partner in a hurry could leave a staircate open. The general debris of daily family life - cups of tea, cosmetics, garden tools - might
cause an accident at any time, simply because this is a home and people are living there. Many of us have steps, corners or uneven surfaces in our homes that we just learn to live with and move around without hazard: to a young child they could mean danger.

All this means that a childminder, rather than becoming neurotic and worried about safety to the point of making everyone nervous, including the children, needs to be sensitive to others' needs and to draw the whole family into a commitment to keep the home safe for everyone. She (or he) needs to set boundaries. That means that there may be some areas of the house where children being cared for may not go; not only for their own safety but also to keep a sense that there are some places, even if it is just one room, which are kept away from the job. A childminder needs to develop a knack of walking into a room and immediately sensing whether there is something out of place or damaged which might present a danger. Above all, she (or he) needs to establish safe working practices that are known and understood by the other people living at home.

Part of the safety of home-based childcare entails fitting safety equipment and making special adaptations. But it is important to remember that many families choose childminding as their preferred option because their children are cared for in someone's home, in a family atmosphere. Childminders are faced with the challenge of providing the safest facilities possible without jeopardising that sense that their home is truly a home, where people can relax and be themselves, and where unexpected things sometimes happen. It is worth remembering that the vast majority of accidents take place in the home. If children can learn safe practices from a safety-conscious childminder, they are learning skills for life.

Use this check-list when you carry out your daily inspection before children arrive

20 tips for a safer pre-school

Tick box when checked

Comings and goings

- Corridors and doorways are free from prams and buggies ☐

- Main entrance door handles let adults in but stop children getting out ☐

- Tasks are allocated to staff:

  - greeting children, parents and carers ☐

  - taking and passing on messages about collecting children, their health etc ☐

  - keeping an eye on siblings not staying for the session ☐

  - checking that children leave with an appropriate adult ☐

  - making arrangements for children left late after the session ☐

Premises

- activities are set up away from doorways and fire exits ☐

- fire exit doors are unlocked ☐

- doors don't slam on children's fingers ☐

- fire extinguishers are fixed securely to the walls ☐

- the toilet area is kept mopped and dried ☐

Equipment

- climbing equipment is placed away from walls/staging/other equipment ☐

- climbing frames are not more than two metres high and have safety mats below ☐

- painting easels and book cases stand secure ☐

- floor toys eg small cars/building bricks, are placed away from doorways and climbing equipment ☐

- dressing-up clothes don't have trailing pieces eg elastic, ribbons, cords ☐

- broken play equipment is removed for mending or disposal ☐

- large unused equipment and containers are stored securely ☐

- carpet pieces are flat and have no frayed edges ☐

Activities

- spills of sand, water and paint are swept up or mopped and dried ☐

- scattered floor toys and small pieces like Lego are returned to designated play area ☐

- ride-on toys are kept away from floor activities ☐

- hot drinks are kept away from children's activities ☐

All information supplied by Child Accident Prevention Trust

Use this check-list as a useful guide on how to make your home a safer place for the whole family and the other children in your care

20 **top** home safety tips

Tick box when checked

1   The floor and stairs are clear of junk or spills in case the family trip or slip. ☐

2   Medicines and chemicals are stored high up and out of reach in case a child drinks something harmful. ☐

3   Safety catches are fitted to prevent a child falling out of the window. ☐

4   Babies or toddlers are never alone in the bath as they can quickly drown in just a little water. ☐

5   The hot water thermostat is turned down to 54°C (130°F) or less in case a child turns the hot tap on and is scalded. ☐

6   Rear hobs on the cooker are used and pan handles turned away from the edge. ☐

7   The smoke alarm is working in case of fire and the family need time to escape. ☐

8   The baby never uses a babywalker - they may fall over or reach for something dangerous. ☐

9   The front door is shut and can't be opened by small children in case they run into traffic. ☐

10 Someone in the family has taken a First Aid course to help cope if an accident does happen. ☐

All information supplied by Child Accident Prevention Trust

Are you confident that all your staff and parent helpers would know what to do in the event of a fire? What fire regulations apply to your premises? Who is responsible for fire safety in your nursery? David Hedley tells you what you need to know

Fire precautions

This guidance is relevant to all pre-school providers - whether you rent a room in the village hall, run a private nursery or are part of an LEA school.

In any nursery, whatever its size, a named individual must be made responsible for fire safety. This job is often combined with health and safety, building management and security. You should have a fire officer even if you are not responsible for the building.

Assessment of risks

But even before considering fire safety, it is essential that all risks are assessed in any premises. The building and what goes on in it should be carefully monitored and the following points set down:

- possible starting points for fires;
- weaknesses in the structure;
- scope for a small fire to spread;
- ways in which people could be trapped or killed;
- the possible extent of losses, both direct and as a result of temporary closure.

Key areas and contents which could be affected by a fire and by fire fighting operations should be taken into account. Insurers, your local fire brigade and, in many cases, the local authority may be able to help you with this assessment; until the appraisal has been completed, the

Action plan

Once you have identified the risks you need to establish an action plan.

Key members of your staff must be designated to liaise with the nominated fire safety manager to confirm their roles. Action to mitigate the effects of a fire should be taken. For example:

- set up duplicate records in a separate location (including attendance registers).

- ensure all visitors sign in and out of the building.

- take an inventory of all contents including, where applicable, serial numbers, receipts for goods.

- prepare an emergency list of contacts, including parents, insurers, building contractors.

- consider how business can continue, for example temporary accommodation.

- ensure that there are written procedures for emergency evacuation of the building, which include special measures to be taken where children are located above or below ground level, known to all staff and fire drills are carried out periodically.

- the registered person is fully informed of fire evacuation procedures for the whole building (shared accommodation).

What is fire ?

Fire is the chemical reaction called combustion (usually oxidisation resulting in the release of heat and light).

For an outbreak of fire to occur and continue, the following are essential:

Fuel: a combustible substance either solid, liquid or gas

Oxygen: usually air which contains approximately 21per cent oxygen

Heat: the attainment of a certain temperature (once a fire has started it normally maintains its own heat supply)

The way to prevent fires from starting is to ensure that sources of heat and fuel are kept apart. Once a fire has started it can only grow bigger if there is a supply of fuel and oxygen.

first steps towards effective fire prevention cannot be taken.

Compliance with the law

Most buildings in the United Kingdom are now subject to statutory fire safety regulations and require a fire safety certificate under the Fire Precautions Act 1971, the Fire Precautions (Workplace) Regulations 1997 and the Fire Precautions (Workplace) (Amendment) Regulations 1999. These regulations apply to all nursery and pre-school provision whether private or local authority. In addition, all day nurseries and creches (both local authority and private) must also comply with the terms of the Children Act. Local authority provision in nursery schools and in nursery classes in primary schools is not subject to the terms of the Children Act.

The Health and Safety at Work Act 1974 applies in all cases.

In shared acommodation the person who has overall control of the building will be responsible for ensuring that

Spread of fire, smoke and fumes

Fire spreads by heat travelling from areas of high temperature to areas of lower temperature. There are three ways in which this can happen:

Conduction

Heat from a fire can travel through the materials in buildings such as walls, wood, metal, etc, causing a rise in temperature until ignition occurs. The ability of materials to conduct heat varies greatly. Materials with low conductivity are used to prevent the spread of fire (eg fire doors).

Convection

During a fire, convection currents move hot gases, produced by fire, upwards, usually via corridors, stairwells and lift shafts. This convection spreads the fire to other parts of the building. In turn currents of cool air drawn towards the fire replace the hot gases rising from it and accelerate the burning.

Fire can spread at alarming rates due to convection currents. For this reason it is essential to close doors and windows to contain fire.

Radiation

Radiation is the transmission of heat between materials which are not in contact with each other. (The sun heats the Earth by means of radiation.)

Many fires are caused by radiation. One of the most common causes is clothing catching fire when it has been placed too close to a radiant heat source.

emergency routes and exits are kept clear at all times. Where a person has, by virtue of a contract or tenancy agreement, an obligation of any extent in relation to the safety of any workplace (a creche leader would qualify in this respect if their contract - tenancy contract rather than employment contract - specified that they were responsible for the safety or repair of that part of the building which they used), that person shall be deemed to be in control of the workplace under the terms of the Fire Precautions (Workplace) Regulations 1997.

All legal requirements relating to fire safety are intended to protect people rather than property. The nominated fire safety manager should, however, aim for far more than the minimum required by law.

Basic procedures

A fire safety plan must begin with a set of procedures which can be followed in the event of a fire and are easily understood by all staff, visitors (including parents and helpers) and contractors. The full procedure should set out, step by step, what should happen if a fire occurs when the building is occupied, including:

- how to raise the alarm;

Smoke - the killer

Smoke is the term used to describe the products of combustion, including gases and particles.

It is smoke and not flames which is the cause of most deaths in fires.

The hot gases produced by combustion are toxic. Individuals who inhale them are quickly overcome.

The hazard increases when polyurethane foam, or other materials which give off highly toxic fumes, are burning.

The denseness of smoke causes a state of panic.

Smoke rises and generates a flow of colder air at lower levels. This lower level of clean air can provide a means of escape.

To prevent the spread of smoke all doors and windows should be closed.

- methods of alerting those on premises and taking early action to fight small fires(waste bins etc only) and limit damage;
- allocation of individual responsibilities to staff concerned.

Staff should know from their first day at

work how to raise the alarm on discovering a fire and exactly what they should do if they hear an alarm. Training in the use of fire extinguishers should be undertaken as soon as possible and staff should be aware of all fire exits, to whom they should report and their assembly points. Fire drills should take place at regular intervals, ideally every three months. These requirements also apply to visitors and contractors.

Fire prevention

Good housekeeping and appropriate storage of combustibles, such as paper, will reduce the possibility of a fire occurring. It is important to ensure that:

- there is no accumulation of rubbish, waste paper or other combustible materials;
- corridors, exits and other parts of the building which are part of a fire escape route must be kept clear at all times and never used for storage;
- combustible materials must not be stored near a heat source;
- electrical wiring, plugs and sockets must be correctly fused, in sound condition and never overloaded;
- electrical repairs should only be carried out by a competent person;
- electrical testing of portable equipment should be carried out on a regular basis, by a competent person;
- electrical equipment should be switched off when not in use, where this is reasonably practicable;
- where smoking is permitted, careful disposal of matches and extinguishing of cigarettes is essential.

Much can be done to prevent the spread of fire, for example by ensuring that fire doors are kept closed and never propped open. Bearing in mind the high incidence of arson, access should be controlled and the building made as secure as possible.

Fire protection systems and fire fighting equipment

In all but the smallest building, an electrical fire alarm is the most effective means of raising the alarm in the event of a fire.

Where one is installed, suitable arrangements should be made to test the function on a weekly basis. The test should be recorded in a Fire Precautions Log Book. Your alarm installer will provide you with a log book. A different call point should be tested each week. Staff should know where all alarm call points are.

Quarterly and annual inspections and tests of the alarm batteries, connections and electrolyte level should be carried out and recorded in the Fire Precautions Log Book. These tests should be carried out by the installer of the system or a specialist contractor. Log books may be inspected by fire brigade officers during inspections.

Fire fighting equipment such as fire extinguishers, hose reels and so on should be checked annually by a qualified engineer, usually under a service contract with the supplier.

The servicing engineer should enter details of this visit in the Fire Precautions Log Book.

In addition, an appropriate member of staff should be nominated to carry out the required monthly visual inspection of fire fighting equipment to ensure, for example, that extinguishers have not been stolen, moved, discharged or damaged. This monthly inspection should also be recorded in the Fire Precautions Log Book. All staff should be aware of the siting of extinguishers and be aware of their operation and be able to select the appropriate extinguisher for a particular type of fire.

Fire escapes and exits

All routes and exits used as a means of escape in the event of a fire must be kept clear of obstructions at all times. Fire exit doors must be immediately openable from the inside and must never be locked. Doors fitted with panic bars or pads should display a notice detailing the operation of the door release mechanism. They should also be tested daily.

The number of fire exits required will depend upon several factors and it is imperative that you seek advice from your local fire brigade. For local authority nurseries, safety officers will provide suitable advice. Fire doors, which check the spread of smoke within buildings, should never be wedged open, even when buildings are empty. It is important that the self-closing devices on these doors are checked on a regular basis.

David Hedley is Principal Officer (Asset Management and Emergency Planning), Newcastle upon Tyne Education Department.

What causes fires?

- Arson
- The careless disposal of lighted cigarettes or matches.
- Children playing with matches.
- The accumulation of rubbish, paper or other combustible materials.
- Electrical faults. Electrical equipment left switched on when not in use (unless it is designed to be permanently connected), not serviced or not correctly serviced.
- Flammable materials left close to a heat source.
- Obstruction of ventilation for example wall heaters, computers and office equipment.
- Cooking.

People are the common denominator - almost every fire can be prevented.

People cause fires by:

- Poor judgement
- Error
- Ignorance
- Wrong attitude to fire safety
- Failure to follow instructions
- Failure to maintain equipment properly

Use this as a guide for a monthly review of your fire precautions

Fire precautions check-list

Name of setting

Date of inspection

Name of person carrying out inspection

Fire alarm

	Yes	No
Is there an effective means of raising the alarm in the event of a fire?	☐	☐
Do all staff and helpers know how to raise the alarm and what the alarm sounds like?	☐	☐
Do they know the drill for fire practice?	☐	☐
Can the alarm be heard throughout the building?	☐	☐
Has the electric fire alarm (if installed) been activated weekly from a different call point or zone and a record kept?	☐	☐
Are records of tests being entered into the fire precautions log book?	☐	☐
Is the electric fire alarm being electrically inspected every six months and the inspections recorded? Check your records.	☐	☐
When was the last practice drill? (They should be quarterly.) Date	☐	

Fire fighting equipment

	Yes	No
Is the fire fighting equipment being serviced annually and records kept?	☐	☐
Check all fire extinguishers to see whether they have been damaged, discharged or stolen and record your findings.	☐	☐
Are fire extinguishers, hose reels and fire blankets readily accessible and unobstructed?	☐	☐
Is there enough fire fighting equipment and is it in the appropriate places?	☐	☐
Are all fire extinguishers marked with standard identification signs?	☐	☐

Fire prevention

	Yes	No
Is there any accumulation of rubbish, waste paper or other combustible materials?	☐	☐
Are corridors and exits which are part of a fire escape route kept clear at all times?	☐	☐
Are fire doors kept closed and never propped open?	☐	☐

First aid and resuscitation

It is important that you know the basics of first aid. Ideally, everyone on your staff should receive basic training to enable them to give the best possible first aid treatment in an emergency. This is for your own peace of mind as well as to reassure the parents of the children in your care. Information about first aid training in your area may be obtained from:

St John's Ambulance,
27 St John's Lane
Clerkenwell
London EC1M 4BU
Tel: 0207 324 4000

St Andrew's Ambulance,
St Andrew's House,
48 Milton Street,
Glasgow G4 0HR
Tel: 0141 332 4031

British Red Cross Society - You will find local numbers in your telephone directory.

ABC check

You may have to deal with an emergency at any time, so familiarise yourself with the most important principle of first aid - the ABC check:

Airway - is it clear?
Breathing - is the child breathing?
Circulation - is there a heart beat?

Airway - Lift the chin with two fingers and tilt the head back. If the child is breathing, place him in the recovery position.

Breathing - If the child is not breathing, start artificial ventilation.

Circulation - Check the child's pulse by pressing on the groove of the neck, in front of the large muscle at each side. If you cannot feel a pulse, then start cardio pulmonary resuscitation (CPR).

If the child is unconscious, ask someone to call an ambulance. While you wait the child should be put in the recovery position as follows:

The child lies on his side almost on the tummy with the arm underneath preventing him rolling forward. The head should be tilted back to keep the airway open.

In an unconscious baby tilt the head back slightly whilst holding the baby securely in your arms. This prevents them from inhaling their own vomit.

Dr Shabde, consultant paediatrician, Northumbria NHS Trust.

There is no legal requirement for there to be a qualified first aider in a nursery. However, the Health Education Guide recommends that a school has one nominated qualified first aider who has undergone approved training for 18 hours. This is renewable every three years. The principles and practice of first aid are included as part of the curriculum for NNEB students and most colleges offer a separate first aid certificate. However, this would need updating regularly.

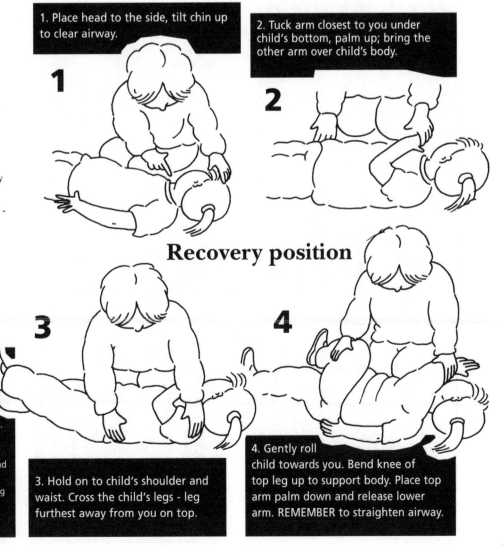

Recovery position

1. Place head to the side, tilt chin up to clear airway.

2. Tuck arm closest to you under child's bottom, palm up; bring the other arm over child's body.

3. Hold on to child's shoulder and waist. Cross the child's legs - leg furthest away from you on top.

4. Gently roll child towards you. Bend knee of top leg up to support body. Place top arm palm down and release lower arm. REMEMBER to straighten airway.

Check your first aid kit. It should contain:

+ **Cotton wool**
+ **Surgical tape**
+ **Sterile dressings**
+ **Absorbent wipes**
+ **Tweezers**
+ **Triangular bandages**
+ **Crepe bandages**
+ **Tubular finger bandages**
+ **Scissors**
+ **First aid handbook**
+ **Safety pins**
+ **Non-adhesive absorbent dressing**
+ **Antiseptic wipes**
+ **Assorted waterproof plasters**

This can vary depending on your local authority regulations. Check with them first

FIRST AID EMERGENCY SITUATIONS

1 Unconsciousness

2 Shock

3 Cessation of breathing and heart beating

4 Burns and scalds

5 Cuts, bruises and bleeding

6 Broken bones

7 Poisoning

8 Choking and suffocation

9 Joint and muscle injury

Resuscitation

If the child is not breathing, you should start artificial ventilation at once by breathing for him.

+ Tilt the child's head back slightly and lift the chin with two fingers of the other hand to open the airway. You may need to clear the airway.
+ Pinch nose shut with two fingers of one hand whilst supporting the child's jaw with the other hand.
+ After taking a deep breath, open your mouth wide and seal your lips over the child's mouth. Breathe into the child's mouth, taking a fresh breath yourself after each of the ventilations. If the procedure is correctly applied the child's chest will rise and then fall. If the child has a pulse then continue artificial ventilation at the rate of one breath every three seconds ie 20 breaths per minute until the child can breathe by himself. As soon as regular

breathing is established, place the child in the recovery position.

Proceed to CPR if the child has no pulse in order to keep the vital organs supplied with oxygen as permanent brain damage can ensue after only three minutes without oxygen.

CPR is a technique which combines artificial ventilation to deliver air into the child's lungs and external heart massage through chest compressions to enable the oxygenated blood supply to reach the organs in the body.

+ Open airway and check breathing (as described above).
+ Give artificial ventilation (as described above).
+ Check for a pulse by placing your two fingers into a groove between the child's wind pipe and the large muscles in the neck, just below the jaw. Feel for five seconds. If there is no pulse then start chest compressions.

+ Place the child on a hard flat surface and find the breastbone (the bone that runs down the centre of the chest).
+ Place two fingers (middle and index finger) at the spot where the ribs meet and then place the heel of your hand over the lower half of the child's breastbone, keeping your fingers off the child's ribs.
+ Press down to a depth of 2.5 - 3.5 cm (1"- 1.5") and then release the pressure
+ Do this five times within three seconds at a rate of 80-100 compressions per minute (counting the compressions 'one and two and three', and so on, as you do). Alternating with one breath of artificial ventilation continue, until the ambulance arrives.

It is important not to apply too much pressure or force as you can break the child's ribs.

Policies and procedures

Professional childcarers have a responsibility to ensure that the health and welfare of the children in their care is paramount. Any facility registered under the Children Act 1989 needs to have a policy on health, safety and child protection, to make sure that everyone involved in the setting - staff, volunteers and parents - is clear about their responsibilities and the procedures to be followed, to promote a healthy safe environment and to protect the well-being of children and adults.

Legislation

Although the Children Act 1989 is the major piece of legislation covering providers of day care for children under eight years, other health and safety legislation has to be complied with.

❑ Health and Safety at Work Act 1974

❑ Health and Safety Regulations 1981

❑ Management of Health and Safety at Work Regulations 1992

❑ Electricity at Work Act 1989

❑ Fire Precautions Act 1971

❑ Food Safety Act 1990

❑ Reporting of Injuries, Diseases and Dangerous Occurrences Regulations 1985

❑ Disability Discrimination Act 1995

It is unlikely that you will have in-depth knowledge of any of this legislation, and you are not expected to. Your local authority under-eights department should be able to advise and help you.

Under the Care Standards Act, which came into force in September 2001, the role of regulation of day care facilities for children under eight in England passed to Ofsted, with the support and training functions being retained in the local authorities.

In June 2001 the D/EE published a set of 14 National Standards for each type of facility: childminding, sessional care, full day care, creches and out of school care. You should refer to the appropriate standards for your facility.

Standard 7, which covers health, states: 'The registered person promotes the good health of children and takes positive steps to prevent the spread of infection and appropriate measures when they are ill'. The supporting criteria cover hygiene, animals, sand pits, food handling, medicine, first aid, sick children and smoking.

Keeping records

Before admitting any child into your care, you should discuss with parents the stage of development their child is at; any health problems, allergies, disabilities, special dietary needs and the child's immunisation records. It is good practice to record all of this on the child's profile, together with the name, address and phone number of the child's doctor, health visitor and emergency contact numbers for parents. In many areas parents are encouraged to share their child's health records with carers. To make sure that details are accurate at all times, it is essential that you ask for the information to be updated at regular intervals.

Make sure everyone knows where this information is kept and remember to take it with you if you take a child to hospital as the doctors will need to know details about immunisation and possible allergies, for example.

When children are unwell

If a child is unwell, they should not be in any care provision - not only to prevent the risk of infection spreading but also because constant nursing and attention may be needed. This policy should be made quite clear to all parents when their child starts with you. Persistent colds, coughs and other infections need to be discussed with parents and children should only be accepted again when they are fit enough. Periods of exclusion for communicable diseases should be obtained from your local health authority department of public health. In the case of vomiting and diarrhoea you should specify how long a child should be kept away - at least 24 hours after the condition has stopped and the child is fully fit.

If a child becomes unwell whilst in your care, it is your responsibility to ensure that the child's parents are informed. The child should be allowed to rest away from other children but within contact of an adult until collected by parents. When other children are exposed to communicable diseases and infections, all parents should be informed as soon as possible but always within 24 hours. This is important for all children but especially for those whose immune systems may be low. Confidentiality must be respected and the child who is unwell should not be named.

Administering medicine

There is no legal duty which requires carers to administer medicine. Medication policies are recommended in all care facilities. Although a child on medication is best off at home, there may be occasions when a child can be re-admitted on doctor's advice but needs to complete a prescribed course of medicine. If you are offering a full day care service, you may be asked to help with this.

You may be asked to care for a child with special health needs, who perhaps is asthmatic or has a life-threatening allergy for which prescribed medicine/procedures must be used. Before accepting any such child

into your care, check with your insurance company that you will be covered and advise your local under-eights officer. Discuss the child's health needs fully with their parents and draw up a protocol to be followed in the case of emergencies. Make sure that you have professional instruction in the administration of medical procedures such as epipens. Confirm whose responsibility it is to check the shelf life of any medication and get both parents to countersign any agreements reached with review dates built in.

In all circumstances parents should have given medicine prior to expecting you to administer it, so that the child has no proven allergic reaction. Parents must also complete a medical consent form which names the prescribed medicine, times and doses of medication to be administered. This should be completed by the carer as any medicine is given and, if you work in group care, get the entry countersigned by a colleague who witnessed it. Confidentiality should be respected and a separate proforma per child used. A new consent form for each course of medicine is needed. All medicines should be kept out of reach of children and refrigerated if necessary.

Accidents and first aid

Everyone involved in caring for young children should carry out a daily risk assessment of the environment and playrooms in which they are working. Do not assume that someone else has already done this! By being vigilant you can minimise the risk of accidents happening to the children in your care.

You should keep at least one emergency first aid box which complies with the Health and Safety (First Aid) Regulations 1981 in a safe place where all staff know where it is and how to access it. The contents should be checked regularly and items replaced as necessary by a designated member of staff. It is especially important for childminders to ensure that the first aid box you use for your

childminding service is separate to that used for your own family. A suggested list of contents is given on page 70 but it is worth checking for local guidance.

A first aid kit should always be taken on outings. Obtain permission in writing to take children out and adhere to the recommended adult/child ratios. If you are a childminder it is important to carry identification that you are a childcarer and an emergency contact number should you be involved in an accident.

First aid is exactly what it says - first aid. All group care facilities should have at least one trained first aider on duty at all times,

---

Medicine: National Standards (for group care)

The registered person has a clear policy, understood by all staff and discussed with parents, regarding the administration of medication. If medicine is to be given it includes the following:

❑ medicines are stored in their original containers, clearly labelled and inaccessible to children;

❑ medicines are not usually administered unless they have been presribed for that child by a doctor

❑ the parent gives prior written permission to administer any medication

❑ written records are kept of all medicines administered to children, and parents sign the record book to acknowledge the entry

❑ if the administration of prescription medicines requires technical/medical knowledge then individual training is provided for staff from a qualified health professional. Training is specific to the individual child concerned.

First aid: National Standards

❑ For group care - at least one member of staff with a current first aid training certificate on the premises or on outings at any one time. The first aid qualifications includes training in first aid for infants and young children.

❑ For childminders - must have completed a first aid course for infants and young children within six months of commencing childminding. A current first aid certificate is maintained.

---

although all staff should be encouraged to undertake training.

Parents should give written permission for first aid to be administered and for medical help to be sought in case of emergencies. This should be included in the formal form filling before the child starts with you.

If an accident occurs, no matter how minor, you as the childcarer should complete an accident report form, ensure that the child's parent has been informed and has countersigned to acknowledge this. Confidentiality should be respected at all times so it is important that details cannot be seen by another parent, and if another child was involved that child is not named. These records should be available for your inspector to see. It is also a good idea to check with your local authority for any preferred proformas and the length of time records should be kept.

For more serious accidents, for example a broken limb, hospitalisation or the death of a child (or staff member) you have a duty to report this under the Reporting of Injuries, Diseases and Dangerous Occurrences Regulations to your local Health and Safety Executive. Advice on the procedures for this should be obtained from your own local authority department.

All children develop at different rates and part of the work of health professionals is to monitor the progress of each child as an individual within the accepted sequence of growth and development milestones. As a childcarer you can work in partnership with parents to reassure, or identify any potential problems and tactfully encourage them to seek appropriate help and guidance. Minor accidents are common in childhood and some can be linked with different stages of development whilst the child is exploring and making sense of the world around them. Usually accidents have a plausible explanation and although possibly could have been avoided are accepted as that.

Child protection

Occasionally, however, injuries are caused deliberately by adults who are responsible for their children - these are known as non-accidental injuries and are a form of child abuse. As a childcarer you have a responsibility to work with the local social services and police to protect children. Procedures to be followed will have been drawn up by the Local Area Child Protection Committee and you should familiarise yourself with their guidance.

Child protection is a complex subject and if you have not had any child protection training, ask your line manager, contact your local authority or the National Society for the Prevention of Cruelty to Children for advice or literature.

If you feel that something is not right with a child or a child discloses that they are being abused, remember that you are not alone. You are part of a professional network which will work together to help the child, and offer support to both the child and their family. If a child makes a verbal disclosure, you should overcome your own feelings, and reassure the child that it was right to tell you. Listen, but do not put words into the child's mouth and never promise that you will keep any information a secret. Tell the child that you will need to discuss anything you see or

hear with your line manager or local social services duty desk. Keep a written record of events, making the report factual, including dates and times. Ensure that you know the routes of referral in operation in your area.

Protecting yourself

In order to be able to provide continuity of care for children, you need to ensure that you are fully fit. As a childcarer, discuss with your own doctor the immunisations that will protect you and if advised to have boosters or additional innoculations, take that advice! Rubella, tetanus, tuberculosis, polio and hepatitis are those that are usually recommended, but only you and your doctor know your own medical history and can make the right decisions.

Check that parents have used items such as teething gel, baby creams and sun protection cream on their child prior to using these yourself. Always use products supplied by parents - do not be tempted to use your own. If you work in a group care setting, follow the guidelines set down in your facilities procedures.

❏ Never administer anything without parents' written consent.
❏ Check your own insurance position.
❏ Ensure that you know the procedures and regulations of your registering authority.
❏ Remember to follow procedures and complete relevant paperwork at the right time.
❏ Make sure that you are up-to-date with current thinking and practice.

This will not only protect you but will ensure that you are giving a professional service.

Sheila Collins

What happens if there is an accident in your setting resulting in personal injury? Would you know the procedure to follow if someone were to make a personal injury claim against you? We outline the important aspects of making a claim and tell you how your claim should be handled by those dealing with it

Handling insurance claims

On 26 April 1999, the Government introduced changes in the law which altered the way in which personal injury claims would be handled by your insurance broker or insurance company.

These changes are the result of the recommendations contained in the Report by Lord Woolf into the handling of personal injury claims and the Government's wish to find a procedure in dealing with such claims that was both speedier and less expensive.

The Civil Procedure Act of 1997 effectively enacted the relevant changes and as a result there are now certain time limitations and obligations imposed on those dealing with your insurance claims in respect of:

a) personal injury, third party, motor and property claims; and

b) medical negligence claims.

As it is the first of these that is likely to be more relevant to you, I will outline the more

---

Are you legal?

❑ It is taken as read that you are covered by appropriate insurance. In January 2000, new regulations came into force regarding employer's liability insurance; these now require a minimum indemnity limit of £5,000,000.

❑ You should have your insurance certificate displayed in a prominent place and also make sure that appropriate public liability insurance is in force.

❑ Some schools also offer parents the opportunity of effecting personal accident insurance cover through a block policy.

---

important aspects of making a claim and tell you how your claim should be handled by those dealing with it.

Complete a claim form

So what happens if there is an accident in the workplace resulting in personal injury? Apart from dealing with it in accordance with the manner contained in your health and safety procedures, your insurers will want to receive details of your claim as soon as possible and for you to complete a claim form without delay. You will be able to obtain a form either from your broker or directly from your insurer. It's a good idea to keep the telephone number of your broker or insurer handy and near to your telephone.

The claim form is normally fairly easy to understand but your broker will be able to help you if you have any difficulties in completing it.

Time limit

Your insurers have a duty to acknowledge any letter of claim made in respect of personal injuries within 21 days of posting and (in the case of a claim against a third party - as in a motor accident, for instance) to give details to the claimant of name and address and other relevant details of the third party's insurer.

If liability is admitted then the insurer will make arrangements to settle the claim within a period of 90 days from acknowledgement of receipt of the claim.

If claims are denied in part then it is a matter for the Courts to decide whether delays have been as a result of any deliberate prevarication by one of the parties. Under

the new provisions anyone who is found to have caused a delay can be fined £100 or, in extreme circumstances, can be liable to imprisonment.

If liability is denied, your insurers have 90 days from the date of their acknowledgement of receipt of the claim within which to respond with full details of the reasons for denying liability.

'The real moral as far as insurance claims in schools or pre-school settings are concerned is to ensure that reasonable precautions are being taken to avoid risks, that proper procedures are in place to deal with accidents if they occur and that all the staff are familiar with their duties and responsibilities in health and safety matters.'

Important records to keep

For accidents at work, your insurers may well ask you for all or some of the following information (so it is important for you to see that proper records are kept):

❑ The accident book entry

❑ Any health and safety committee minutes

- ❏ Accident risk assessments

- ❏ Any internal investigatory reports

- ❏ Statements of witnesses

- ❏ Details of any similar accidents

- ❏ First aid or surgery records

- ❏ Repair maintenance records

- ❏ Training records

- ❏ Copies of correspondence with your health and safety authority

All this may seem somewhat intimidating but unfortunately it may be very relevant in assessing the value of the claim and your potential liability.

Expert witness

On dealing with a claim in order to speed up the process, you (or your insurer) will be required to accept a single mutually agreed expert witness and their evidence will usually be in the form of a written report (any further expert evidence will normally be at the expense of the party requesting it and can only be given in evidence with the approval of the Court).

New channels

If a claim is not settled then, depending on the amount of the claim, it will be 'tracked' into one of the new county court channels. These are:

Small Claims Court - claims up to £5,000 (£1,000 for bodily injury)

Fast Track - claims up to £15,000

Multi Track - over £15,000.

Extra vigilance

All these procedures are intended to reduce both the time taken and cost involved in settling claims. In practice, most of the claims you are likely to be involved with will relate to children in your care. For this

reason alone, extra care will need to be taken both in avoiding accidents and reporting to your superiors any circumstances which you anticipate might give rise to an accident or which you believe to be an area of risk.

If an accident involving a child does occur, the potential for a large claim is enhanced because of the life expectancy of the claimant and the claimant's physical weakness, so it is essential that staff report accidents as soon as they occur and always follow your health and safety procedures. Make sure that staff are confident about these procedures and organise regular training or refresher sessions for those you feel need it.

At least one of your staff should be trained in first aid (regulations vary - check with your local authority), so make sure that all staff know who that person is and where the first aid kit and accident book are kept.

As soon as practicable following an accident, it is important that you make a note of the circumstances and, where appropriate, obtain as much evidence as possible from witnesses. All of this information may be vital to your insurers in assessing both the amount or value of the claim and the legal liability.

The real moral as far as insurance claims in schools or pre-school settings are concerned is to ensure that reasonable precautions are being taken to avoid risks, that proper procedures are in place to deal with accidents if they occur and that all the staff are familiar with their duties and responsibilities in health and safety matters.

Alistair Pinnock, independent financial adviser

Related articles:

❏ Inspection and maintenance of play equipment - see pages 83 - 86

❏ Playing safely - accident prevention - see pages 61 - 64

A photocopiable accident form can be found in our book, *A-Z of Child Health* (Step Forward Publishing).

'In practice most of the claims you are likely to be involved with will relate to children in your care. For this reason alone extra care will need to be taken both in avoiding accidents and reporting to your superiors any circumstances which you anticipate might give rise to an accident or which you believe to be an area of risk'.

Most children today do not have the freedom to play outdoors and explore unsupervised, to experience the thrill of adventure and take risks. Yet taking risks - and learning from them - is a vital part of growing up. Jennie Lindon suggests some strategies for helping children recognise and deal with everyday risk

Taking risks -
or learning life skills?

You are responsible for the safety of other people's children. You are also responsible for ensuring that children gain from their time with you. Children need to add to their skills and knowledge in a way that helps them to feel not only more competent with their current skills, but also keen to face new learning challenges.

The right balance

A balance between protection and experience of an acceptable level of physical, intellectual and emotional risks for children has to be part of an enjoyable early years setting, just as in any family home.

Of course, you should work to avoid those accidents that are genuinely preventable and keep alert to what children are doing in the light of individual capabilities and understanding. A safe setting needs sensible health and safety guidelines and checks on equipment. But we all need to focus on childhood as a time of growing competence. It is responsible to watch children with great care around water, to have effective covers

for any pond or paddling pool. However, it is unhelpful to remove any craft tools that could even remotely be used by children to hurt each other or to ban boisterous games without any proper discussion with the children (who may have taken much time and imagination to create the games).

Children react to excessive and unexplained restrictions in different ways. Some children believe the anxious adults and worry unduly; others dismiss parents or early years workers as tedious fusspots and lose vital opportunities to learn important safety lessons. Any child can be bored in a setting dominated by calls of 'Be careful!' and 'Don't do that!', or when valuable time is wasted watching an adult do a task that they could manage on their own, if those skills had been patiently shared with them.

Supporting children's learning

Children's learning stretches over all the years of childhood. Many useful skills are learned a bit at a time, so you are not trying to pass on everything in your relatively short

period with individual children, nor are you in any way taking over from parents.

However, there are genuine risks for children if a whole series of key adults take the over-protective route, perhaps assuming that somebody else will help children learn important life skills. Older children can get into danger because they have no idea of real risks and the window of opportunity has passed when they are more willing to take advice and guidance from adults.

Children do not learn about recognising and dealing with everyday risk just because they have passed a certain birthday. They learn because:

❑ Adults have shared useful skills, techniques and tips, such as how to hold the wood properly when you are sawing or watching out for where the needle is going when sewing.

❑ Children have been helped to weigh up and deal with risks in a situation where adults are on hand to support, talk and listen. For instance, 'This is a safe place to cross the road because . . .' or 'The monsters game is crashing into other children. What can we do about it?'

❑ Children have been able to practise skills in the company of friends and to discuss problem-solving strategies with their peers as well as adults. For example: 'Our obstacle course is wobbly. How can we make it safe?' or 'We've got too many children on the climbing frame. Can we use the sand timer, please?'

❑ Where appropriate (which is much of the time), adults have talked about everyday risks in such a way as to involve the children and extend their understanding.

'We do young children no favours if we try to protect them from learning about all risks.'

Brief explanations and reminders such as, 'We wash our hands before cooking because ...' or 'How do we carry our spades safely?' help children to take part in their own well-being and that of others.

Risk assessment

The wariness felt by many adults can be sharpened when you care for disabled children or those with a continuing health condition. However, disabled children have the same motivation and needs to learn and grow in competence as their peers. They are not helped by excessive protection. The organisation Kidsactive (previously HAPA) has many years of experience in offering play, especially adventure play, to disabled children. Their approach is definitely one of risk assessment. In brief, you evaluate the genuine risk for each individual child and take the necessary steps for sensible protection: sometimes special equipment but more often appropriate adult support. Then you accept that disabled children will gather some bruises or scrapes and get in a mess, just like any other child who is having fun playing with their friends.

Coaching through tell-show-do

Children learn safe behaviour because adults have taken the trouble to go through the steps of tell-show-do:

❑ You tell children about what you do in an activity or routine and explain the safety aspects without going on so much that you become boring.

❑ Then you show them what to do, for example how to use the scissors, how to approach heat safely or wash your hands after handling any pets.

❑ Now children need plenty of opportunities to do the tasks, to practise as much as they want and to ask for more help as and when they judge they need it.

This supportive pattern of tell-show-do is just as relevant to disabled children, because the approach always needs to tune into individual children, their pace of learning and any sources of confusion.

When children apply their skills, you need to be encouraging, enthusiastic about what they can manage and supportive in reminding them of safety or good technique. You can revisit any safety issues in individual conversation or sometimes in circle time. So long as your comments acknowledge children's successes and are well grounded in activities, you will not sound as if you are nagging or criticising.

Early years settings can have woodwork or needlework tables and develop lively gardening projects with proper tools that work (unlike most so-called 'child safe' versions). The lessons from such settings are to be generous with tell-show-do time for each child who comes new to the activity, enabling them to gain confidence in the relevant skills. Such activities do not then need extra adults to supervise, because the children know what they are doing. It is also important to discuss any such activities with parents who express concern about the safety angle.

Children who feel involved and trusted are far more likely to follow a small number of safety guidelines and to understand the point of ground rules. Perhaps it is that only adults handle the 'big' scissors, the milk crates are never built more than two high, the superheroes game is just for the garden and woodwork tools are always put back on the tool board.

Children learn a great deal through play, but play is not their only vehicle for learning. Some groups are beginning to recognise the great value of involving children in daily routines (not only tidying up). Children show how they want to be part of the domestic activities involved in running an early years setting. They can learn how to take messages and carry items safely, help with drinks and make snacks, take turns to deal with the rabbit or be supportive to a child who either feels unwell or whose disability means they appreciate some focussed help.

The point of childhood is that children

'Children cannot learn to anticipate and weigh up ordinary risks unless they have been enabled to learn with supportive adults nearby. Parents and workers are often most aware of physical risks, but all children also need to handle the emotional and intellectual risks of childhood.'

emerge into young adulthood as competent and confident individuals. Children cannot learn to anticipate and weigh up ordinary risks unless they have been enabled to learn with supportive adults nearby. Parents and workers are often most aware of physical risks, but all children also need to handle the emotional and intellectual risks of childhood. They need experience that reassures them that something new can be an enjoyable opportunity, that not knowing how to do something is just the beginning and that they can make a mistake and not have it treated as a disaster.

We do young children no favours if we try to protect them from learning about all risks. It is vital that any early years team, in partnership with parents, is ready to reflect and discuss the important questions. Be ready to ask 'How can we make this safe?' and not just, 'This will have to be stopped!'. Work out how you can replace 'We can't let the children do that!' with 'So let's look for ways that we could enable them to be involved'.

Jennie Lindon

Kidsactive is a national charity providing information and training on inclusive play. You can contact them at Pryor's Bank, Bishop's Park, London SW6 3LA. Tel: 020 7731 1435.

It's never too early to start teaching good road safety habits. Rose Johnson takes you through the steps in organising a street walk and the lessons that can be learned from one

Organising a **road safety** walk

The importance of good road safety habits cannot be over-emphasised. It is one of the few areas of teaching which could save children's lives. You can provide safe and purposeful practical experiences which are valuable to both children and their parents.

Let parents know that you are planning a practical road safety activity. Encourage as many of them as possible to come along and join in. If they are not able to you should get written permission for their child to take part. Make sure that there is an adult to accompany every child. The leader of the expedition should not be amongst those with charge of children. Before leaving the pre-school building, make a list of everyone who is joining in the walk - children and adults.

Be safe - be seen
If possible, each child and adult should wear some sort of fluorescent clothing. Your local road safety officer (contacted via the council offices) should have some available for loan. Use this to introduce ideas about 'Be safe - be seen'. Emphasise how important it is for children to hold an adult's hand at all times. There are good reasons for this. Firstly, in terms of sensible restraint, but also in terms of visibility. A lone child presents a very small moving object, whilst a child and adult together are much more easily seen.

Care in car parks
On leaving your building, walk in crocodile formation, with the activity leader in front. If you have a car park, stop and use the opportunity to discuss safety around parked cars. The number of accidents in supermarket car parks makes this aspect of safety very relevant. Choose a safely parked car. Stand the group in front of the car and take one small child to the back of it. Ask the group in front of the car to look through the windscreen towards the back. (You might

have to lift them up!) Can they see the adult? Can they see their friend? This is a highly effective way of showing how difficult it is for a driver to see children who play behind vehicles.

Where to walk
Talk about places where it is safe to walk. Introduce the vocabulary of the roadside: kerb, pavement and footpath. Many children have confused ideas about the meaning of the word 'traffic'. Talk about safe behaviour on the roadside. Why do children think it

The Green Cross Code
Look to the right and listen,
Look to the left and listen,
Look to the right and listen again.
If it is safe to do so walk across
Looking and listening all the time.

is important not to run ahead of an adult? (It is useful to explain to parents that many accidents involving children are caused by cars pulling out of driveways.)

Where do the children think is a safe place to cross the road? Where is it not safe? (between parked cars, at bends and at road

junctions) Why? Encourage children to discuss their ideas and explain their thinking. If possible, show children crossing places such as zebra or pelican crossings. However, most accidents occur where there is no such provision. You cannot repeat too often that they should never attempt to cross the road on their own.

If it is safe to do so, ask the children to close their eyes and listen to the sounds of traffic. Can they identify whether a sound is from a car or lorry? Is it going fast or slow? Which direction is the sound coming from? Is the vehicle getting nearer or going away?

The Green Cross Code
Although children of pre-school age are extremely unlikely to be confident in identifying left and right it is still a good idea to introduce the Green Cross Code at this stage. The rhythm of the phrases used will be memorised even though the meaning of the words is as yet insecure. Encourage the children to teach the words of the code to the adults with them.

Show the children how to stand at a safe distance from the kerb. Holding their adult's hand they say together the words of the Green Cross Code. This should be done with just a few children and adults at a time, or the sound of the rhyme will drown out the noise of the traffic, and children will fall into the road as they lean forward to see around each other! Explain why it is important to walk not run across the road. If they run they could easily trip and fall.

When you get back, encourage the children to talk about their own experiences, enact some activities, such as crossing an imaginary road, and make models such as 'stop-go' lollipops, traffic lights or vehicles.

Rose Johnson, Road Safety Department, Uttlesford District Council, Essex

Disabled children have a right to play and be included in their local communities. Thanks to new disability legislation this right is now law. Rachel Scott examines the implications of the Disability Discrimination Act for play providers

The Disability Discrimination Act:
how it affects you

Disabled children need and want to play as much as and alongside their non-disabled peers. Yet as a result of social and environmental barriers, many disabled children are missing out on this essential part of growing up.

Play and early years workers are in a position to make a difference, and can begin to lead the way in promoting good practice in inclusive play. Disabled children have a right to play and be included in their local communities. This right is now firmly enshrined in disability legislation.

The Disability Discrimination Act 1995

The second stage of Part III of the Disability Discrimination Act (DDA), introduced in October 1999, requires service providers to ensure that disabled people (including children) are not discriminated against. Although buildings don't have to be physically accessible to wheelchair users until 2004, when the final phase of the DDA is implemented, everyone is now expected to think about and make 'reasonable adjustments' to the way in which they provide services. This includes providing auxiliary aids and services (such as sign language interpretation or information in Braille) to enable, or make it easier for disabled people to use the service.

Part III of the Act covers all aspects of services to the public including private companies, public sector organisations and voluntary and community groups. In terms of play and recreation services, the Act covers leisure centres, indoor and outdoor playgrounds, play areas in public parks, playgroups and some private

nurseries. Although, according to a D*f*EE spokesperson, 'the new regulations are very complex and something of a grey area where play and the early years are concerned. As education is exempt from the DDA, any nursery or playgroup, which receives funding from a local education authority, is not currently covered by the Act. However if a school hall is hired out for "non educational use" to a playgroup or facility then it is covered by the Act'.

It is difficult to say at this stage what the full implications of the legislation will be until cases are brought to court. Nor does the legislation spell out in detail what is meant by 'reasonable adjustments'. However, despite its shortcomings, there is no doubt that the DDA is beginning to raise awareness of disability issues. At the very least a marker has been put down on the principles of

equality of access and opportunity; and all play and early years providers (whether or not they are covered by the Act) should be looking towards developing inclusive services which have at their heart a policy of equal opportunities.

Inclusion defined
So what are the main areas that need considering when looking at the development of inclusive early years or play services? The starting point has to include reaching out to parents of disabled children, spending time building up relationships, and listening to what they have to say. It is only through working in partnership with parents, carers and disabled children that good quality inclusive practices can be established.

To be truly inclusive a play environment must address three fundamental components - access, participation and activities - and we will examine each of these in turn. Many supposedly inclusive play environments provide access but fall short on participation. It is no good allowing disabled children to attend if you do not have the appropriate resources to enable them to participate. Making play environments inclusive means that we must examine the types of experiences available to the majority of children and ensure that those experiences are also available to disabled children.

Access
Clearly physical access for children with mobility difficulties is an issue although the majority of disabled children do not use wheelchairs. In most cases minor alterations can be made

which are relatively cheap and can improve physical access. Organisations such as the Centre for Accessible Environments can help in this process. Most pre-school settings can already accommodate pushchairs and so need no adaptations in terms of level entrances. In some cases more permanent physical alterations will be required - such as the provision of suitable toilet facilities.

Access is not just about physical access to buildings but also about ensuring that the needs of visually impaired children are taken into account, and that signs and information is provided in large print and Braille. Colour codes and picture symbols can also be used for children with learning difficulties.

Over and above this, access is about having the will and the commitment to include disabled children. This is far more important than ticking off points on a check-list and declaring your project accessible. Dealing with needs as they arise and making every effort to include and welcome all children is central to this process.

Participation

Some children will undoubtedly need extra support or help with communication in order to participate - children with challenging behaviour and children with physical disabilities such as cerebral palsy in particular. Children who will not participate or whose behaviour seems inappropriate or obsessive may also need to be encouraged and supported to try out new activities. But you don't need to be an 'expert'. Rather you need practical information from parents such as 'How does the child communicate?' 'What are her likes and dislikes?' 'Does he need any special equipment for feeding?', and so on.

In order for children with speech and language difficulties to participate they need to be able to communicate. There are many methods of communication apart from the spoken language (British Sign Language and Makaton, for example) and it is important for staff and for non-disabled children to be aware, and have some knowledge of these

Organisations to contact

Kidsactive (formerly HAPA), Pryor's Bank, Bishop's Park, London SW6 3LA. Tel: 0207 731 1435. National charity providing information and training on inclusive play.

Parents for Inclusion, Unit 2 , 70 South Lambeth Road , London SW8 IRL Tel 0207 735 7735. An organisation set up by parents of disabled children to provide support and advice to parents and to campaign for the inclusion of disabled children in mainstream education.

RNIB, Tel: 020 7388 1266. Can advise on many aspects of play and leisure for visually impaired children.

National Deaf Children's Society, 15 Dufferin Street, London EC1Y 8PD. Tel/Minicom: 0207 250 0123. Can advise on communicating with deaf children.

MENCAP, 123 Golden Lane, London EC1Y ORT. Tel: 0207 454 0454. Can advise on working with children with learning difficulties.

Centre for Accessible Environments, Nutmeg House, 60 Gainsford Street, London SE1 2NY. Tel: 0207 357 8182. Information on access and design.

methods. This can be encouraged by, for example, involving children in games and songs which involve signing - all children seem to love this!

It is also important to provide some training for staff. The charity Kidsactive (formerly HAPA) provides training nationwide on inclusive play and can adapt training packages to suit the needs of early years workers in pre-school settings. There are also a number of organisations offering disability equality training. However, most nursery staff will find that they already have many of the skills needed to work with disabled children, the essential attributes being sensitivity, adaptability and imagination.

Activities and resources

Play environments must support play experiences that are matched to children's developmental levels and are also individually appropriate. Thus activities and resources must offer a variety of active learning experiences which are geared to the needs of disabled children as well as children

from ethnic minorities.

Special play equipment is rarely needed - although some toys for disabled children are useful. Far better to use ordinary toys and equipment with some small adaptations, or toys with sensory stimulation which are naturally inclusive. The RNIB, for example, has a toy catalogue which includes a wonderful range of toys for visually impaired children but which all children can enjoy. The organisation PLANET can advise on all aspects of toys and resources that are appropriate to varying ages as well as disabilities. The other alternative to buying is to borrow - in the UK there are around 1,000 toy and leisure libraries for disabled children run by Playmatters, the National Association of Toy and Leisure Libraries.

Challenging discrimination - overcoming barriers

Setting up an inclusive play project is not easy. It presents many challenges, and there are many barriers to overcome - not least barriers of attitude and how society views disability. Negative attitudes from parents and carers of non-disabled children is not uncommon. They may be wary about their own children mixing with disabled children or be ambivalent about the idea of inclusion. Then there are the concerns of parents of disabled children who may worry about the level of care their children will receive, the safety of the environment, and the reactions of other children.

Most of these attitudes arise from fear and ignorance, and it is only through challenging discrimination and awareness raising with parents that we will begin to change attitudes. As for the children, the most common reaction to difference is one of curiosity and acceptance - particularly in the early years. Let's capitalise on this and start the process of moving towards a society where all children, regardless of disability, ethnicity or any other difference, can play together in a supportive environment without fear of prejudice or discrimination.

Rachel Scott, Information co-ordinator, Kidsactive

There has never been more choice of early years equipment and the variety grows with every new catalogue. If you find yourself with the funds to invest in some new furniture, it pays to give some serious thought to what you need and how it will be used.

Buying **tables** and **chairs**

The Children Act 1989 refers briefly to the style and provision of tables and chairs within early years settings, but the implications of these basics can be much greater than you think - the shape of the table and its impact on the arrangements for the peace talks at the end of the Vietnamese war, for example, was cause for much debate.

Table shape has an impact on behaviour and on personal dynamics. In the nursery, it has implications for personal and social development. Different shapes lend themselves to different activities. It may seem obvious, but it is also important to remember that one size does not fit everyone; children need to sit on chairs and at tables that are the right height for them. (A 30cm high table would be suitable for three- and four-year-olds, with a corresponding chair of 13cm.) Many early years settings have storage problems and whether tables and chairs stack may have to be a prime consideration.

Round versus square
In the past, schools used to have rectangular or square tables arranged in a uniform pattern. Since the 1970s, circular tables have slowly crept into early years provision They create a more active flow of traffic and introduce variety into floor plans. A round table encourages interaction between children. Lines of communication are easier and children can relate to each other on an equal basis. This makes circular tables good for more social activities such as games or activities that involve conversations.   In language work circular tables are used to foster discussions and collaboration.

Groups working at a circular table often find it easier to focus around the table and interact with each other; there tends to be more eye contact. Resources placed in the middle are within arm's reach of everyone - making it easier to share or take turns.

Dough play and construction can be sociable activities. Children tend to appear engrossed in what they are making but are often engaged in conversation with themselves or others. There are often exchanges in tools or materials and these are moved to and fro around the table. Some

suppliers produce tables with a central area bowl for such items.

Sometimes a square table is helpful to get children to focus on their given task. Four children, one sat on each side, can work better as individuals. If too many children are placed around a circular table, especially with creative activities, sheets of paper overlap, pencils get mixed up, and opportunities for disruption are greater. It is also easier to cover a square table with newspaper for creative work!

Square tables are useful to promote focused paired tasks and foster problem-solving. Encourage pairs to consider a problem and then later to share ideas with the opposite pair on the table.

Board games on a square table can bring about more formality and organisation - the shape of the table tends to bring about clarity of turn taking if there are only four

players, though games played on a square or rectangular table tend to be more competitive and confrontational.

Ideally, you will have a combination of square and round tables and use different ones for different activities. 'Fitness for purpose' is the key to achieving the desired learning and behaviour of young children.

Layout

Just as important as the type and style of furniture is how it is arranged within your setting. The basic shape of the room, organisation of activities and location of resources will all play a part in the overall layout, but it is worth remembering that the layout of tables does have an impact on the provision. Put them too close and they can cause points of confrontation, leading to poor behaviour and possible accidents.

Placing tables in a regimented fashion can bring about formality in an early years setting too soon. You can create some interesting bays and shapes with square tables that divide into two by placing them against a wall.

Other shapes

Another table shape to look at is the trapezoid (a quadrilateral with no sides parallel!). This in some ways is a good compromise between the square and circular table - it gives the benefits of collaboration and co-operation and yet children have a defined place. A group of six can use the table in comfort, perhaps working as two trios, which is another interesting grouping!

Another option is the half-circular shape, sometimes known as the horse-shoe table, where an adult can sit within arm's length of the child. Even more unusual is the clover shape table now being produced by some suppliers.

Seating

The various surfaces and floorplay that is on offer to your children will inevitably have an impact on the provision of chairs. With the present focus on literacy, book corners are of key importance. The Children Act 1989 states, 'Providers may wish to supplement chairs with beanbags and floor cushions which help to create a friendly and informal atmosphere.'

Another area of design growth is the computer centre - an integrated table and bench seat on which a computer can be placed and two children can sit. However, a bench style chair does not provide proper back support.

You will need to think about the design of chairs in terms of the support it offers physically - the back support on a chair and its height is of great importance. A seat that is too high causes unnecessary thigh pressure by not allowing the feet to rest on the ground. If you're buying chairs to go with existing tables, check how much leg room there will be.

The Children Act also refers to the need for adults to have appropriate seating so that they are comfortable yet at a level which makes eye to eye contact with children possible. Some suppliers call these 'low height adult chairs'; they have a seat height of 28 centimetres or 11 inches.

Materials

The life of a chair depends on the material it is made from. Chairs tend to be made in either polypropylene or wood. Many settings have wooden chairs that have lasted a life-

The writing table

In many settings the 'emergent writing table' where children can experiment with early writing can be found placed against a wall where an alphabet frieze or other prompt can be displayed to encourage children to write symbols or letters. It may be found behind a storage unit which juts out from a wall. The writing table is like a work station for children; they need to have easy access to it all the time. Perhaps only a maximum of two chairs are necessary. Table and chair height is important to encourage children to sit correctly when writing.

time. Some of the polypropylene ones are fire retardant. Some wooden chairs are made from a laminated maple so that they are as easy to wipe clean as plastic. (This is also the case for some tables.) Look out for features such as rounded vinyl edges for safety on table tops.

Tables and chairs are important investments, so it pays to do some research and check prices with several suppliers.

Ann Roberts

Main suppliers

One of the market leaders in the field of wooden furniture is Community Playthings. They even have a research unit in New York where they investigate furniture design and factors such as table shape. They provide many early years settings with their furniture.

Other educational suppliers have catalogues with sections on furniture with recommended height charts - NES Arnold, Galt, Hope, to name but a few.

It is your duty to ensure that any equipment you have is safe and in good condition. David Hedley outlines the steps you should take to ensure the safety of your charges and protect yourself from any legal action

Inspection and maintenance of play equipment

The inspections recommended below are intended to apply to new playground equipment made in accordance with Parts 1 and 2 of BS5696. Other equipment may require different maintenance, and some situations require a more frequent and higher level of inspection and maintenance. The frequency will depend on the type of equipment, its condition and history of maintenance, the environmental conditions, degree of use and the likelihood of vandalism. It's important that these factors are assessed and used to prepare a maintenance schedule for all play equipment which should be reviewed regularly in the light of experience. You should keep records of all the inspections.

Photocopy the forms on pages 85 and 86 and keep them in a ring binder. As you acquire new equipment ensure that a relevant form is completed for each piece. Inspections must be carried out as follows:

Daily inspections

A daily visual examination of all equipment, fixed and mobile, should be carried out by a nominated person. If parents or volunteers are used as nominated persons, it is important to ensure that they are reliable, and that the load is shared between a number of people. There is no laid down requirement for the training of those undertaking daily inspections, although all of the points on the inspection schedule provided should be checked

Regulations

BS 5696 : Part 3 : 1979 lays down the recommendations for the inspection and maintenance of 'play equipment intended for permanent installation outdoors'. There are no equivalent regulations for mobile play equipment, whether it is used inside or out. Therefore, for safety, you should only use mobile play equipment which bears a kite mark or a CE mark. You are legally obliged to inspect your play equipment. If it is carried out as recommended here, it could form a defence in a claim for injury. Failure to carry out inspection could lead to prosecution by the Health and Safety Executive or local authority.

daily. Particular attention should be paid to the list of typical faults and defects. When equipment is first installed, the daily inspection should take account of 'running-in faults'. Any equipment which is considered unsafe should be secured against use or, in the case of mobile equipment, locked away. Details of the fault and action taken to repair/rectify should then be entered onto a daily record sheet (specimen provided).

Recorded inspection (one to three months)

At intervals of between one and three months, a more detailed inspection of equipment is required. The results of this and any remedial action should be entered onto a permanent inspection record (see specimen provided), which should be kept for future examination. In addition to the defects checked on a daily basis, particular attention should be paid to the effects of corrosion or other deterioration, wear and vandalism, all of which will be particular to individual locations. Again there is no requirement for trained personnel to undertake this inspection. However, I would recommend that the nursery's building inspector or maintenance contractor should carry out this survey and complete the inspection record.

Certified inspection (six to twelve months)

At intervals not exceeding 12 months, and preferably twice yearly, coinciding with the end of the winter and the end of the summer, a detailed inspection should be carried out by a specialist inspector and the results entered onto the permanent record. The Royal Society for the Prevention of Accidents (0121 248 2000) and the National Playing Fields Association (0207 8335360) will carry out inspections at reasonable rates. Arrangements may be made with manufacturers and installers. In the case of local authority nurseries, health and safety officers will be able to recommend a suitably qualified inspector.

Defects

When a defect is discovered it should be reported immediately and the equipment secured against use. The defect should be rectified as soon as possible. Details of all defects and any remedial action taken should be recorded in the permanent record.

To ensure that inspections are systematically and thoroughly carried out a check-list detailing all items of equipment to be examined should be drawn up. This check-list can be used as the basis of a permanent record. It may be worth displaying a notice where reports of any defects noted by parents or helpers should be made.

Reminder

You should also be in the habit of checking other nursery equipment on a regular basis - wooden furniture for splinters, chairs and tables for wobbly legs or loose screws. Every day as you set out equipment for children check for broken or damaged toys.

Maintenance

General

Maintenance and repairs to equipment and replacement of components should always be carried out in strict compliance with the manufacturer's recommendations.

Replacement of components

Components and fasteners should be replaced whenever necessary with the correct part. Substitute parts should not be used unless you get the approval of the manufacturer or the certified engineer. If the components are fixed with screw fastenings which are rivetted over, they should be fixed in the same way when replaced.

Coated surfaces

All coated surfaces should be regularly maintained in accordance with the provisions laid down in BS 5268, BS5493, CP118, CP231 and CP3012 as appropriate. Non toxic materials should always be used. If only minimum surface protection is specified, it is important that equipment is regularly inspected and repaired before serious deterioration takes place. It is usually more cost effective, in the long term, to specify a better and more durable surface protection which protects the equipment and reduces maintenance costs.
Note: It is recognised that after a period of use it is inevitable that components will have coatings, such as paint, worn off.

Impact absorbing surfaces

Natural impact absorbing surfaces such as Cambark should be cleaned and raked over and/or replaced at regular intervals. Artificial surfaces should be regularly inspected and replaced when excessively worn or damaged to avoid the introduction of further hazards.

David Hedley, Security Manager, Newcastle upon Tyne Education Department.

Outdoor play equipment

Daily inspection / maintenance sheet

Week ending

1. Check each item and tick box if satisfactory. **2.** If a minor repair is carried out which then renders the equipment /item safe (eg replace screw, sand or remove sharp edges), tick box and enter details below under action taken. **3.** If a repair/defect cannot be rectified, put an X in box and enter details below under action recommended. Following reporting procedure, disable equipment and put up warning sign.

	Mon	Tues	Wed	Thurs	Fri
Equipment					
Time of inspection					
Safety surface					
Paths					
Steps					
Daily maintenance (time taken)					
Comments/ Action taken					
Action recommended					

Signature of person carrying out inspection .... Position ....

Date ....

Print name ....

Defects check-list

Equipment should be checked daily for superficial faults. The following are typical defects which can be identified during a visual check:

Structure — bending, warping, cracking, loosening, breaking

Surface finish — protective coating missing, rust or other

Consumable items — missing, bent, broken, loosened, worn, open hooks

Edges — protrusions, sharp points or sharp edges

Pinch or crush points — exposed mechanisms, junctures or moving components

Mechanical devices — worn bearings, lack of lubrication, seizure or other moving parts, excessive motion, unduly noisy motion, incorrect clearances, missing covers

Guard or hand rails — or swing barriers missing, bent, broken or loosened

Access — missing or broken rungs, steps or treads, loosening

Swing and other seats — missing, damaged, loosened, sharp corners, insecure fittings

Foundations — cracked, loose in ground

Protective surfacing — compacted, displaced to ineffectual level, not extensive enough to cover possible impact area, insanitary, missing

Drain holes — blocked, covers cracked or missing

Outdoor play equipment Inspection record

A record should be kept for each individual piece of equipment

Year _____

Name of equipment .... Description of equipment ....

(reference number if applicable) .... Nature of ground area beneath/beside equipment ....

Three-monthly inspection

Date carried out		Comments/Action recommended	Name	Signed
Jan - Mar				
Apr - Jun				
Jul - Sep				
Oct - Dec				

Annual inspection

Date of inspection	Inspection carried out by	Action taken	Signed

Given the choice, some children prefer to be active outside rather than playing indoors. If they have constant access to an outdoor area you can make sure that there are opportunities to explore all areas of learning - and that includes Literacy

Literacy in the **outdoor play area**

All children enjoy talking about things which are relevant to them. They like talking about their immediate environment and enjoy a real-life approach. The outdoor play area can provide opportunities to develop this in a context.

Developing a nature centre

You could set up a small area in the playground which includes a pond, a grassy area, a dark/damp area and a plant area. Once it is established you can add labels which reflect the dangers and fascinations of the area. A label by the pond may say, 'No fishing!' Signs in other areas may say, 'Keep off the grass!', 'Digging in progress', 'Worm turning left', 'No stamping: woodlice easily shaken!' or 'Please be quiet!'

This nature area could also have a map for the children to use in order to find the places mentioned, like you find in large shopping malls. The map would have all the areas labelled for the children to read and use - pond, plant and shrub area, planting area, grassy area, dark and damp area. All the areas pinpointed on the map can include a small amount of information about them underneath the headings.

The children can be taken out in small groups to read these maps. You can discuss the orientation of print, sound/symbol relationships and that print has meaning in a context, so children can see the purpose of print and how it relates to the world they are living in.

The bike park

Most nurseries have an area where children can ride bikes. Put up some notices to develop literacy skills: 'Bike park', 'Drive carefully'. You could make number plates for the bikes. The discussion about what is written on them will encourage the children to recognise letters and numbers. You could discuss registration numbers and their purpose. On the playground where the children are riding the bikes you could paint lanes and speed limits - 5mph in one lane, 10mph in another.

You could also have a colour ticket system where different bikes have different tickets depending on how popular they are. These tickets could be made from card and laminated, and say, for example: 'Bring back in: 3 minutes'. The child would have this ticket and the adult on duty would need to make sure that the children kept to the time on the tickets. This helps children to see

literacy used within their own situation.

A rectangle could be painted on the ground to make sure children put the bikes in the grid: 'Please keep bikes inside the rectangle'.

Games on the playground

Another great idea is to have a game painted on the playground which can be played in all seasons. It could have a 4 x 4 grid numbered appropriately (see below). It might include pictures and words to convey instructions or left free to develop a variety of games. The children will need a large die. (You can get dice where instructions are inside the die - this would support the flexibility of use.)

Take a small group out at a time to play the game. At first, you will need to guide them around the game. All the children will enjoy trying to work out what the writing says. Parents can become involved by playing with the children when they come to drop them off and pick them up.

Children will be able to pick up letters/ sounds relationships and build up some sight vocabulary, but crucially will see the importance of the text as giving meaning.

Rubina Din

1 Start here...	2 Go to six	3 Hide	4 Pick up the key
5	6	7 Wild fish - run!	8 Go forward to 12
9 Go back to 5	10 Go back to 6	11	12
13 Go forward 1 space	14	15 Have you got the key?	16 Wow! You got the treasure

A camera is one of the most valuable resources you can have in your nursery, says Ann Clay. Buy the best you can afford and keep it to hand at all times for staff - and children - to use

Every nursery **needs a camera**

Cameras are becoming essential in early years settings. If you don't have one, it's certainly something you should think about buying.

There are so many different types of camera on the market - from the basic point-and-press varieties to the latest digital cameras which can be used with computers - that it can be daunting when you first start to shop around. Our theory is, buy the best camera that you can afford with a zoom lens and built-in flash. Try to choose one that is simple enough for every member of your team to use. If you are working to a tight budget, buy a good basic model, but do buy one! A camera is now most definitely one of our essential resources.

There is a variety of children's cameras available, but you'll find that most adult ones are child-friendly. Alternatively, buy the disposable ones and the children can use them anywhere - within reason!

Polaroid cameras are still fascinating to use with children. It is worth photographing a child's reaction to the Polaroid photograph developing before their eyes!

Why do you need a camera?

Many of the day-to-day activities taking place in our nurseries are difficult to record - the child who has made a beautiful lighthouse from junk, a large-scale construction with wooden blocks and imaginative play both indoors and outdoors.

Photographs are essential in these situations as they can:

- show evidence of the work and learning taking place;

- enable assessment to continue after observation;

- give you the opportunity to inform others about your work in the nursery, for example visitors, parents, children - and inspectors!

- be used to illustrate your weekly planning;

- be used to illustrate your policies;

- enable you to show parents how children learn through play. For example, you could produce a photographic display in your entrance area to show parents the learning which comes from playing in the sand tray. Change this display at regular intervals until you have covered all areas of learning within your nursery.

How using a camera can improve your work

There are many ways that photographs can be used in teaching. Here are a few ideas you might try:

- Make books of photographs showing all the nursery activities and take them on home visits as a talking point for parents and children.

- Take photographs of geographical landmarks in your area and make a book of these to use as a teaching aid and to have in your book corner.

- Use photographs of staff to help children and parents name and identify them in the early stages and then use them to pin point where the key worker will be in the nursery, developing matching and geographical skills.

- Use photographs of activities as specific teaching aids at small group times to encourage children to plan their own work and develop their geographical skills through locating the chosen activity within the indoor or outdoor area of the nursery.

- Use photographs for matching and sequencing activities to illustrate familiar objects and settings.

- Photographs of equipment in the home corner, laminated and used as labels, will help children tidy up, knowing that everything has a place and again developing matching skills!

- Use photographs to look at the seasons changing in the nursery garden and help the children to develop an understanding of science in a familiar setting.

- Use them as a stimulus for both indoor and outdoor play. Have photographs enlarged to A4 size and then laminate them. Not only are you using familiar stimulus for the children, you've got them forever!

Using photographs to help record a child's progress

Photographs are essential to illustrate children's work you are unable to document or keep.

Use photographs:
- as part of developmental records on each child;

- in ongoing records of achievement folders which, when transferred to the child's next stage of education, help to form the basis of a lifelong record of work;

- to celebrate a piece of work. Children love it when we photograph them during or after an activity!

- to recall work that children have done over the last week, months or year, helping to develop an understanding of the passage of time;

- as a 'visual memory' of events and visitors to our nurseries, for example Diwali, a visiting circus or theatre group - and the day that the hedgehog walked into the nursery garden!

Have the camera available to hand at all times - you never know what is going to happen next! Plan to take photographs of certain activity areas and work going on but always be ready for that moment of spontaneity. If the camera is locked away in the filing cabinet, you have missed it forever!

Ann Clay

How the children benefit

- They gain hands-on experience of holding and using a camera to follow on from role play using an old camera in the home corner.

- They increase their understanding of technology - how the camera works, the correct terminology for parts of the camera and the development process.

- They develop an understanding of the whole process from taking the photograph, to finishing the film, taking it to be developed and collecting the photographs.

- Through the above process they develop links with the wider community.

- They can celebrate their own work by asking to take a photograph of it.

- It improves skills in socialisation and organisation especially when photographing their friends.

- They develop creativity and an appreciation of the world around them and can capture moments of awe and wonder, for example dew on the spider's web, blossom falling from the trees, the duckling hatching from the egg.

- Taking their own photographs really helps the children come to terms with past, present and future.

Have the camera to hand at all times - you never know what is going to happen next!

What form of supplementary heating is safest and best? How warm do you need to be? And what about ventilation?

Keeping warm in winter

To work and learn and play children need a warm and well-ventilated environment. All settings, whether in a purpose-built classroom, a church hall or a modular building (mobile), will have some form of background heating which is normally sufficient to maintain a reasonable temperature. However, when the cold really strikes many settings will need supplementary heating to maintain the ideal temperature.

Guidance for the working environment

Guidance on the ideal condition for working environments is given in the CIBSE Design Guide, published by the Chartered Institute of Building Services Engineers, under the section 'Environmental criteria for design'. This gives the suitable temperatures for people in active or sedentary occupations. The guide also gives approximate ventilation rates for the dispersal of smoke and body odours from people within a room. Children under 14 are regarded as being high in the body odour department - so a room of 16 four-year-olds is soon likely to become polluted.

Specific guidance for pre-school premises is lacking so much must be done by common sense.

Ideal temperature

Because we are talking about activities taking place within a short time-scale in a variety of settings and premises it would be unreasonable to attempt to provide different temperatures and ventilation rates. Children are sometimes sedentary - sitting down at story time - and at others active - jumping up and down for physical development. So it comes down to achieving

a sensible temperature of around 20°C at the child's body level - that is at their height. Temperature is usually measured at 1.5 metres from the ground - higher than most small children - so bear this in mind when reading any guidance about heating.

The modest requirement of 20°C can be quite difficult to achieve when you consider the ventilation that is also required, particularly with the standard hot water or electric convector/panel radiator system.

The problem is that warm air rises from the radiator or heat source and cooler air falls

(including the cold fresh air from outside for ventilation) and so the room becomes very warm at high level but noticeably cooler at floor level. You can feel this effect at home - put your hand up towards the ceiling and then down at floor level - 3-5°C difference is not unusual.

Remember this when you or your staff feel warm. Test exactly what the temperature is at the child's level.

You should also remember this temperature difference when children sit on the floor in winter - the coldest place. You might want to encourage them to sit on chairs - or a sofa. Make sure that warm socks and shoes are worn - even if it feels warm higher up in the room.

You are aiming for a mean temperature of 20ºC. The accepted temperature for 'alert' active work - such as in school gyms - is 18ºC. So it is not unreasonable to start the day at this temperature - when children are engaged in active play. When it comes to story time the temperature should ideally be around 21-22ºC. So if your session starts active and ends with story time then you should aim for a gradual warm-up of the setting.

Suitable heaters and safety considerations

The ideal systems for warming at low level are floor heating and overhead radiant heating. Many premises will already have this as background heat. But in the cold weather you may be tempted to turn up the thermostat on the boiler to increase the temperature of your radiators. Portable electrically heated radiators (and even the standard, hot water, central heating radiators) should not have a surface temperature higher than 43ºC or there is a real risk of skin burning on contact. This is especially so with small children and the elderly. A child falling onto a radiator at a temperature above this is in danger of suffering burns.

You may well need temporary supplementary heating for the coldest days.

When considering what heating to choose, the overriding consideration must be safety. Floor-standing, portable, electric fan heaters are unsuitable in an area where children are going to run around, but wall-mounted, with the air stream directed forwards and downwards, they can provide a suitable

means of supplementary heating. However, they can be a little noisy and are perhaps not suitable for sitting under for any length of time.

Similarly, wall-mounted electric radiant heaters offer an excellent means of warming at lower levels. These are the infra-red type of heaters which are often used in bathrooms. Because it is radiant heat it does not lose its effectiveness as it travels through the air. It gives off its heat when it meets a surface - the floor or children's faces and body. If you have a particular problem with cold in your setting, a wall-mounted heater over the book corner will ensure a snug audience for story time. Although moderately expensive to run its use can be monitored to make the cost more reasonable.

Portable, LPG (Calor), cabinet radiant heaters release all of their combustion gases and a good deal of moisture into the room. Although they can be a useful back-up in an emergency they are really not suitable for long-term use. The moisture will cause condensation and the combustion gases will also have to be vented so even more ventilation will be required. They are safer to use in large volume, well-ventilated rooms but less effective as a heating means in these circumstances.

Electric bar fires are not suitable.

Ventilation

Those of you in large, Victorian classrooms or a church hall with a high ceiling will find that heating is the greatest problem. Exchanging the air will not be a priority as the warmer air will rise and self-ventilate the room.

However, if you're in a modular building or smaller, low ceilinged, modern room, you will also have to maintain ventilation as well as heat.

We have already pointed out that small children can be smelly. Smells can build in an enclosed atmosphere. As we work in the room we become less aware of the smell, but newcomers - and that includes children - will be aware of it. It may be worth asking any visitor who you know well about whether they can smell the room. Tell them you will not be embarrassed by their answer and increase your ventilation if need be.

A window should be kept open at all times - no matter what the weather. If you operate two sessions it is worth opening more doors and windows before the next group arrives. You will lose some heat but not as much as you might think. There is residual heat in the walls, floor and ceiling, which will soon bring you back to the ideal temperature. The smaller the room the more ventilation it will need but it will also warm up quicker.

Norman Jones, Sutherland Associates, Building Services and Energy Consultants

Useful address
Institute of Domestic Heating and Environmental Engineers, Dorchester House, Wimblestraw Road, Berinsfield, Oxon OX10 7LZ

Tel: 01865 343096
Email: info@idhe.newnet.co.uk

Excessive energy use diverts precious funds away from enhancing the learning experiences of children. This check-list suggests some ways of reducing the energy drain on resources. Some cost nothing to implement, it is just a matter of changing procedures. Others require a small investment that will normally pay for itself within a couple of years. Major upgrading schemes are not considered because they are expensive and only pay for themselves over many years

How to save **energy** – a check-list

Look at lighting

Sunlight is free. Electricity is an expensive form of energy. It makes sense to use the former wherever possible.

- Make sure windows and roof lights are clean.
- Don't block out natural light by attaching excessive amounts of display materials to windows.
- Switch off lights nearest the windows as soon as natural lighting is adequate.
- Switch off lights in unoccupied rooms or areas.
- Check the need for any electric lighting after 10 am.
- Fit time-delay switches or lights controlled by occupation detectors in corridors without natural daylight.
- Regular cleaning of the diffusers around lamps can significantly increase lighting levels.
- Make sure cleaners only light the areas in which they are working.
- Encourage out-of-hours users to use lighting wisely while maintaining safety and security.

Investigate:

- fitting reflectors behind fluorescent tubes;
- using 26 mm diameter fluorescent tubes when 38 mm types fail;
- using compact fluorescent lights instead of intensively-used filament bulbs;
- refurbishing strip lighting over 15 years old with high frequency ballast units;
- fitting modern fluorescent lights.

Home in on heating

Over two-thirds of the energy you use will go on heating rooms and corridors. Action can both reduce costs and increase comfort.

- The target temperature for comfort and health in classrooms is 18°C. If it gets hotter than this during winter, then take action. Start by checking the setting on thermostats. If altering the thermostats has no effect, call in a heating engineer to investigate. Every 1°C above the target temperature adds about 6 per cent to heating bills.
- The target temperature for corridors, washrooms and toilets is 15°C. Other targets apply to special schools and sick-rooms.
- Make sure that air is free to circulate round radiators and hot air grilles.
- Fit tamper-proof thermostatic radiator valves (TRVs) when the central heating system is next drained for maintenance.
- Check the louvre, fan, thermostat and manual over-ride mechanisms of night-storage heaters. Find out how to use the controls effectively.
- The time clock controlling electric heaters (storage, radiator or fan types) should be telling the correct time. Check that the on and off times suit the present pattern of occupation.
- During winter, make sure that the blinds or curtains are closed at night.

Evaluate ventilation

All buildings should be warm but without becoming stuffy or humid. The average school loses about a quarter of its heat through excessive ventilation and draughts.

- Check that window frames and panes are tight-fitting. The seals on opening windows should be intact.
- Install draught stripping if this is not already present. It may not affect the temperature, but it will make a room feel warmer.
- Check that automatic closers are installed and working on all external doors.
- Make sure everybody knows that opening windows is not the ideal way of dealing with over-hot rooms.
- Only run extractor fans when they are really needed.

Work on water

All but the smallest schools pay for water by volume. Significant savings can be made by simple measures.

- Hot water tanks should be at a temperature of 60°C to maintain sterility. They should be well insulated.
- Hot water pipes should be lagged, provided that the water is no hotter than 43°C at wash-basins.
- Fix dripping taps.
- Fit flow restrictors and push taps when ordinary taps need replacing.
- Switch off auto-flushing urinals at night, over weekends and during holidays. However, a daily hygienic flush is required.

Keys to reducing energy costs

1 Know what is going on. How much equipment is used, by whom and why?

2 Log electricity, gas and water meters at least monthly. Investigate unexpected changes. They could indicate problems.

3 Check meter readings in bills against your own readings.

4 Take steps to reduce energy consumption. Involve the children in this process.

5 Find out more about energy management and the ways in which savings can be identified and quantified.

6 Contact national organisations for guidance and local bodies for support when starting to bring your energy bills under control.

The open market in gas and electricity

There have been many changes in the energy market in the last few years. Under delegated budgets, most state schools in England and Wales are now responsible for paying their own energy bills. Climate Change Levy has been applied to these bills since April 2001.

To attract or retain customers, many suppliers are now providing packages that can include anything from a few educational goodies, through energy audits and advice, to total energy management contracts. These cover monitoring and reporting on consumption, identifying problems, recommending improvements and upgrading controls.

Independent energy management consultants are also offering their services. They will offer to negotiate tariffs in addition to monitoring, and so on The best will support teachers in the educational aspects of energy and its management.

Suppliers of gas and electricity can be changed without altering any of the pipes, cables and meters that bring gas and electricity into your building. All that happens is you get your bills from a different company.

It is a wise precaution to note down all meter readings on the day of change-over and then check that they have been used correctly in calculating the last bill from the old supplier and the first from the new.

State nursery schools may find that negotiations with energy suppliers are done on their behalf by their local authority. Find out what they are charging you for this service together with what other benefits they are supposed to be providing (for example, energy efficiency advice or talking to groups of children and their parents.) Always obtain the permission of your landlord (the LEA) before taking measures to improve energy efficiency, entering into contracts with new suppliers or appointing energy consultants. If problems arise under arrangements that you have made independently, the LEA may not provide support.

Private nurseries

Independent and grant maintained schools must make their own arrangements. It could be worthwhile joining a purchasing consortium or using the local authority scheme. If you run a pre-school that rents a church hall or similar building, there is little you can do about changing energy suppliers or physical measures to improve energy conservation. However, you can raise these issues with the owner, suggest improvements and make sure that you are not being overcharged for energy.
Whatever your situation:
- Make sure that what you buy is what you actually need and can afford.
- Don't enter into long-term contracts.

John Rodway,
Education and Training Officer,
Centre for Research, Education
and Training in Energy (CREATE).

Where to get help

For state nursery schools, the first point of contact should be your local authority's energy management unit. Unfortunately, there is no consistency across the country as to its title, or its position within authority departments. Officers within the LEA should know if it operates as part of the architects', building services' or engineers' department.

The Department for Education and Skills has several publications dealing with managing energy in schools. A good introduction is *Managing School Facilities: Guide 3 - Saving Energy.* (ISBN 0-11-270880-3).
Details from HMSO Publications Centre. Tel: 0207 873 0011

Building Energy Efficiency in Schools: A guide to a Whole School Approach: This is the key publication in a government series for schools. It is free from BRECSU, Building Research Establishment, Garston, Watford WD2 7JR. Tel: 01923 664258.

Energy - a Source of Wonder is a workbook to help teachers introduce pre-school children and their families to basic concepts of energy. A supporting video case study is available on free loan. NEA, St Andrew's House, 90 Pilgrim Street, Newcastle NE1 6SG. Tel: 0191 261 5677.

Openings! is a guide to quality education and energy management materials together with a list of organisations that can provide support and advice. It is published by CREATE on behalf of the Energy Education Forum.

SchoolEnergy Programme - Rebates for schools throughout the UK to make improvements to their heating, lighting and boiler controls, etc. The scheme is managed by CREATE on behalf of the Energy Saving Trust. Tel: 0870 7000 457.
Website:www.schoolenergy.org.uk

The Centre for Research, Education and Training in Energy (CREATE) provides a free enquiry service for teachers, pupils and school managers on all aspects of energy education and management, including the availability and appropriateness of teaching resources.
Free newsletter available.
CREATE, Kenley House, 25 Bridgeman Terrace, Wigan WN1 1TD.
Tel: 01942 322271. Fax: 01942 322273.
Web site: www.create.org.uk

Chapter 4

Unit C3: Promote the physical development of children

About this unit

This unit is all about how you can help children to develop physical skills appropriate to their age and stage of development. At first, babies have no control over their physical movements, but by placing stimulating objects such as rattles, dangling objects, play mats and play gyms within their reach you will help them to begin to develop physical control. Soon they will be able to hold, pat, tap and shake objects. They will also put everything in their mouth, so you must make sure that toys are safe, with no small or sharp pieces, and hygienic. As they become more mobile they will need moving toys to encourage them to roll, crawl and eventually walk. After that, there's no stopping them! They don't have the experience yet to know what is dangerous, so the adult needs to make absolutely sure that the environment is safe for them to explore.

There are currently concerns that even young children are not as healthy as in the past because they are not getting enough physical exercise. There are several possible reasons for this:

◆ Busy working mothers tend to drive their children to school or nursery.

◆ Children don't always go to school or nursery in the immediate neighbourhood, so it's too far to walk.

◆ Parents don't feel that it's safe nowadays to let children play outside on their own.

◆ Some children spend a lot of time watching television or playing computer games.

◆ The strong emphasis on literacy and numeracy and other academic subjects in schools means that time allowed for physical activities has been cut down.

Consequently, it's important that children have the opportunity for a variety of physical experiences in the early years setting, both indoors and outside. Children need the freedom to experiment with movement under the watchful eye of a responsible adult. Good progress in other areas of development is dependent on sound physical development.

Have a look through the unit and read the notes on each element, to get a picture of what evidence you need to cover. You may have already covered some parts of the unit. For instance, Element 4 is all about fine manipulative skills, which you may have evidence of in C10, perhaps as part of developing creativity in C10.4. You may have evidence in C2 of how you have encouraged children to develop manipulative skills in routine situations such as getting dressed. Check your cross-referencing sheets to see whether you have included evidence from those units.

You will notice that you need to use large apparatus with children for part of the unit. If you work in a school, you are unlikely to be allowed to take a class on your own because of the safety and legal requirements. You will need to ask your class teacher if you can lead a session while she watches, or if not, be responsible for a group within the main lesson. You should also show evidence of giving children the opportunity to use physical activity outside as well as indoors. Perhaps you can play some singing games with the children at playtime, or join in an outdoor PE lesson. In other settings, physical play often tends to be going on alongside other things, so you will be able to provide evidence more easily.

Values

The welfare of the child and keeping children safe is particularly important in this unit, as there are many potential dangers in using large and moveable equipment. You must ensure that you position equipment safely, make use of safety equipment such as mats and supervise children closely, especially outside.

There is also a strong emphasis in all the elements on promoting children's learning and development and of being a reflective practitioner (thinking about why you do things, what the children will gain from them, and how you can make them better).

You need to ensure that all children have equal access to physical activities. This may mean taking positive action to encourage less confident children to join in, and being alert to the fact that the more confident children may monopolise the more energetic activities or most popular equipment. Make sure that you don't stereotype boys and girls into particular activities, such as boys playing football and girls skipping. Throughout the unit you will also need to think about how you will provide equipment and support for children who have difficulty with physical skills, especially if you have children with special needs or disabilities in your setting.

You need to take account of the religious beliefs of some cultural groups. For instance, some Muslim children are not allowed to undress in public or bare their arms and legs. Depending on your status in your workplace, you will need to discuss this with your supervisor or the parents. The setting will probably have made arrangements with parents already if there are issues like these to consider.

Getting started
In this unit you're going to show how you help children to develop:

◆ confidence in movement

◆ skills of locomotion and balance

◆ gross motor skills

◆ fine motor skills

Read the notes on each element to see which activities you need to cover. If you need to, use the personal skills check-list in Chapter 1 (page 21) to identify which activities you feel confident about, and where you need to gain further experience or training. The articles at the end of the chapter will give you much of the information you will need, and a lot of good ideas for activities.

C3 is one of the child development units. The others are C5, C10 and C11. For the knowledge requirements for each of these, you need to show that you have a good understanding of child development. You may like to write one assignment to cover all areas of development at the same time - physical, intellectual and language, emotional and social - and cross reference it to each unit.

If you're in a setting where the activities described in Elements 1, 2 and 3 are separate (this often happens in a school), you may have a music and movement session on one day, large climbing apparatus on another, and small apparatus such as bats, balls and skipping ropes on another. In this case, you will need separate observations for each element. If your setting has a more informal approach, you may be able to cover more than one element at once. For instance, you could start a session by encouraging the children to do a variety of movements such as running, walking, jumping and skipping (Element 2). Then give the children the choice of a range of apparatus, including climbing apparatus, wheeled toys, bats and balls and so on (Elements 2 and 3).

Once you are confident, plan how you will gather your evidence, with your assessor if possible. Try to plan the whole unit together, so that you can avoid any unnecessary repetition. If you plan carefully your assessor may be able to observe more than one element in one observation.

Don't forget
Check your cross-referencing sheet for evidence from other units.

Element C3.1 Develop children's confidence in movement

Key issues
A good way of developing children's confidence in movement is through movement to music. As suggested in the notes for the element, you should aim to use a whole range of songs and music - from different cultures, classical, pop and children's songs - and also percussion and home-made instruments. Use other ways of helping the children to move imaginatively, like streamers and ribbons, or use a story as a starting point, or a topic such as the wind blowing, machines and so on. There are so many exciting ways to encourage movement, and the children will love it.

If you work with older children, try some simple country dance sequences with the traditional music, and make up your own little dances. The music is really lively and great fun! Here is a simple one to try:

Hold hands in a circle and
circle left
circle right
four steps forward
four steps backward
Hold both hands of the person next to you and skip round in a circle
Start the sequence again

As with all aspects of promoting physical development, you need to be aware of safety. Make sure you've got plenty of space to move in, and have strategies for calming the children down if they get too carried away! A good tip is always to finish with something quiet and calm.

It's also a good idea to have a change of clothes for physical activities, or at least to remove outer clothing, and to do the activity in bare feet. Remember to check whether this will cause a problem for any of the children because of religious beliefs or health reasons.

Which type of evidence?

Your assessor will need to **observe** the whole of this element. You can also write an **activity plan** to show that you have planned the session carefully. A **child observation** of physical play will help you to identify what stage of development the children are at, and whether any of the children lack confidence and may need additional help. Are there any children with physical disabilities you need to provide special equipment for? There are some useful articles later in this chapter which will help you.

You need to show evidence of the whole range, and you can do this through a **reflective account** or a **candidate diary** describing other activities you have carried out with the children. You could ask your supervisor or colleague to write a **witness testimony**. You may keep **development records** of the children in your setting, so include an example if you can. Remember to remove the surname, and ask permission, first.

Remember:
Any child observations you do will be evidence for C16: 'Observe and assess the development and behaviour of children'.

The **knowledge evidence statements** which are relevant to this element are 1, 2, 3, 6, 7, 10, 15, 17. You will easily be able to cover some of these in your other evidence. Some of them overlap with other elements too, so check, and write about them all together. Remember, if you have already written an assignment to cover child development, some of it will be relevant for this unit. If you have any gaps when you have completed your other evidence, write a short assignment, relating it as much as possible to your own work practice. If you are confident that you can give your assessor the information orally, arrange that with her.

Element C3.2 Develop children's skills of locomotion and balance

Key issues

For this element you need to show that you can use a range of large and small, fixed and moveable equipment with children, and also encourage movement which involves no equipment, such as running, jumping and skipping. Read through the range and PCs, and the notes on the element to see which sort of movement to encourage, and the equipment to use. With the right sort of equipment and careful planning, you can include all of these activities in one session. Safety is paramount, so you need plenty of space and a suitable floor surface, or protective mats around the climbing equipment, and close supervision.

You also need strict rules about the number of children on each piece of equipment, allowing each other space to move with no fear of being pushed, and a signal for everyone to get off the apparatus and sit down immediately if you request it. If you follow these rules, the children will be able to get the most out of the session and be safe, too. Children will not usually attempt more than they feel confident to do, so you don't need to worry unduly if a child climbs high or tries something quite difficult. Be close at hand if they need you but don't show you are nervous. They need to be given the freedom to try things out. On the other hand, some children will need help and encouragement to do the smallest task.

Which evidence?

As we said earlier in the chapter, if you work in a school, you will not be allowed to take a PE session on your own, so you will need to discuss with the class teacher and plan with your assessor how you can get sufficient evidence for this element. Your assessor will need to **observe** you for all PCs except two, and for one aspect of each category of the range. She will need to inspect the setting and check on how much responsibility you have for setting out equipment. If you cannot be responsible for the whole session or group, arrange to be responsible for setting out, and for taking part of the session or a small group. Prepare an activity plan with the layout you intend to use, and safety measures you will take.

If you are not able to cover the whole range in the activity your assessor will observe, write a **reflective account** or **candidate diary** of activities you have carried out previously, perhaps if you have worked in another setting or with a different age group. For each group of children, include a description of the different sorts of equipment and activities you have used to suit their level of development.

It would be useful to observe children taking part in a PE session, or during physical play. Of course, you will need to make sure that there are enough staff to supervise the activity while you are observing. Choose a confident and a non-confident child and carry out a **child observation**. Compare their abilities, then decide how you can plan for both of their needs.

The **knowledge evidence** statements for this element are 3, 6, 8, 9, 11, 12, 16, 17. Remember to look for links with the PCs and range, and cover as much as you can in your other evidence.

note:
Although we have taken each element separately, remember that one reflective account, child observation or other piece of evidence may be enough for more than one element and for some of the underpinning knowledge. Don't write more than you need to.

Element C3.3 Develop children's gross motor skills

Key issues

This element concentrates on skills like throwing and catching, kicking, bouncing and so on, using small equipment such as bats, balls, hoops and bean bags. Read through the range and PCs, and the notes on the element, so that you're clear what evidence you need. You can use small apparatus both indoors and out - for some activities outside is better because the children have more space.

Again, safety is really important. Children should be taught how to use equipment safely. Outside, grass is safer than tarmac, because children can fall without hurting themselves. However, there may be other hazards such as animal droppings and broken glass which cannot be seen so easily, so you will need to check the area carefully. Also, it is not always possible to use grass in wet weather. Safety surfaces are good but tend only to be used for areas under climbing equipment because they are so expensive.

The activities recommended in this element are ideal for encouraging co-operation and team work - for instance, in order to catch a ball your partner has to throw it quite skilfully, and football requires sharing the ball and passing to each other. The way you organise the activities will determine whether they promote competition, too. You need to think about what sort of emphasis you put on these two aspects, and what effect it will have on the children who are less able if you emphasise competition too much. You also need to ensure that you are giving all children an equal opportunity to take part in all sorts of activities, and challenge stereotypical attitudes such as 'football is for boys' and 'only girls skip'.

Which type of evidence?

You will see from the evidence requirements that your assessor needs to **observe** all PCs and one aspect of each range category. Other types of evidence can include an **activity plan** to show how you prepared for the activity. Your assessor will find this useful in helping her to judge whether you are fully aware of the issues involved, and would be able to adapt the activity to meet the needs of different ages and abilities of children. To cover areas of the range your assessor was not able to observe, write a **reflective account** or **candidate diary** to describe other activities you have carried out in your work, or get a supervisor or colleague to write a **witness testimony**. You may wish to do a **child observation** to check individual children's gross motor skills.

The **knowledge evidence** statements for this element are 2, 3, 8, 11, 13, 14, 15, 17. Don't forget to include them in your other evidence. The articles later in this chapter contain some useful ideas and information to help you with your activities.

Element C3.4 Develop children's fine motor skills

Key issues

This element deals with fine motor and manipulative skills. It involves activities such as drawing, painting, modelling, threading, cutting out, writing, jigsaws, table toys, and small construction. Get the children to use playdough and clay without tools sometimes, because the squeezing and kneading helps to strengthen their finger muscles.

Finger rhymes are a fun way of helping children with fine motor control. Here are a few suggestions: 'Tommy Thumb', 'Roll the bobbin', 'Five fat peas' and 'Incy wincy spider'.

Every early years setting has their own favourites, and there are some lovely collections available in books such as *This Little Puffin*.

You also need to encourage the children to use fine motor skills in routine activities such as getting dressed, doing up buttons and so on. Your assessor may have been able to observe many of the PCs for this element while she was observing C10.4, or during routine activities, but you will probably need to cover some of the range in other ways.

The development of fine motor skills is crucial in order that children develop the ability to write when they are older, but it is neither necessary nor desirable to push children into writing when they're very young. Getting children to trace their name and fill in worksheets at two and a half is not appropriate.

> **Don't**
> push children into formal writing before they're ready. Give them lots of opportunities to use pencils and crayons in their play.

There are so many other interesting and enjoyable activities which help children to develop their fine motor skills, such as those listed above, and in the notes on this element. You will be able to think of many more. Give children access to pencils, crayons and paper in the different play areas such as the home corner and the shop, and have a writing and drawing corner, to encourage first attempts at mark making and writing. Praise their efforts, and write for them if they ask you to. In this way, writing is part of their play, and they don't have to worry about getting it wrong. If you work with older children in school, they will of course be beginning to learn how to form letters correctly, and some children will be ready to do this earlier, but don't push children who are not ready.

Which type of evidence?

Your assessor will need to **observe** you working with the
children unless she has covered it through another
observation, such as in C10.4. There is a great variety of
activities relevant to this element, so make sure that your
evidence is wide enough. You could organise a whole morning's
activities to show the range. Or write a **reflective account** or
candidate diary to show other activities you have carried
out. You may like to make a **work product** for the children,
such as threading cards.

The knowledge evidence statements related to this element
are 1, 4, 5, 7, 8, 11, 13, 15. You will probably have already
covered most of them, if you referred to them when you were
writing your other evidence. If you have any gaps, write a
short assignment to cover them.

The following pages have some articles to help you. You will
find a list of books recommended for further reading on page
24.

Whether children are playing on a see-saw or pushing a pram they are learning about themselves and how their bodies move. Gay Wilkinson explains what the Early Learning Goals for Physical Development set out to achieve

Physical Development

Young children's physical development contributes to all other aspects of their development. It is about large and fine motor activity - running, walking, jumping, climbing and dancing as well as cutting, drawing, painting, writing or gluing.

Sense of self

When playing on a climbing frame, slide or with wheeled toys children can learn and practise a variety of skills. They develop their personal and social skills as they learn to wait and take turns and consider other's feelings. They develop their language skills as they negotiate who should go first, listen to each other or decide what should happen next. Mathematical skills are used as they look and count how many bikes there are or match them to the children there to see if there are enough. They use the language of position, which relates to both mathematics and reading, to describe their movements as they climb on the climbing frame. As they play on the see-saw or rocking horse they begin to think about weight and balance and the relationship between them. Outdoors they explore the world around them and wonder at its many marvels. As they ride bikes and scooters or push a pram they experience different speeds and relate these to effort and energy. Above all they develop a holistic sense of self - an awareness of the shape and movements of their bodies, the spaces and other people around them and how they relate to them as they move - and their feelings of self-esteem and self-worth are fostered. They learn about themselves. That is why you should be making sure that the children have opportunities every day for all aspects of their physical development when you plan your programme.

The importance of outdoor play

Young children need to be able to move vigorously and freely - it is part of their natural development. They also need to be able to make choices, follow interests and

exercise their growing independence. That's why purpose-built early years provision is normally designed to include a safe and secure outdoor play space where children can spontaneously develop their physical skills as they play. In this space children can move freely without worrying about bumping into objects and can exercise their voices without being told that they are being too noisy! No matter how generous your hall or

room spaces the children cannot move and play as they do outdoors. They cannot exercise in the way that they do outdoors. Outside they are subject to the effects of weather - sunshine and cold - which affects the body's movements and they learn to make adjustments. They can feel what it is like to be part of a much larger space than that indoors - where walls, ceilings and furniture constrain movement - and begin to experience the immensity of the natural world and their place in it.

This sort of physical activity and play is of special importance today because many parents feel unable to let their children play outdoors, even in the garden, because of fears for their safety. Many children live in

flats or maisonettes and do not have access to a garden area unless they are taken there. The place of physical activity and exercise is therefore vital in the early years curriculum if our children are to develop as healthy and happy individuals.

If your provision has its own outdoor space then you need to think how you are going to incorporate this space into your daily planning. What sort of activities will you make available to challenge every aspect of the children's physical development? How can you make sure that they have easy access to this area for most of each session and how will you enable staff to interact with and contribute to the children's play? If you don't have immediate access to this area from your room you will need to work out how children can use the outdoor space as much as possible.

Finding alternatives

If you do not have an outdoor area you will need to think about how to overcome this. Is there a local nursery or primary school that would let you use some or all of their outdoor play area? Is there a parent with a reasonably large garden who might let you use this with either all or some of the children on a regular basis? What equipment will you need to take with you - for example, a first-aid kit? Make sure that the place you choose is within reasonable walking distance for young children and that you have enough adults to supervise the children safely as they walk. If none of these options are possible then you could build into your programme regular opportunities for the children to go for short walks. This is particularly important today since many families rely upon the car for most of their journeys and many young children have too few opportunities to develop a healthy lifestyle.

Useful tip for safer walks

A useful aid when taking a group of very young children out for a walk is a length of strong rope that has shorter lengths knotted across at regular intervals. With an adult holding each end the children then walk either side of the rope holding onto the cross-pieces. The rope gives the children a clear visual signal of what they are expected to do, they feel safe and secure and the adults supervising can see each child easily since they are spaced out along the rope.

Adapting space indoors

Does your provision have a reasonably large indoor space, without furniture, that you could use in addition to the classroom? If so, it might be worth thinking about letting the children use this space more often for spontaneous play. Although it cannot offer the same challenge as that outside the extra space will allow them to incorporate larger physical movement into their play. You will need to plan which activities and resources you could move into this space to encourage the children to incorporate   large movement in their play without   being directed.

Organising space outside

If you do have an outdoor area, take a long hard look at it. Is it attractive and interesting? Just as you organise your indoor environment into clearly defined spaces so

that children can make sense of it, so you need to do the same with your outdoor area.

- Are there larger spaces where the children can ride wheeled toys, run around safely or play with balls?

- Are there smaller spaces where children can role-play?

- Is there a space where they can write, draw or paint if they want to?

- If you have slides and swings is there a clear space around them?

- Are there tree trunks on which children can climb and balance or from which they can jump on and off?

- Can the children move indoor activities and resources outside?

- In planning your curriculum do you plan for both the inside and outside spaces as one area?

There are many ways to provide focused activities outside that parallel those inside and challenge children's large and fine motor skills. For example, painting easels inside can be complemented with painting outside on large sheets of paper and using large decorating brushes. Indoors children can fill and empty using small containers and plastic tubing in the water tray. Outside they can use buckets and pieces of guttering and drainpipe. Planting bulbs or cress inside can be complemented with gardening outside. You can even take children outside for planned gymnastics, dance or games lessons for most of the year, although you might want to make sessions shorter during the winter months.

Planned activities

As well as the spontaneous opportunities for physical development provided in the indoor and outdoor environment you will also want to provide planned opportunities specifically to develop the children's physical skills and abilities, particularly those related to dance, gymnastics and games. It is important to remember when planning any focused games, dance or gymnastics sessions that such activity is probably well outside most

young children's experience, as is working and responding to precise adult instructions, either yours or those accompanying a music and movement tape. They may well be unused to working in a large hall or outside play area. For some children, getting undressed or changing into other clothing can be daunting. Children from some cultural backgrounds are not allowed to show their arms and legs and you need to respect this. Some may prefer to undress in

'Physical Development in the Foundation Stage is about improving skills of coordination, control, manipulation and movement . . . It helps children gain confidence in what they can do and enables them to feel the positive benefits of being healthy and active'.

private. You will therefore need to be sensitive to the different needs of the children and give them time to become accustomed to these new demands.

Keep it simple

Children need to enjoy the experiences you offer and so you should build on what the children are already familiar with when planning activities. Many of them will be familiar with simple songs and action rhymes and you will be extending this repertoire daily. Rather than launching into separate gymnastic, dance or games lessons, which may well require the children to use skills they have not yet developed, start with what they can do. Choose a known action rhyme into which you can incorporate movement that the children can do - running, walking, galloping, hopping, skipping - and let them move to this while you all say the rhyme together. They will be able to concentrate on and respond to your instructions - for example, stop, start and change - more easily since they do not have to think about other things.

Introduce the words associated with different parts of the body and actions during this period and begin to encourage them to think more carefully about their own movements - running softly on their toes or making themselves tall like a giraffe by stretching up as they walk. As they become more confident, introduce a different but familiar stimulus. Well-known stories often lend themselves to movement/dance interpretation. Perhaps having read one at story time you could talk to the children about how the story might be interpreted in this way. Remember to set realistic targets that build on and extend those loco-motor skills you have been working on already. Only when the children are secure and confident in the space you use and can respond to your instructions should you think about using percussion instruments or taped music, particularly if the tape also gives movement instructions for the children to follow. These early lessons will also provide a starting point for the separate elements of games and gymnastics.

Games to play

The children will already know about playing some games from home. At this age the emphasis should not be upon competition but rather upon enjoyment. At first choose games that do not need any equipment but give further practice in responding to signals and becoming more aware of spatial language - up, down, under, on, over, high, low, and so on. Most children enjoy playing games such as 'Simon Says', 'Statues' or 'Grandmother's Footsteps'. There are many others that help them to learn spatial language, the names of body parts, and to respond to instructions. Introduce equipment such as balls, hoops, quoits and bean bags gradually and only when the children are confident about using the space. Give them plenty of opportunities to experiment with each type of equipment. Young children need time and practice in order to develop their skills.

Large apparatus

Don't be tempted to use large gymnastic apparatus too soon. Give children time to explore and begin to control and co-ordinate their own body movements first. Learning how to balance yourself is hard enough on the floor without adding the further difficulty of doing this on a raised bar or plank! Always let the children practise their movements on the floor before asking them to transfer these to apparatus.

When you feel that the children are ready to use the large apparatus only use that which will support your learning objectives. For example, if your objective is to help the children to develop their balancing skills you may only need one or two benches.

You may feel that getting out any apparatus half-way through a lesson is not possible with young children because of the difficulties of supervision. This should not be seen as a problem since from the beginning you should be training them to handle and move apparatus. This might mean that in the early stages you feel that they take so long getting the apparatus out that there is little time to actually use it! Be patient and remember that they will only get better through practice!

Your role

In all the physical activities that you provide for the children, both spontaneous and focused, it is important to think about your role. What sort of interactions will help and encourage them to begin to consider the movements more carefully? How can you balance praise with comments that will provide an appropriate challenge to improve? Remember that how you talk to the children, the comments you make and the questions you ask play a significant part in ensuring that they develop all their physical skills as they should.

Gay Wilkinson

Assessment and record keeping

Even if you observe and assess children throughout each session, there is a need to find time on a regular basis to make specific observations of children and record what they are doing with regard to particular aspects of their development.

Staff should agree the categories within children's physical development for their setting. These can then be used as headings in a written record. Draw up a duplicated master sheet with three columns, like the one below. List the agreed categories in the left-hand column. The other two columns are for staff comments and parents' comments. Each recorded entry should be dated so that progress can be evaluated.

Categories	Staff comments	Parents' comments
Fine motor skills		
Holds pencil and paintbrush correctly		
Can thread beads and buttons onto a lace		
Can grasp and manipulate small items of equipment, eg fitting pegs into a pegboard		
Can use scissors and cut both safely and effectively		
Can use a hammer and saw		
Uses a range of equipment, materials and toys with increasing control and co-ordination		
Has established hand-eye dominance		
Gross motor skills		
Runs with some degree of control and confidence		
Walks steadily		
Jumps over or off an object with both feet together		
Can hop on one foot and maintain reasonable balance		
Can skip		
Able to throw a bean bag, ball, etc		
Able to catch a ball, bean bag, etc		
Can pedal a bike		
Can lift and arrange blocks		
Can push and pull toys or objects		

This is not a definitive list. Staff must consider their own children when identifying the categories for the record sheet.

Teaching a child to recognise the changes that occur in their body when they have been active is a simple first step onto the more complex stages involved in the evolution of independence and self-sufficiency

Recognising **changes** in **our bodies**

Understanding that things that happen to your body usually have causes and solutions is a source of fascination and reassurance to young children. Removing the fear of the unknown is a great gift and one which education exists to provide. Primitive peoples the world over and throughout history have learned about their bodies by reading the signs given by them and developed complex solutions (such as modern medicine) by applying this knowledge. To a lesser extent, your children are doing the same thing!

No single activity can help meet the requirements of the Early Learning Goal which states that children should:

❑ Recognise the changes that happen to their bodies when they are active.

It is a question of raising awareness at appropriate times and reinforcing understanding on a regular basis.

Raising awareness of children's bodies is essential in the development of balance, coordination, self-esteem and social skills. For a child to be active is essential for the development of healthy bodies and the understanding of a child's relationship to the world around him. Risk taking begins with a young child's physical relationship with his world. So do confidence and creativity - there is a great payback for a small investment at this early stage!

Reading the signs

If a child is hungry her tummy will rumble; the solution is to eat. If a child is cold she will shiver and the solution is to put on a coat or jumper. Obvious? Why then do so many pre-school children simply stand and suffer? Because they have not learned yet to read the signs, trust their interpretation and act appropriately upon it. That is why you are there! Explaining how to deal

independently with problems at this early stage, even when you are actually doing it for the child yourself, will help the child develop their independence and self-esteem.

Explain what's happening

Young children should be physically active frequently! After a child has run enough to make themselves hot and breathless you could explain that exercise makes the muscles work hard and that warms us up; because their body needs more air it is asking the lungs to breathe harder for a short while. Wearing lots of warm clothes for running around is going to make us too hot. Not wearing enough clothes is going to make us uncomfortably cold. Help the child to come to a decision about appropriate clothing for whatever activity they are doing.

Making the most of learning opportunities is a great skill. It is the difference between a satisfactory early years experience and an

excellent one. Using what is happening around you to focus the child's mind and to support her development is a rewarding and effective policy. If a child is hungry, explain what is happening and then discuss solutions. If a child is hurt, explain that the body has to find a way to let you know that something is wrong - what would make it better? Understanding these basic physical functions at this age paves the way for a more complex understanding of emotions and empathy as the child grows older. It encourages the child to take control of her own needs.

Making a targeted activity out of this learning goal is a simple exercise in observation. Sit the children down and ask them to be aware of their breathing and the temperature of their body. Run around for five or ten minutes and ask them to describe the changes. Vocabulary such as 'breath', 'temperature', 'breathless', 'puffed out', 'sweaty', 'achy', 'hot' will all encourage the child to be aware of these changes. A quick plug for healthy living is appropriate at this point, too. Teaching children the importance of caring for their bodies starts at pre-school level. Encourage physical activity, exploration, a range of movements and discussion about these activities and you will be building the foundations for a healthy and balanced approach to life.

Physical development is the corner-stone for so much else that we owe it to pre-school children to help them understand the importance of play and exercise and to incorporate it into the curriculum very regularly indeed.

Sara Stocks

Young children need opportunities to develop an awareness of space and of others around them. Jean Evans explains why and suggests some activities suitable for both large, open spaces and smaller, restricted ones

Developing spatial awareness

As they take part in planned physical activities in small and large groups children will become aware of those around them and how their own movements affect others. They will begin to challenge their own bodies and extend the range of movements they can make. If you give them appropriate opportunities, as their confidence develops they will use the space around them to express their feelings and imaginary ideas.

In order to provide activities which ensure progression of movement skills, present challenges to those who are more able and security to those who are less confident, it is essential to plan carefully. Begin by listing the different movement skills you wish to develop, such as running, jumping, hopping, skipping, crawling, striding, curling up and stretching. Next consider the space available and how you can make the best use of it. Is there direct access to a hall and outdoor area? Are the times when you can use these

facilities restricted?

Look at your timetable and decide when you will introduce activities which are directed by an adult and when children will have time for free exploration. Remember that both forms of physical activity are important. Whilst carrying out your activities make observations of children's achievements and record them so that you can adapt future plans to meet the needs of individual children.

Planned activities in a large space

❑ **'Find a space'** Children need introducing to ways of finding a space of their own. Start by working in a large space, indoors or

outdoors, until children are more competent and then gradually reduce the space available. Suggest a simple activity such as going for a walk alone. Once all the children are walking around tell them to stop and stretch out their arms. Can they touch anyone? Tell them to shuffle about until they have their own space. Get them to turn around slowly with arms outstretched and then to sit in the space they have made for themselves. Develop the activity by asking the children to make themselves as small as possible in their space and then as big as they can. As children become more competent they can run, jump or take giant steps to their own spaces.

❑ **Playground markings** Use chalk to draw out train tracks, snakes and other shapes for children to move along, and stepping stones for them to move across.

Planned activities in a smaller space

If space is restricted for movement activities children can still explore the space around them. Move as many obstacles as possible to create a clear space.

❑ **'We're going on a bear hunt'** Dramatise the action of this popular story so that children move as a group 'over', 'under' and 'through' imaginary obstacles as they follow the story. Extend the activity by adding

challenges, such as crawling through a tunnel or scaling a high mountain. Work closely with timid children who may be overwhelmed by the possibility of an encounter with a bear!

Action songs and games

Action songs and games create opportunities for children to become aware of how their movements affect others in the group and for them to co-operate as they move in a designated space. Try some of the following: 'Hokey cokey', 'In and out the dusky bluebells', 'Here we go round the mulberry bush', 'I went to school one morning' (all in *This Little Puffin*).

Number rhymes

'Five little speckled frogs' Let the children

sit in a circle and choose five 'frogs' to sit on a 'log' made from chairs. They can then jump off the 'log' into the 'pool' as others sing the song.

'Five little ducks' Work in groups of six with 'five ducks and a mother'. Let one duck at a time swim over the pond and far away.

'Ten in the bed' This one is great fun! Work with ten children lying in a row on a carpet or blanket.

Jean Evans

Dance
❑ Let the children move freely to a range of taped music.
❑ Play musical statues.
❑ Wave ribbons on sticks and dance to Chinese music.

Drama
Move imaginatively to appropriate music, for example, pretending to be dinosaurs, elephants or Jack-in-the-Boxes.

Down's syndrome is a condition we have all heard of and perhaps think we know something about. Sarah Rutter explains the facts and makes the point that we should not make generalisations about people with Down's syndrome but look at each person as an individual

Including **the child** with Down's syndrome

What is Down's syndrome?

The human body is made up of cells. Each cell is like a tiny factory, which makes the materials needed for growth and maintenance of the body. Contained within each cell is a set of 46 chromosomes (23 pairs), half of which come from the person's mother and half from the father. The chromosomes carry the genes that are inherited from a person's parents.

Down's syndrome is a condition that occurs at or around the time a baby is conceived. Most people with Down's syndrome have an extra copy of chromosome 21 in every cell, making 47 in all. It is not yet known what causes this to happen. However, it is something that occurs in all races and all social classes. It is known that the chance of having a baby with Down's syndrome is higher in older mothers, although, because more babies overall are born to mothers in the 25- to 30-year-old age group, the majority of babies with Down's syndrome are born to 25- to 30-year-old women. We do know that, in the vast majority of cases, Down's syndrome is not passed down from generation to generation.

The presence of the extra chromosome has the effect of disrupting the growth and development of the baby. Quite how much effect the extra chromosome has varies from person to person, although all people who have Down's syndrome have a certain degree of learning disability.

People with Down's syndrome are as different from each other as any other unrelated members of the population. Like the rest of us, they get all their genes from their parents, so they look and act much more like members of their family than someone else with Down's syndrome. Their abilities and skills, strengths and weaknesses are just as variable as they are amongst the rest of us.

It is important not to make generalisations about people with Down's syndrome, but to look at each person as an individual.

How common is Down's syndrome?

In every 1,000 live births, one baby will be born with Down's syndrome. That is about 600 babies every year in the UK.

Diagnosis

In most cases, it becomes clear quite soon after birth that the baby has Down's syndrome. Doctors and midwives are usually alerted by certain signs that are more common among babies with Down's syndrome than among other babies. For example, if doctors detect a heart disorder it may alert them to the possibility of Down's syndrome because about 40 per cent of

babies with Down's syndrome also have a heart problem. Diagnosis can be confirmed by a blood test to analyse the chromosomes.

It is important to stress that it is not possible to tell how disabled a child will be at this early stage. The number of physical characteristics of Down's syndrome a child has bears no relation to his or her degree of developmental delay.

Developmental delay

For a variety of reasons, such as poor health and/or hospitalisation at an early age, some young children with Down's syndrome will be more delayed than others. By the time children reach three or four, it may be apparent that they are not as advanced as their ordinary peers. Nowadays, most young children with Down's syndrome will have benefited from an early intervention programme (sometimes known as Portage) designed to help them gain the skills that other children learn naturally. Such programmes can be encouraging to parents who feel they can be actively involved in promoting their child's development. An early intervention worker will help parents to teach their child by breaking down tasks into small manageable steps. In some areas of the country, Portage is available from the age of six months; in others it starts later.

Speech and language delay

Speech and language difficulties are common in young children with Down's syndrome. Most children will be under the care of a speech and language therapist who will give parents and carers (including early years workers) guidelines on how to encourage the speech and language development of the child according to an individual programme.

Most parents of a child with Down's syndrome will have become experts on their child's condition and needs. They need to feel that their views and knowledge are being respected and taken into account. Communication is the key to successful inclusion and many potential problems can be avoided by both parties keeping the other informed.

Common health problems

Children's development can be delayed because of health problems that are more common in Down's syndrome.

Hearing

Many children with Down's syndrome have hearing problems caused by a condition called glue ear, which can be a consequence of repeated upper respiratory infections such as colds, or infected or enlarged adenoids. The fluid in the ear becomes thick like jelly and cannot drain away and hearing is affected. This can happen in all children but it is more frequent in children with Down's syndrome. Glue ear can cause deafness, infection, pain, delayed speech development, and temporary behaviour problems. Glue ear can be successfully treated, but early years workers need to be aware that the effects of hearing impairment can be reduced by a few simple steps outlined below:

❑ Always give the child plenty of time to respond to anything you have said - they will get frustrated if you start saying something new before they have had time to respond to the first thing you said. (This applies to most children with Down's syndrome whether or not they have any degree of hearing loss.)

❑ Try to face the child when speaking to them.

❑ Don't shout but speak clearly.

❑ If the child does not understand, don't just repeat what has been said but try to rephrase it.

❑ Make sure the child is paying attention before you start speaking.

❑ Give the child lots of visual clues - signs and gestures - to help them understand what you are saying.

❑ Keep your hands and any visual aids away from your mouth.

❑ Don't use exaggerated lip movements.

Vision problems

Some young children with Down's syndrome need glasses to correct their vision and, just as with other children who wear glasses, you may need to make sure that the child does wear them when necessary.

Lack of muscle tone

Where to go for help

Your local education authority's Special Education Department should be able to provide advice and support to staff who are involved in including a child with Down's syndrome in a pre-school setting.

The Down's Syndrome Association has an information service and also a number of advisers it can call on for specific information about such things as speech therapy, medical and behaviour problems. Lists of the DSA's leaflets and recommended reading are available to anyone who sends in a stamped addressed envelope to:

The Down's Syndrome Association,
155 Mitcham Road,
Tooting, London SW17 9PG.
Telephone: 0208 682 4001.

E-mail:
information@downs-syndrome.org.uk

Web site address:
http://www.downs-syndrome.org.uk

Many babies with Down's syndrome have poor muscle tone and tend to be 'floppy'. In most cases, this improves as the child grows. However, it can contribute to delay in learning how to run, skip, throw and catch (gross motor skills) and affect the development of skills such as writing (fine motor development). Most children will master these skills eventually, but may take longer than their peers to do so. Many young children with Down's syndrome will have regular physiotherapy sessions either at home or at a child development centre. These sessions are designed to give parents exercises to do with their children to help them achieve particular skills.

Monitoring development

The developmental progress of children with Down's syndrome will usually be monitored by staff at the local child development centre. In the early years, parents are often offered extra support by a specialist health visitor or a social worker who is able to keep them

---

informed of facilities for children with special needs in the area.

How to cope with questions about difference

Pre-school children in general tend to accept differences in colour, behaviour and so on much more readily than older children might. Most of the time, if children in a group ask questions about a child being different, it will be enough to point out that we are all different - 'You have blonde hair but Jessica has black hair'. The Down's Syndrome Association (see box) has a list of recommended reading books for children which deal with issues of difference.

Relationships with parents/carers

Most parents of a child with Down's syndrome will have become experts on their child's condition and needs. They need to feel that their views and knowledge are being respected and taken into account. Communication is the key to successful inclusion and many potential problems can be avoided by both parties keeping the other informed. It may be helpful to remember that a child with Down's syndrome is a child first and foremost and that his or her condition is secondary.

Sarah Rutter, Information Officer, The Down's Syndrome Association.

When a small child with cerebral palsy (cp) joins a pre-school group staff may have little or no specific previous experience to draw on. They will, however, already have a broad range of experience and this will form a firm foundation, but it is important for staff to have a basic understanding of what cp is and how it affects children

Including the child with cerebral palsy

From the moment of birth, or soon after, children with cerebral palsy (cp) have very different learning experiences than their able bodied peers.

Babies experience a short, frustrating period of helplessness quickly followed by an increasingly active exploration of their world. They experience their world through lying, sitting, reaching, rolling, crawling and standing. In a few months they are up and away. Babies born with cp do not explore their world independently at the same times as their peers, if at all. Many, in addition to the physical difficulties, also have altered perception of space and altered sensations of touch. The picture they build of their world may well be a very different one to others of their age.

When a small child with cp joins a pre-school group where staff have little or no previous experience to draw on staff will be unsure of their ground. They should be reassured that their experience of working with and understanding the needs of a broad range of children will stand them in good stead. However, it is important for pre-school staff to have a basic understanding of what cp is and how it affects children.

What is cerebral palsy?

Cp is caused by abnormalities in the brain usually before, during or soon after, birth. Fifteen hundred babies are affected each year, roughly one in 400 children in the UK. Cp is not infectious and, although the disability may become more noticeable with age, it is not progressive. Cerebral palsy jumbles up the messages going from the brain to the muscles causing them to behave oddly. There are three types of cerebral palsy

corresponding to the three areas of the brain that can be affected. The first is spastic cp which occurs when the part of the brain controlling thought, movement and sensation is affected. 'Spastic' means 'stiff' and the stiffness can affect the arms and legs and possibly the neck and trunk. The terms quadriplegia (four limbs), diplegia (both legs) and hemiplegia (one side) are used to describe this type of cp. The muscles are very tight and limbs get pulled out of line.

The second type, athetoid cp, results in children having floppy muscles and uncontrolled movements of their legs and arms. When messages are sent to move muscles the floppiness can rapidly become tightness causing the limb to fly outwards. Children may also have difficulty with the fine movements of the mouth and tongue, causing problems with speech, chewing and swallowing.

The third type, ataxic cp, causes shaky jerky movements and particularly affects fine motor control. Children with ataxia may also be unsteady when walking.

Children may have some effects and not others. Some children are only mildly affected while others are profoundly affected. Some may experience two, or all three, types of cp. There is no treatment or cure but some of the effects can be helped by therapy and teaching. Because the muscles pull abnormally they can cause the child to sit or lie in odd ways which can result in stiffness and pain. Correct positioning in sitting, standing or lying can go a long way to helping prevent pain and can really make a difference to helping the child get involved in learning.

Four out of ten babies born with cerebral palsy have other difficulties. Some children have great difficulty unscrambling the messages they receive from their eyes. In the most severe cases children may appear blind but more commonly will have difficulty making sense of pictures or writing.

Spatial awareness

Many children have difficulty with spatial awareness. If they are walking or moving their own wheelchair they bump into things; they cannot judge the speed of cars when crossing the road. In the group they may find it difficult to judge how much space they need and may 'push in'. Commonly they find it difficult to hold the picture of an object in their head with consequences for copying and mathematics.

Hearing difficulties

Hearing difficulties are commonly associated with the athetoid form of cp but colds and glue ear affect all children. Many children are sensitive to sounds and startle at loud noises. Usually they become more tolerant of noise as they become used to the group.

Speech problems

Speech problems are common. Speech and language therapists will suggest the best way to help the child communicate and also help with chewing or swallowing problems. Most children will use speech to communicate but some will need an alternative form either to help them make their meaning clear or as their best way of talking. If children get speech aids early it can help reduce frustration. Speech aids might come in the form of a picture book or symbols, like little cartoons, that the child points to in order to clarify meaning. For some children the speech aid will be in the form of a speech synthesiser with pre-recorded messages activated by pressing switches. Using a speech aid will never prevent speech and it can help the child take part in group work and shout out with the others. Speech and language therapists will recommend what the individual child needs.

Epilepsy

Epilepsy is the additional problem most commonly associated with cp and is usually easily controlled. The medicines may affect the child's behaviour and learning and the likely effects should be recognised. Where children may have a fit in the group it is important to reassure staff by doing a thorough risk assessment and gaining confidence in how it will be handled.

> *It is vital that staff other than the child's support assistant become confident in handling, positioning and communicating with the child. A child may visit the group without this happening, a child may be made welcome, but for the child to be included everyone has to feel confident.*

Assessing the child's needs

Many youngsters with cerebral palsy have odd sleep patterns that can affect their readiness to learn. They will be frustrated by their disability and may be angry. Many children, even those with average or above average ability, will have difficulty with speaking, reading, drawing and mathematics. When the children are young it can be difficult to know whether the learning difficulty is because of ability or because of the barriers. One useful way to assess a child's needs is to spend time observing him in different situations. Watch the eyes and watch for signs of anticipation. Does he laugh at adult-to-adult humour? Does she get angry with herself when she can't complete her task? These signs will help you to gauge the level of ability.

Each child is an individual but most children will benefit from the early learning experiences provided. They will enjoy the chance to experience messy play and to be part of a larger group. Most pre-school toys will have additional uses to stimulate listening or speech. Toys that react to voice are often particularly useful, as are cause and effect toys that react to touch. Toys that have interesting smells or textures are useful and can help staff to develop an understanding of the child's range of expressions of pleasure and dislike!

Supporting parents

In most cases the parents have already become the experts on the way cp affects their child but in some cases, where the child is more mildly affected, the parents may only suspect that there are difficulties and staff may have to help them to get a diagnosis. If parents suspect that their child might have cp they should discuss it with their GP and may find it helpful to contact a local group.

Where the child has already been receiving support, parents and therapists or other carers can give a great deal of information before the child joins the group. It is vital that staff other than the child's support assistant become confident in handling, positioning and communicating with the child. A child may visit the group without this happening, a child may be made welcome, but for the child to be included everyone has to feel confident.

Lindsay Brewis, Education Officer, Scope.

Action songs hold a place in all our childhood memories. A wet afternoon can be turned into something special by using them with our children. Chrys Blanchard celebrates action songs

Action songs

Action songs draw us together from our earliest days right through to our final fling down the old folks home. Remember the Birdie song and that holiday in Spain? You'll find them at weddings, social events and parties all over the country. Even father-in-law, who hates singing, can be seen absent-mindedly jerking his elbow and nodding his head along with the rest.

So, what is it about action songs? Why do they play such a big role in our culture? I think it's because they are so accessible. They usually have the vital ingredients of repetition and familiar or comical actions to mime.

Many years ago a TV comedy duo did a sketch which parodied children's entertainers. They sang in 'sugary' voices that all you needed to be a children's entertainer was 'brightly coloured dungarees, a fixed smile, and a song in which you sing everything three times'. I'm not sure whether children today would settle for the image, but the three times over rule is a sure bet. You only have to listen to any advertiser or politician to know that they are aware of the success of this technique.

Magic recipe

This is why so many of the songs we sing with children today have stood the test of time. They have been passed from generation to generation because they use the 'magic' recipe. Songs such as 'Here we go round the mulberry bush' have been sung for decades and while most of us wouldn't recognise a mulberry bush if we tripped over one, we can all 'brush our hair', 'stamp our feet' and 'go to school'. 'Wind the bobbin up' also gives an opportunity to introduce topics that cover the past. There is a whole history project in this song. And what about the more modern songs such as 'If you're happy and you know it clap your hands', 'The bear went over the mountain' and 'Brown girl in the ring'. They all have the three times over rule along with their actions.

All join in

'The wheels on the bus' has the ideal ingredients for an action song of our time. Simple, recognisable actions and the 'three rule'. Doing it three times over gives you more of a chance to join in. First time...Aha...there's an action here; second time...let's try it...oops missed; third time...there...done it!

Songs such as 'Wheels on the bus' can involve even the youngest child, who will be able to participate with a very simple action, long before he or she is able to speak clearly. The other important quality of this song is that it can become an 'everlasting song'. If you tire of the same old lyrics, add your own verses. The song will soon become a 'family possession'. What about the verse that goes 'The wheels on the bus go phssss, phssss ...' because of the time we had that puncture on the way to Nana's?

These days, every child in early years education will find themselves doing a topic on 'Me', 'My Body' or 'Myself'. Parents and teachers will be able to find plenty of songs on these themes. There are some excellent publications available. I still wouldn't be without my *This Little Puffin* compiled by Elizabeth Matteson ISBN 0-14-030-300-6, or the PLA booklet of finger rhymes. Oxford University Press do *Round and Round the Garden* ISBN 0-19-272132-1 and *Oranges and Lemons* ISBN 0-19-272171-2. A & C Black also have many publications of children's songs, including songs from different cultures, many of them with actions. A trip to any children's bookstore or music shop these days will probably provide you with enough material to find an action song on any theme you need.

So, don't undervalue the action song. Enjoy them, invent them, play with them and share them - have fun!

Chrys Blanchard, composer and music consultant

In these games, everybody wins, no-one loses and the children play *with* rather than *against* each other. Vicky Hislop explains

Non-competitive games

How many times have you heard young children say, 'I can't do that' or have seen children stand at the edges when it comes to competitive physical games? Have you ever wondered why?

I have had these concerns and, following a discussion some years ago with an American kindergarten teacher, she introduced me to a series of non-competitive games which encourage co-operation and not competition. This will come soon enough!

In these games, everybody wins, no-one loses and the children play *with* rather than *against* each other. The games help to eliminate the fear of failure and reaffirm the child's self-confidence.

In some cultures, co-operative games have been played for centuries and this sense of comradeship has been maintained right into adulthood, unlike the Western culture of competition. If the importance of winning is conditioned too early, the child can no longer play for fun and enjoyment. We do not want our children to experience consistent failure at this tender age. In co-operative games the child has a part to play and as a result is partly responsible for the game's success.

These games require little or no equipment and can be used in a variety of settings. They can involve everyone (even the visiting parents!) and they also make a great backbone for 'fun days' involving the community.

You don't need to stick to any given rules.

Once you are familiar with the concept you will be able to create your own games and adapt the ones given here.

The tortoise
The idea is to carry the tortoise's 'house' around the room/garden by co-operating with each other.

❑ A small group of children get on their hands and knees under a 'shell'.

❑ They have to move together in any direction to a given point.

The 'shell' can be made out of anything that will cover the children. To begin with you can make it easy and use a blanket and later more difficult with a large piece of card (this will fall off more easily if the children don't co-operate). You can also increase the number of children in the group. Should

you have access to a gym mat, this makes a very difficult 'house' to move and helps to build strength in the child's arms, legs and back.

'By the end of the Foundation Stage, most children will be able to:
- *move with control and co-ordination*
- *show awareness of space, of themselves and of others'*

You can make it more difficult again by introducing obstacles to negotiate and by asking another group of children to issue instructions to take the children under the 'shell' to a given point.

Don't worry if at first some of the children are a little reserved about joining in. It does help if all the adults including yourself are involved, but it does take time to build up the trust required. Be patient and take your time with the children but most of all enjoy the adventure.

Tiptoe through the garden
❑ First, create a long winding garden using paper. Paint objects on a long piece of corrugated paper (stick together sheets or ask local packing firms for their rubbish - we found ours in a skip!) If you can do this outside the children can have great fun creating the garden first.

❑ When it's finished, the children have to tiptoe through the flowers and objects. If you are feeling very adventurous, you might let the children paint their feet to do this as it leaves great patterns and they can see where they went! If you paint their heels as well as their toes, you can see if they have managed to stay on tiptoe!

❑ This enhances balance, builds strength in the legs and develops co-ordination skills.

Vicky Hislop

Young children in pre-school settings are still mastering gross motor skills using the whole body. This form of physical activity is essential if they are to strengthen bones and muscles and increase manual dexterity, say Carol Boylin and Linda Henderson

Balancing activities

All improvements in physical skills depend upon practice and young children need the opportunity to repeat the movements they know and the ones they are learning in order to improve their skills and control.

It is important to realise that physical education underpins children's future development in other curriculum areas. Large muscle development precedes small muscle control, so mastering control over large body movements will help children when they are involved in activities which demand the use of fine motor skills, as it takes much physical effort to sit still, listen to instructions and then carry them out, especially if children have poor muscle tone.

Balance is the ability to sustain control of the body and its movements. It derives from the gross motor movements of the body and it is essential for all children to develop these gross motor skills to achieve their full learning potential.

Types of balance
There are two types of balance:
❑ Static balance, where children attempt activities when not moving;
❑ Dynamic balance, where the activities require movement whilst still maintaining the child's steadiness.

Whatever the activities the children are engaged in, they should be guided and encouraged, allowed to work at their own pace and never put in a dangerous position. Their confidence will grow and their skills develop through practice not through maturity alone.

Activities: large apparatus
1 Sloping plank attached to a climbing frame.
The use of this demands some degree of balance and also lower leg strength.

The child will progress from crawling up/down the plank using hands to grip for added security to gradually walking up/down the plank on feet only in an upright position.

2 Balance beams - the same width as gymnastic forms.
Suspended from two tripod frames a short distance from the floor the beams provide excellent practice for children to move along and increase their balance control.

Activities: small apparatus
Bean bags
1 Walk forwards/backwards/sideways with bean bag on head. Increase speed to make more difficult.
2 With bean bag on head, slowly lower body into a sitting position.

Activities: floor work
1 Musical statues: children walk/skip/run around area, stopping and holding position when music stops.
2 Children balance on one leg then the other.
3 Children hop around the area, changing feet.
4 Children rise up on tiptoes (balls of feet), arms by sides, lift arms above head and balance.
5 Children rise up on tiptoes (balls of feet), arms by sides, lift arms out to side to help balance and slowly bend knees until in a crouching position.

6 Children on all fours, lift one limb and take body weight on three limbs, return to starting position and move a different limb.
7 Sit on bottom, knees bent, feet on floor, arms on floor, children lift feet and hands and balance on bottom.
8 Children lie on backs, arms by sides, lift legs and arms off floor and balance on backs.

The above suggestions are not an exhaustive list and many of the activities will be familiar to staff in pre-school settings. They may, however, act as a prompt or starting point for further activities.

Many of the activities show progression and a varying degree of difficulty to aid differentiation and can be used by anyone who is involved in furthering young children's physical development.

Carol Boylin and Linda Henderson

Settings should plan for a range of balancing activities so that they can challenge the most adventurous children and encourage those who lack the necessary confidence and physical co-ordination. Jean Evans shares some ideas

Improving **balancing** skills

The bodily control demonstrated by pre-school children varies enormously. Some have no difficulty in climbing to the top of a climbing frame or balancing along a narrow beam. Others may be reluctant to venture from the safety of solid ground because they lack the appropriate skills and confidence. By ensuring that planning for physical development covers a range of balancing activities we are able to challenge the most adventurous children, and encourage those who lack the necessary confidence and physical co-ordination to gradually progress in simple manageable stages until they, too, can enjoy the satisfaction of achievement in this aspect of their physical development.

Movement activities
- ❑ Play games involving balancing, such as musical statues and 'Follow my leader'.
- ❑ Enjoy rhymes involving different movements, such as hopping, jumping and walking on tip-toe to the verses of 'I went to school one morning' and 'Here we go round the mulberry bush'.
- ❑ Work with a partner as you move to favourite rhymes, such as 'See-saw Margery Daw' and 'Row, row, row your boat'.
- ❑ Try balancing on different body parts. Stand on one leg, then the other. Lie flat and lift legs off the floor, then head. Walk along on all fours. Is it possible to lift one limb and still balance ?

Imaginative balancing
Children love pretending to be something or someone else. Stimulate their imaginations and interest with dramatic movement.
- ❑ Pretend to be stiff wooden puppets on strings, lifting arms and legs and nodding heads. Contrast this stiff movement by

singing 'I'm a dingle-dangle scarecrow'.
- ❑ Fly around like aeroplanes with arms outstretched, sometimes leaning on one leg as the aeroplane lands.

- ❑ March like soldiers, changing on command to march on heels and tip-toes.
- ❑ Pretend to be different creatures, waddling like ducks, crawling like crabs, jumping like rabbits, hopping like birds.

Large equipment
Climbing frames and slides enable children to choose to work at different heights according to their ability. Try adding planks and ladders, either horizontal or sloping, to increase the choices and challenges available. Less confident children enjoy pulling themselves along or up and down using their hands before they gradually progress to balancing along planks. A tunnel is a comfortable and safe piece of equipment to crawl through. Children show great satisfaction as they manage to balance from one end of a beam to another. Even the most timid child will try with a friendly adult hand to steady them.

Wheeled vehicles
From when a child first tries to walk unaided equipment with wheels can provide the

stability they need. Push-along toys, pedal cars and sit-and-ride toys encourage early confidence and control. Children can then progress to tricycles and scooters. Bicycles, with and without stabilisers, are excellent for developing balancing skills but unsuitable for pre-school settings for safety reasons.

Small equipment
Bean bags and quoits can be balanced on different parts of the body. Get the children to lie down flat and try to lift their legs in the air with a bean bag across their feet or a quoit hanging from a foot.
- ❑ Hoops, small mats or carpet squares can be spread across the floor as stepping stones and children can jump, or take long strides from one to another. Get them to try hopping in and out, tip-toeing around the edge or stepping into a hoop held by an adult. Jump on and off carpet squares.
- ❑ Ropes and long ribbons can be spread along the floor in straight or wiggly lines and children can tip-toe or hop along them or jump over them. Put them in parallel lines and try crawling along the lines on all fours. Chalk lines can be drawn and used in the same way. Get two children to hold a rope just above the ground while the children crawl or wriggle under.

Jean Evans

Be aware of the needs of all of the children in the group. Children with mobility problems may need extra space to move and use apparatus. Activities may need to be adapted, perhaps by working on the floor or at a lower level.

If your group has access to an outside play area, then no doubt you will possess a number of tricycles and other large wheeled toys. But do you get the best use out of them? Matthew Jarvis gives some pointers

Using wheeled toys

Tricycles and toys which need to be pushed or pedalled can build muscle strength, and improve fitness and co-ordination. With a little planning and preparation they can also be used to stimulate imaginative play and enhance areas of learning from other parts of the curriculum.

Layout

Trikes move fast and may be a danger to pedestrians. You should therefore have an area designated to wheeled toys and so have other areas which are trike-free where children may play without fear of being knocked over. A physical barrier, such as a line of tyres, will remind children of the boundaries.

To make the layout more interesting, mark out paths and roads using paint or chalk. Although chalk will need renewing regularly, it does mean that you can change the layout frequently.

Include features such as junctions and crossroads to avoid a procession of children and to allow for some decision making.

Curves and bends encourage controlled steering. Arrows, road signs and traffic lights stimulate the imagination and provoke discussion. Allow children to have some input into the design, getting them to consider issues such as size and safety.

Do not limit yourself to roads. Paths can become rail tracks with the children riding on trains through stations to different destinations - painted boxes for shops and a sand tray to represent the seaside. Alternatively, trikes may become boats sailing down rivers, avoiding crocodiles!

Equipment

Toddlers or children with mobility problems need toys which encourage them to stand up and push. This includes prams, pushchairs, baby walkers and push-along animals. Children may also be leaning on these toys for support so check that the handles will bear some downward force without toppling over.

Sit-on toys fall into two categories - those which are scooted, Flintstone style, by the child's feet, and those propelled by pedals through leg and arm power. Younger children are more suited to trikes without pedals since they need less muscle strength

Early Learning Goals

❏ **Creative Development**
Have a carnival - allow the children to decorate the bikes with streamers and balloons. Junk (cans and plastic bottles) tied to the axles will make noise as you parade. Add hats, masks and bright clothes whilst the other children provide a musical accompaniment. On dry days, soak wheels in water and 'paint' with the tyre marks.

❏ **Mathematical Development**
Draw arrows on the ground for the children to follow: introduce the words left, right, forwards and backwards.
Have races: introduce ordinal numbers such as first, second, third. Include slow races as well as fast. Stress that everyone who finishes is a winner and give them all a cheer.
Play at being postmen or women. Chalk houses on the ground. Give each a number and encourage children to deliver parcels to the correct house.

❏ **Physical Development**
Practise controlled steering by weaving through obstacles.
Allow children to chalk lines on the ground for their friends to follow.
Draw abstract patterns and shapes on cards - waves, zigzags, and spirals. Give the cards to the children and let them interpret them as a bike journey.

❏ **Personal, Social and Emotional Development**
Talk about road safety. Add zebra crossings to road layouts, make a crossing patrol lollipop. Local accident prevention officers may be able to lend you working models of pedestrian crossings.

to be operated. As most of these toys have handlebars, children will need to learn how to steer them - a skill requiring hand-eye co-ordination, spatial awareness and plenty of trial and error and practice to learn how the trikes perform. To encourage children to steer their trikes, place obstacles in the bike areas. Old car tyres are ideal as they are large enough to withstand collisions. Beanbags or cones are so small and light that younger children are unlikely to swerve to avoid them. Include plenty of obstacles so that children's attention remains fixed on steering rather than building up speed.

When children move onto using pedals, they will require sufficient leg power to turn them through a complete circle, otherwise they tend to rock backwards and forwards on the same spot.

Include trikes of various sizes - too large and children will not be able to reach the pedals, too small and their knees will be tucked up under their chins.

As they learn to pedal encourage children to raise the pedal on their dominant side to a position about one o'clock for as large a first stroke as possible. You may have to push children on the trikes while they have their feet on the pedals to get used to the rhythm and motion of pedalling. A final larger push should be sufficient to send the children away under their own steam.

There are never enough bikes to go around, so it is worth mentioning sharing. A system you may wish to adopt is to group the children by giving them different coloured sashes to wear. Allow those with red sashes a certain amount of time to play on the bikes before swapping them for another group, and so on.

Matthew Jarvis

Children need lots of experience playing with a ball to become reasonably competent with the basic skills of rolling, throwing, catching and bouncing. Pam Taylor shares some ideas

Improving **ball skills**

We need to provide plenty of opportunities for children to master new skills using a ball in various ways. What is a simple straightforward skill to us will need to be broken down into many stages before a child will become competent at it.

It's always sensible to give young children the opportunity to throw and catch a bean bag before introducing a ball. Bean bags are easier to handle and do not bounce or roll away! When you start using balls, make sure you select the right size ball and give the children plenty of space to practise in.

Here are a few simple ideas that will help the children to improve their skills in rolling, throwing, catching and bouncing a ball.

With their partner they can play roll, chase and stop. One child gently rolls the ball for the other to chase and stop it. Children then swap places. This part of the lesson can get quite exciting and noisy but remember there is nothing wrong with a 'working' noise.

Throwing and catching

Catching is a much more difficult skill than throwing because of the amount of co-ordination involved. Children have to be able to watch the ball as it moves and use their hands without looking at them! They start off by being afraid of the ball and you can see them physically flinch as the ball comes towards them. You need to spend time demonstrating how to catch a ball. Stretch arms in front of you, fingers

spread wide. Tell the children that when they catch the ball they will need to bend their

arms and pull the ball into their chest.

Let the children have a ball each. Tell them to gently push the ball into the air so that it goes past their nose and just higher than their head. (Be ready for the over exuberant ones that launch the ball to the ceiling.) Tell them to keep their eyes on the ball all the time and let the ball drop back into their hands and clutch the ball to their chest. If

this part of the lesson gets too noisy, with balls going everywhere, use the commands ready, throw, catch, stop. You will be able to see instantly the children who are mastering the skill and be able from your observations to position yourself close to a child that might need 'hands-on help'.

Make this into a game by asking the children who drop the ball to sit down until you have a few children left. This does make the children focus more on what they are doing.

Next, throw and catch with a partner. Again, start close together then increase the space between them as they get more skilful and confident.

Bouncing

Children should stand on a 'magic' spot holding the ball in front of them. They need to place their hands either side of the ball, fingers spread and arms fairly straight in front of them. Drop the ball and catch it again making sure eyes are on the ball.

Develop this by telling the children that as the ball comes up to meet them they need to put their hands on top of the ball and gently push it down to the ground again - a bounce. See how many times they can bounce the ball without moving off the spot.

Bounce the ball to a partner. Place a small hoop on the floor between the two children. Tell them to aim to bounce the ball in the hoop for their partner to catch. The children need to be told to push the ball down and forward directing the ball towards their partner.

Pam Taylor

Rolling
Roll the ball along the ground to a partner. Tell the children to bend their knees and swing their arms as they let the ball go. The child catching the ball must keep their eyes fixed on the ball and bend down to meet it. As children become more skilful, extend the space between them.

Most pre-schools have a few small balls in their store cupboard. Don't be frightened to use them - they don't necessarily have to be thrown! Kate Wright shows you how to make them a valuable part of your PE programme

Using **hand** apparatus

A successful PE programme needs variety. This can be achieved by presenting a number of skills in many different ways. Hand apparatus is an excellent way of providing variety.

Hand apparatus can help to develop:
❑ Physical skills, for example balance and co-ordination.
❑ Body management, such as alertness, timing, and manual dexterity.
❑ Social awareness, for example working with others.
These skills are not just important in physical education but are an essential foundation for a child's general development.

You may already have a number of small balls as part of your equipment. If you don't, then most children will be able to bring a small ball from home, providing you make it clear that it must be small and light - Dad's cricket ball is a definite no, even tennis balls are quite hard when thrown enthusiastically. Airflow, foam and ball pit balls are ideal and are inexpensive to buy.

A group of nursery teachers looked quite alarmed when I suggested that they might like to use small balls in their PE class. We have all met the boisterous four-year-old eager to show off his hardest throw, and his friend who wants to do even better! But balls do not necessarily have to be thrown! Here are some ideas to show the variety of ways in

which small balls can be used. You could plan your complete session around all four headings or choose just one section for four different sessions.

Warm-ups
Egg and spoon
Children put ball on outstretched hand and move round the room weaving in and out of each other. Stop! Change hands and move again. Try walking backwards! Try walking on tip-toe! Avoid one hand being

outstretched for too long! Keep palms flat and thumbs off the ball!

Football
Children use feet to tap the ball around the room. Use lots of little taps to keep ball in control. Use both feet. Look to see where you are going.

Noseball
Children go on hands and knees and push ball along ground with nose. Try to keep in touch with the ball all the time.

Chase ball
Needs a big space - a good playground activity. Children roll ball along the ground and then chase it. Look where you are going!

Individual activities
Sit in a long sit (long straight legs, knees and feet together).
1 Hold ball in between two hands and roll it round and round as if manipulating playdough.
2 Roll ball up and down hands.
3 Turn ball in your fingertips - first one way then the other.
4 Foam balls can be squeezed tightly in both hands or in alternate hands.
5 Roll ball down body. Start on head, over forehead, down nose, under chin. (Can you hold it between your chin and chest? Try putting your arms out wide at the same time.) Roll ball onto tummy, round and round tummy, roll it round to your back, swap hands and bring ball back to your tummy. Roll ball down onto your thighs, over your knees and down to your toes.
6 Keeping toes pointed, and ball balanced on feet, ankles and knees together, and legs straight, lift legs off ground so ball rolls back into your lap!
7 Hold ball on floor by thigh, lift legs as in (6), roll ball under legs from one hand to the other.
Sit in a short sit (bend knees and sit in tuck position). Roll ball under knees from side to side. (Could be done in conjunction with (7) in long sit.)

How many places can you hold the ball whilst in a short sit?

Some ideas are:
❑ in backs of knees
❑ between knees
❑ between feet
❑ between knees and tummy
❑ under chin
Grip the ball in any of these positions and try rocking backwards!

Kate Wright

Small balls and targets

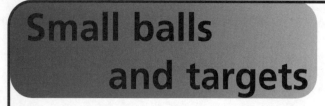

These activities could be set up as a circuit. Give children two minutes on each activity.

Useful objects are: carpet squares or chalk marks, cardboard boxes or plastic baskets, skittles, cones or even lemonade bottles filled with sand, lengths of rope, wooden plank.
If possible, place your targets in front of a wall or some sort of barrier so children do not have far to retrieve a ball which has missed.

1 Kick ball from square set 2m from two cones 1m apart.

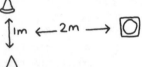

2 From square throw ball into basket 1m away.

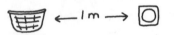

3 From square roll ball to knock down several skittles 1.5m away. (Ropes laid on ground and a box behind the skittles will prevent ball from straying too far.)

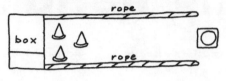

4 Roll ball along a plank into an upturned box.

5 Place two cones 3m apart and using both feet dribble ball round cones.

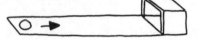

6 Kick ball through a tunnel of chairs.

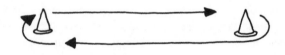

Partner work
(or working with parents)

If working with children only, demonstrate the activity first ideally with another adult or with an adult and child.

1 Both sit in wide sit facing each other (long straight legs, wide apart).   i Roll ball to each other
ii Throw and catch ball with each other

2 A sits in short sit, B sits in wide sit. A places ball on knees and lets it roll down legs over feet and onto floor. B catches it in wide sit. B sits in short sit, A sits in wide sit and the activity is repeated.

3 A sits in long sit, B sits in wide sit. A tucks ball into lap then lifts hips, keeping legs straight. Ball rolls down A's legs onto floor. B catches it in wide sit. B sits in long sit, A sits in wide sit and the activity is repeated.

4 A and B stand one behind each other facing same way. A bends over and rolls ball between legs. B squats to receive. A stretches, B stands to place ball in A's hand. Repeat activity several times then change over.

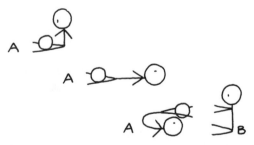

5 A sits in long sit with ball between feet. Lies down. Lifts ball over head and gives to B. A sits up again and B returns ball to A for further turns. Then change over.

Long sit - long straight legs, knees and feet together
Short sit - bend knees and sit in tuck position
Wide sit - long straight legs, wide apart

Kate Wright

Parachute canopies are becoming increasingly popular items of equipment in all kinds of settings. If you're thinking of getting one but not sure how you'd use it, Jean Evans has some ideas

Parachute **play**

Parachute play can make a valuable contribution to the programme for physical development. It is an excellent way of increasing children's large movement skills, particularly those of the upper body.

As they lift and lower the canopy children are using the muscles of their arms, chests and shoulders and developing greater confidence and co-ordination as they do so. Many activities involve whole body movements, both on top of and underneath the canopy. The children become aware of the space around them and of others in the group as they take part.

How to begin

Begin all parachute activities in a large space and have some simple warm-up activities. Spread the parachute on the ground and position the appropriate number of children and staff around the edge so that each person has a handle to hold. Make sure staff are spaced evenly amongst the children. Hold the handles, pull the parachute taut and lift it up and down. Try raising it as high as possible to form a mushroom before lowering it to the ground. Waft it up and down until the children can feel the air movement. What sound does it make? Try flapping it slowly and gradually increasing the speed. What happens to the sound? Now walk slowly around in a circle holding a handle with one hand, perhaps singing as you walk.

Let's go under

Develop the parachute session with games involving moving under the canopy as children hold it up and waft it gently.

❑ Call the names of two children and ask them to run underneath the canopy and change places. Repeat until all children have had a turn.

❑ Hang coloured cards around the children's necks making sure that there are two of each colour. Call out a colour and ask the children wearing the appropriate cards to change places. Try the same game with numbers or letters.

❑ Have half of the children lying on the floor with their heads to the centre of the canopy like spokes in a wheel. Let the rest of the children waft the canopy close to their heads like waves. Change round and repeat the game.

Let's go over

❑ Spread the parachute on the floor and ask some children to sit on it. Get the rest of the children to waft it up and down to create waves which go over the children's heads.

❑ Ask some children to sit in the middle and hold the edges of the parachute over them. Pull the handles back suddenly to reveal the hiding children.

❑ Walk around in a circle with several children in the centre of the parachute to give them a 'ride on a roundabout'. Older children will love to twist the parachute around one child and pull it so that the child spins.

❑ Create a dome of air by lifting the parachute up, pulling it down quickly and kneeling on it. Choose children to try to climb up the dome. This is especially effective outdoors on a windy day.

Ball games

❑ Put some foam or plastic balls in the centre of the parachute and try to bounce them up and down.

❑ Use small balls and try to roll them towards the hole in the centre until they drop through.

❑ Let some children lie underneath and try to kick or punch the balls on the parachute above them until they fall off. The children holding the parachute should try to stop them from falling off.

Jean Evans

Parachutes can be obtained from most early years catalogues. They come in two different sizes and prices start at around £60. The smaller version is for groups of around 10 children and the larger version for groups of 20 to 30 children. They have strong handles and are made of nylon which allows them to float easily. Some catalogues also supply accessories and booklets with suggested activities.

Young children are constantly using their hands, but you still need to make detailed plans for the development of manual dexterity or fine motor skills. Jean Evans suggests some suitable activities

Developing fine motor skills

Providing appropriate opportunities for children to develop their manual dexterity, or fine motor skills, is an important aspect of the planning of your physical development programme. Children need to develop their manual dexterity in order to cope with their personal needs, such as dressing and keeping themselves clean. Children who have enjoyed activities involving exploration of a wide selection of tools and materials are also more likely to approach directed activities related to drawing and writing with confidence.

Children need time to practise the movements they have already mastered, and the chance to try out and repeat new movements. If you offer a stimulating variety of activities the children will be attracted to them, they will be interested for longer and have fun as well. It is essential, therefore, to produce detailed planning for the development of fine motor skills, which includes opportunities for children to handle a range of equipment, tools, everyday objects, construction equipment and malleable materials.

Planning for every child depends on knowing them really well, being aware of their likes and dislikes, understanding their level of skill and being aware of their ability to concentrate. This knowledge depends on having a successful assessment scheme which is understood by all staff members.

Small equipment
Beads and pegs - children enjoy the challenge of threading beads onto laces. Make patterns using alternate colours or copy sequences from cards. Make number tags to attach to the laces and let them count the beads on. They like to create patterns by arranging coloured pegs on boards.

Tools
Scissors - cut around pictures from catalogues to create a collage; practise cutting lines along the edge of a strip of paper to create a pattern.

Spoons of different sizes - choose from a selection of spoons the best one to fill a container with rice. Include a tiny spoon from an ice cream tub, a set of measuring spoons and a ladle.

Mark making tools - experiment with pencils, crayons, chalk and felt-tip pens to create observational drawings.

Miniature worlds - children love to work with tiny items. Create a miniature beach for small world figures using a shallow plastic dish. Use thimble buckets and mustard spoon spades to create tiny sandcastles.

Objects
Buttons and zips - experiment with different fastenings on children's clothes and dolls' clothes.

Shoes and gloves - sort into pairs. Try putting on gloves of different sizes.

Recycled materials - let the children make their own models with a selection of plastic and card containers and small objects, such as buttons and ribbons. Provide different tools to add glue, such as spreaders, lollipop sticks and twigs.

Construction equipment
Bricks - build a tower of five bricks using as many different types as possible. Which tower is tallest ?

Train track - try making a straight track and a curved track across a short piece of carpet. How many pieces did each track need? Were they the same ?

Malleable materials
Clay - create small pots as presents or divas to celebrate Diwali.

Dough - roll out snakes and compare lengths.

Jean Evans

Differentiation
When planning activities try to think of an easier way and a more complicated way to complete a task as a basis for your extension ideas for younger and more able children. For example, when cutting pictures from a catalogue to create a toy collage younger children could simply tear around a large picture. More able children will be able to cut around the edge of quite small shapes. To glue the picture to paper the youngest children will probably find spreading glue all over the base paper easiest. They can then press the picture onto the glue. More able children will derive great satisfaction from gluing every bit of the back of their picture before sticking it down.

Handwriting/pencil control is an art form, which children will achieve at differing levels, according to their ability, talent and interest. But it is an important part of the holistic development of any child, says Janet Jenkins

Good **pencil** control

Good pencil control forms the basis for neat, readable, well-formed handwriting. However, a child will not automatically be able to hold a pencil correctly and scribe easily. These are skills which have to be learned and then practised regularly. There is a wide variety of activities which can help to encourage the development of these skills. These tasks are all used to encourage improvement in hand, finger, thumb and wrist movements. These movements are known as fine motor skills and form part of the requirements for the Early Learning Goals - Physical Development. The greater a child's dexterity in this field the easier pencil control will be for them.

Alongside this we must remember the importance of vision, as eye and hand co-ordination are vital in these activities, one being totally dependent on the other.

Before going further with our planning, it may be as well to recall the saying, 'practice makes perfect', because that is true in this aspect of the curriculum. Only by regular practice and exercise can movements become more refined and controlled so that precision needed for future handwriting can be accomplished. As dexterity increases, so the movements need to become more relaxed. Then writing flows without tension and the writer can scribe for lengthy periods without suffering hand cramp. This is essential, for as children get older they will be expected to write for longer and longer periods.

There is no particular order to work in. All activities can be easily organised, some during free flow play sessions, some as structured play and others as directed tasks.

Free flow play activities such as bead threading, peg pictures, small world play, magnetic pictures and push and connect construction kits will encourage finger and thumb grip movements, as will more directed activities like scissors work and playing finger cymbals.

Construction kits which have a screw type connection or with cogs and wheels, finger and hand puppets, sewing cards, brush painting and wet sand building all encourage finger and wrist movements.

Planning with progression

By structuring children's play many of the activities can be planned with progression. Do this by being more specific about positioning, for example, give children a coloured pattern drawn onto a workcard for them to copy using pegs, beads and so on.

The smaller the items the more dexterity is required and so work can be progressively planned by starting with larger items and slowly reducing these in size to make the task more difficult and demand finer control.

Direct activities, such as finger tracing in fine sand on a tray, or following over given drawn lines of pattern, finger painting, shapes posting, collecting tiny items in a small box or collage work using small items such as matchsticks and buttons will all give extra practice.

Children are keen to copy and follow the example of others. This applies in handwriting. If adults (parents/pre-school staff), become the role model for writing then children will copy and want to write as well. Leave children to copy in this way and experiment for themselves in holding a pencil before you intervene. Many will have watched adults' pencil grip techniques and not need any direct guidance.

However, do not allow a child who doesn't cotton on in this way to continue too long before helping them. Bad habits can soon become embedded, making correction difficult.

Thin round pencils are often difficult for small hands to grip but in my experience the fatter so-called 'first pencils' also cause difficulties, particularly in quite small hands. I would recommend triangular shaped ones which positively assist in positioning fingers in the correct place.

Pencil grips

It is possible to buy plastic triangular grips which slip onto an ordinary pencil so that they can be introduced for children who are experiencing difficulty in this task.

Beware of pencil grips which are not well defined in shape as it is easy for children to ignore the planned finger/thumb position points (see right) and use them in their own way. The definite triangular shaped ones make this not impossible but more unlikely.

Paper position

Often great attention is paid to the pencil grip whilst the just as important paper position is ignored. Fine flowing pencil movements can only be achieved if the book or paper to be written on is in a position for this to happen. It should be tilted slightly to the right or left (again depending on the hand used), and placed slightly up the table, not directly in front, upright and close to the body.

Whilst I have stressed the importance of developing good pencil control, I firmly believe that for pre-school children the most over-riding and important factor is the encouragement of writing or putting marks on paper and that these efforts are valued and not always receiving interference or criticism about their pencil grip. To this end a range of writing implements should always be freely available for the children to use.

Confident, free flowing, relaxed but controlled pencil movements are essential to future development in handwriting and establishing not only an individual style but one which can move easily to joined letters.

Janet Jenkins

How can you help a child who is having difficulty holding a pencil correctly? Here are some step-by-step instructions which have been used successfully with children.

1 Begin with the pencil laid on the table, point facing towards them, but turned to the right or left depending on the hand used.

2 Ask the child to pinch the pencil about two cm from the point.

3 Lift the pencil above the table.

4 The pencil is then swung up and over the hand to rest in the 'cradle' between the first finger and thumb.

5 You will usually find that the second finger automatically supports the 'grip point' but it may need some directing.

Using scissors is a complex skill that we as adults take for granted. It is best taught on a one-to-one basis. Pam Taylor explains how

Using scissors

Using scissors provides opportunities for developing fine motor skills, manipulative skills, improving hand-eye co-ordination and developing logical thinking. Any child who can use scissors competently by the time they arrive in Reception class will be at an advantage not only within the art/craft/technology areas of the curriculum, but will probably have better pencil control than a child who has not had experience of this activity.

At first, just talk to the child about scissors. Explain the opening/shutting action as a crocodile opening and closing its mouth. Get the child to watch you using the scissors, talking all the time about the crocodile's mouth. You don't need any paper or card at this stage, just the scissors.

Let the child experience the feel of the action by placing your fingers with theirs through the holes. Open and shut the crocodile's mouth. Let them feel the tension. Small children have weak wrists and will find it hard to hold the scissors firmly.

Next, let them snip at old greetings cards. (Paper is thin and offers no support - avoid using it in the initial learning process.) Give the child time to sit quietly and just snip. You'll soon see for yourself if they are mastering the skill - there will be bits of card everywhere! Encourage them to use their other hand to hold the card firmly on the side with thumb on top and fingers underneath. Another good idea is to let them practise scissor action by cutting playdough or pastry.

Once children are competent at holding scissors and snipping, they are ready to move on to cutting *through* the card. The open/shut action is important here because unless the crocodile opens

his mouth wide enough he won't be able to cut the card easily. It's quicker if the crocodile opens his mouth wide. If you are using plain card, draw lines up the card and encourage them to follow the line. This improves hand/eye co-ordination.

The next stage is learning to cut around things. Start with a shape such as a triangle. Children then have to consider how to tackle the corners. Again, offer support by putting your fingers through the scissors with them. Talk all the time about what you are doing and help them to manipulate the card. Tell the crocodile to cut close to the lines. When they have successfully cut out the triangle, reward them by drawing a smiley face inside the triangle - make them feel they have achieved something.

They are now ready to move on to cutting out a circle. This is so hard for little ones. Draw a circle around an illustration/picture on a greetings card. It's far more fun cutting out a picture than just a circle drawn on a piece of card. They will really have to concentrate to cut around this circle and use a lot of manipulative skills. Practice and experience is the only way of achieving this step.

Children love using scissors. Don't stop them because you are afraid of the consequences! Set the ground rules - only use the scissors with an adult - and watch their confidence grow and their fine motor skills improve. Remember, you are introducing them to a skill for life!

Pam Taylor

Left-handed children must use left-handed scissors. They are available from outlets such as the Early Learning Centre.
Special scissors are available with an extra set of finger holes for a helping adult. Contact Hands On, Unit 11, Tannery Road, Tonbridge, Kent TN9 1RF. Tel: 01732 773399

Working with playdough is a relaxing, soothing and sociable activity as well as providing a wide range of cross-curricular learning experiences. Sue Fisher explains

Working with playdough

Playdough provides many opportunities for the development of manipulative and creative skills but equally helps develop a range of skills across all areas of the Early Learning Goals, in particular in the extension of language and communication.

It is a valuable activity for introducing and settling children into new environments as well as encouraging shyer children to join in. Conversations at dough tables often stimulate a shy child to take part as the experience helps children to relax.

Making and learning
Dough can be made in a variety of ways with recipes producing cooked or uncooked mixtures. Whilst ingredients vary, salt should always be added as a preservative and oil improves texture and pliability. Cooked dough should last well in a sealed plastic container kept in a cool place.

Involve children as much as possible in making the dough, in particular in weighing and measuring, pouring and mixing ingredients.

Achieve differing kinds of elasticity and texture by adding a variety of materials, for example, cornflower, rice, lentils or glitter. Providing more than one kind of dough extends opportunities for the children.

Make sure enough quantities of material are available to encourage children to share and

to work alongside each other co-operatively.

Give them opportunities to explore the dough itself before using tools, then provide a range of tools for children to select from to cut, mould, shape or make imprints.

Encourage children to work effectively in comfortable and appropriate positions such as sitting, kneeling or standing at a table. Support them by questioning and extending thought and language and offering encouragement to try out new ideas, suggesting and demonstrating new techniques.

Developing vocabulary and language
Descriptive language: lumpy, bendy, soft, warm, squidgy, sticky, silky, smooth.

Language of manipulation: squeeze, prod.

Mathematical vocabulary: relating to weight and volume as dough is being made and to size and shape during play.

Questioning and experimentation
Conservation: learning that the same piece of dough can take on many shapes yet remain the same amount. For example, a ball of clay rolled into a snake can become a ball again.

Questioning on cause and effect: for example, what will happen if we add more flour, water, rice?

Experimentation: What will happen if I hold this big stretchy piece up by one end? What will happen if I keep rolling and rolling this ball of clay?

Fine manipulative control
Working with playdough can fulfil the Physical Development Early Learning Goal - 'Handle tools, objects, construction and malleable materials safely and with increasing control.' Try providing scissors to practise cutting skills on dough.

Occasionally, provide a limited number of tools or none at all and encourage and support the children to achieve a planned effect by using their hands to manipulate the dough.

Balance opportunities for free expression with modelling from observation.

Children need to learn to investigate, experiment and solve their own problems as well as ask questions and learn new language. They should receive positive encouragement to try out new ideas. Even when it is likely these will not work, it is important that children are encouraged to experiment and to take risks. Our role as adults is to support and encourage children to have fun, express themselves creatively and learn from playing with this versatile material.

Sue Fisher

Tools to try:
Rolling pins, knives, forks, spoons, garlic presses, pastry cutters, scissors, spatulas, moulds, dough machines.
Good for patterns and imprints:
Cotton reels, pine cones, buttons, shells, coins.

Physical Development

Chapter 5

Unit C5: Promote children's social and emotional development

About this unit

Unit C5 is a key unit in your NVQ because it's about ensuring that children have a secure environment which will promote their emotional and social wellbeing. If early years workers don't get this right, it doesn't matter how wonderful the environment is in other ways - if children are not happy and secure, they will not develop to their full potential. It's crucial that staff have a common philosophy on how they promote children's social and emotional development, and that they share that philosophy with the parents.

> This unit is best completed over a period of time, to show your assessor that you consistently promote children's social and emotional development.

If you leave this unit until you have completed some of the others, you should be able to cross reference a lot of it. For instance, if you have already completed C10 and C11, you will have shown your assessor how you gave praise and encouragement, how you encouraged children to relate to each other, share and take turns.

The first element is about how to help children settle into the early years setting. The next four are about how to enable them to develop emotionally and socially. The final element is about preparing them to move on to school or other new settings.

Read through the elements and get a feel for the requirements. There is some overlap between the four middle elements, and you may already have some evidence from C10 and C11, but it's important that you cover all of the different aspects of social and emotional development. The settling-in element is obviously best done at the beginning of a new intake of children, if you work in a setting which usually takes children once a year. If you work in a setting which takes new children all the year round, look for appropriate opportunities as they arise. Similarly, helping children to move on will normally need to be done in the term before they start school.

Values

The values statements place particular emphasis on the welfare of the child across all elements, and on working with parents, learning and development and safety across most elements. Elements 2, 3 and 4 have a strong emphasis on equality of opportunity, anti-discrimination and celebrating diversity. It's particularly important that children from other cultural backgrounds are made to feel accepted. Going into a care setting for the first time is daunting for any child, but if a child's home language and family practices are completely different to those of the majority in the group, they will find it even more difficult. Working closely with parents is a key issue for this unit, because consistency of care is essential for the children's emotional wellbeing. You will need to take account of different family and cultural expectations throughout the unit. There will be opportunities to cross reference some of the evidence to P2 – 'Establish and maintain relationships with parents'. You might like to look at this unit before you start, to give you an idea of where you will be able to cross reference.

> **Useful tip!**
> Fill in the unit assessment records with each piece of evidence as you collect it, starting with your assessor's observation. That will prevent you doing too much.

Getting started

In this unit you are aiming to show how you can:

- ◆ Help children to settle in
- ◆ Help them to relate to others
- ◆ Develop their self-reliance and self-esteem
- ◆ Help them to recognise and deal with their feelings
- ◆ Prepare them to move on to new settings

If you find it helpful, use the personal skills review to identify where your strengths lie, and where you need to gain more experience or do some training, reading or research.

Have a look through the units you have already completed, and cross reference all appropriate evidence to this unit. You may need a bit of help from your assessor to do this. If you have used the cross-referencing sheet it should be easier. Then plan with your assessor, using an assessment plan, how you will tackle the rest of the unit. You may have to leave the first and last elements until an appropriate time, unless you have been really efficient and covered them already! When you're planning, think about any work products you can use from your setting, such as policies, progress reports and so on.

Element C5.1 Enable children to adjust to the setting

Key issues

You need to be absolutely clear about what your setting's policy is on settling in, but also do some reading and research to ensure that what you are doing is best practice. In some settings, it's difficult to have the ideal settling-in arrangements because of working parents, but it's essential that you do the best you can for the child. You need to be particularly careful with children between the age of about eight months - when they start being wary of strangers - to about two and a half - when they are beginning to enjoy being with other children. Of course, children's ability to cope with separation will vary a great deal, regardless of age, and you need to be sensitive to this. You also need to be sensitive to the parents' feelings, because it is often a traumatic time for them, too.

You need to get as much information as you can from the parents about their child. You will need the official information, like medical details, emergency contact numbers and so on. Check which documentation your setting uses if you don't know already. It's also useful to ask about things the children like and things which worry them, any particular words they use which you might not understand, whether they speak another language at home, and so on.

Invite the parents and child in for a visit before they start, so that the child gets a little familiar with the setting within the security of his parents being there. Encourage the parents to stay with the child as long as they are able when he first starts, and never let a parent sneak out without saying goodbye. I've seen it done frequently, but it's the worst thing you can do. The child might be upset, but at least they don't feel as if they've been abandoned. The parents should always say they'll be back later, so that the child knows. If possible, make the first stay a short one, and increase the length of time gradually, especially with young children who don't understand the concept of time. Always let the child have something from home, to give them a bit of security.

Which type of evidence?

Read through the PCs, range and notes on this element to make sure you understand what is required. You will see from the evidence requirements that your assessor needs to **observe** all but one of the PCs for this element, and one aspect of each range category. You might need to keep her informed about an appropriate time to do this element, when you have a new child starting. If she is not able to be there at the appropriate time you may have to get a **witness testimony** from your supervisor, employer or a colleague. Use the format suggested by your centre, or the one in the first chapter in this book.

If you can, observe a number of different children, preferably of different ages, when they first enter the setting, and record their reaction using the **child observation** format and one of the methods of recording suggested in C16 in Book 1. Or write a **reflective account** or **diary** account of how you have dealt with particular children - those who settled in easily and those who had difficulty. Think about why this might have been. You may like to include your setting's policy on settling in, and comment on how you have used it and how effective it was. Remember to include as much knowledge evidence as you can in these accounts. The related **knowledge evidence** statements for this element are 2, 15, 27, 29. You should easily be able to cover all of these in your other evidence.

Remember
Cross reference this evidence on to your P2 cross-referencing sheet.

Element C5.2 Enable children to relate to others

Key issues

It's important that children see adults being caring and co-operative. If the staff are calm, friendly and caring, the children are more likely to be. If the staff are always shouting at each other, the children probably will, too. Adults must treat the children with respect if they want the children to treat them and other children with the same respect.

If you have children with English as a second language, they may find it much harder to relate to others. Some may be fluent in both languages, but others may have limited English. In this case, try to get someone who speaks their language to spend at least some time with them, to help them with the transition period as their language is developing. Find out if your local intercultural support service can offer help, or encourage a parent to spend some time in the nursery, working with the child in their home language. If this is not possible, you will need to give them individual support, using body language, gestures and visual aids, and reassuring them, because they are likely to feel very insecure.

The way you organise your day will help children to learn how to relate to others. Think about how you can get the children to share tasks such as preparing for activities and meals or snacks, tidying up, helping each other. Choose games and activities which promote co-operation rather than competition. Competitive games make winning the all-important thing, and where there's a winner there's always a loser. Ask yourself what that does for the young child's self-esteem. Co-operative games encourage children to work together, and it doesn't matter who wins. The articles later in the chapter, and in some of the other chapters, give many examples of co-operative play.

Be aware of children who may have additional needs. For instance, how would you support an autistic child? Look out for the child who always plays alone, or watches others playing but doesn't join in. Think about what strategies you will use to help her to relate to others.

There is a strong emphasis on anti-discriminatory practice in this element. You can help children to be positive about difference through the activities and experiences you give the children. It's also vital that you deal with racist, sexist or abusive language and behaviour if it occurs. You must never ignore it. We would recommend that you attend some specialist training on this important issue, if you haven't already done so. Check with your assessment centre or your local Early Years Development and Childcare Partnership whether there is anything available. You will also find the BBC video and booklet *Children without Prejudice* very helpful (available from BBC Education, PO Box 7, London W3 6XJ).

Which evidence?
Read the PCs and range, and notes on this element, for some examples of activities and experiences which will help children to relate to each other. One activity will not normally be appropriate to cover this element. It's more about the overall experience you are giving the children. Look through your cross-referencing sheet for this unit. You may have appropriate evidence from C10, C11 and C3. This element will probably be built up from several *observations* your assessor has done, so that she can judge that you are helping children to learn how to relate to others in all situations.

It's also useful to collect *witness testimonies* to cover things which happen while your assessor is not there - like how you dealt with an incident of unsociable behaviour or a racist or sexist comment. A *diary* is particularly useful for this element, too, so that you can jot down relevant evidence as it happens. If you don't keep a diary, carry a little notebook with you, and write up your notes later into a *reflective account*. You may

like to do a *child observation* on children's ability to relate to each other. Remember that any observations which you do will also be cross referenced to C16: 'Observe and assess the development and behaviour of children'.

Don't forget to look at the requirements for the knowledge evidence before you write up your other evidence, so that you can cover as much as you can. The related *knowledge evidence* statements for this element are 1, 3, 4, 23, 24, 30, 31. Some of the articles later in the chapter will help you to ensure that you understand the importance of being a good role model and of establishing a positive, caring and secure environment for the children in your care.

Some of the evidence you collect for this element may be appropriate evidence for C7: 'Provide a framework for the management of behaviour'. Write anything you think fits onto the cross-referencing sheet for that unit.

Element C5.3 Develop children's self-reliance and self-esteem

Key issues
Children need to be given the opportunity to make their own decisions, make choices and have a say in the decisions you make in the nursery. They need to become self-reliant and independent. You need to think about whether you are giving them this opportunity. Are you doing too much for them, and not allowing them to develop self-help skills? A few minor changes in the way you organise your day can make a lot of difference to children's self-reliance, and the more confident they become, the better their self-esteem will be.

The notes on this element suggest appropriate activities and experiences to develop children's self-reliance and self-esteem. You probably already allow children to choose in some situations - such as choosing books for story time and songs they enjoy singing. How much choice do you give them in the art area? Are they able to help themselves to different materials, or do you have out a particular activity for that day? Do you set out the toys that you want them to use in the morning or do you let them choose equipment from the cupboard during free play? Think about how you can incorporate more choice and decision making.

You need to be aware of those children who have difficulty with this, and give them a lot of encouragement but help them where necessary. Don't expect too much of them at first, or else you will make them less confident rather than more so. Remember that in some families and cultures, children are not expected to be self-reliant, so you need to take account of this when you are working with the children, and you may need to discuss it with the parents.

Which evidence?

Again, your assessor is likely to want to **observe** this element over a period of time, while she is observing other more specific activities and routines. She needs to observe six of the ten PCs and one aspect of each range category. You will probably find that your **witness testimonies, diary** or **reflective accounts** will provide other appropriate evidence. The element builds on C5.2, in that you are now looking at ways of helping children to be more independent, and at the same time, building their self-esteem, both of which are a natural progression from relating well to others. **Child observations** will help you to identify how self-reliant individual children are.

The related **knowledge evidence** for this element is 4, 5, 6, 17, 18, 24, 32. Try to cover as much as you can within your other evidence.

> ### Remember
> You don't have to have all of these types of evidence in every element. Just make sure that you have enough, and try to cover different types of evidence across the unit. This is why it's good to plan a whole unit together, because you can get a good range of evidence without having too much.

Element C5.4 Enable children to recognise and deal with their feelings

Key issues

Some young children find it hard to express their feelings in appropriate ways, and this is why they may become unco-operative, aggressive or withdrawn. This is particularly true of children around two years old, because they want to do so much, but they don't have enough language skill to express themselves adequately. They also haven't much idea of danger, and are unable to understand the concept of waiting or sharing. Put all of these together, and no wonder they have tantrums! It's important that you have a good understanding of children's development, so that you can deal with them effectively. It's no use telling a two-year-old that they must share, because they haven't reached the stage where they are able to.

Children can become quite frightened by the strength of their own feelings. It's crucial that you stay calm in situations where children are having an emotional outburst. If you lose your temper and start shouting, it will make the situation worse. You need to find out why the child may be having negative feelings at that time - it could be some sort of family difficulties, in which case the child will need a lot of reassurance. You may need to call in an expert to help the child if the problem is serious. Of course, this would need to be discussed with the parents by the person in charge. If there is a suspicion of child abuse, your setting will have a procedure to follow. Make sure you know what it is.

As an early years worker, you need to enable children to learn how to express their feelings through words, actions and play. Don't wait for emotional outbursts to happen before talking to children about feelings. Talk to them about what makes them feel unhappy or angry, and help them to see that if they are unkind to others, it will make them feel unhappy, too. Use stories, role play, puppets and dolls to illustrate the points you are making. This element is also about positive feelings, and it's important that as adults working with children, we don't lose that sense of eagerness and enthusiasm, joy and wonder about the good things in life, and that we point out to them the exciting and interesting things we see as we listen to a bird, see a beautiful flower, feel the sand in our toes, or talk about something a child has achieved or enjoyed doing.

The articles later in the chapter are helpful for ideas for this element, and also parts of the BBC video, *Children without Prejudice*.

Which evidence?

Your assessor will need to **observe** all but two of the PCs and one aspect of each range category, but again, she is likely to do this over a period of time. Read the PCs, range and notes on this element to get a picture of the evidence you need to provide. Check your **diary** for appropriate evidence, or write a **reflective account** of some of the times you have helped children to express both their positive and negative feelings. If you have a child in your setting who is having difficulty with controlling his feelings or has emotional outbursts, you will find it useful to carry out a **child observation**, and evaluate what may have caused it and what is an appropriate way to deal with it. Use an event sample to observe the child over a period of time. You will find guidance on this in C16 in Book 1. Ask a supervisor or colleague to write a **witness testimony** about a situation you dealt with successfully.

> ### Don't forget
> Fill in relevant evidence for other units on your cross-referencing sheet.

The related **knowledge evidence** statements for this element are 7, 8, 9, 14, 19. Try to cover them in your other evidence. Where necessary, do some reading, research or training to ensure that you have the necessary understanding of the issues. The articles later in the chapter and the recommended reading list on page 24 will help you.

Element C5.5 Enable children to develop a positive self-image and identity

Key issues

Children will come to the early years setting with very different levels of self-image and identity, depending on their experiences in their first years of life. Children quickly pick up negative feelings about themselves if they have not been valued as individuals within their families or in the wider community. If they and their parents have been subjected to racist or sexist remarks, or if their parents have been over critical of them, or not praised their efforts, they will have been affected by this. Children from minority ethnic groups and cultures, bilingual children and children of mixed race, children with special or additional needs and abused children are more likely to have a low self-image.

It's absolutely vital that early years workers take account of children as individuals in all of their planning and work. It should be written in the setting's policies that all children are respected and treated as individuals, but you must be confident that this is really happening. It's not enough to say, 'We treat children all the same'. This element is about celebrating diversity, and giving children access to equal opportunities to achieve their full potential, regardless of their gender, culture, colour or ability.

> Children are individuals, with their own talents and needs, their unique family and cultural background, gender role, and level of ability, and all must be valued and respected for who they are.

There are specific activities you can do to develop a good self-image, such as games with mirrors and children talking, drawing and writing about themselves and their family, but it has to be more than that - it should be integral to the ethos of the setting. Look around your setting at the displays, books and other resources. If a child comes into the setting, and sees no images from her or his cultural background, or if children from a predominantly white area never see positive images of people from other cultures and with a different colour skin, what message is that giving? Your local intercultural support service will probably be able to give you information about successful people from different ethnic groups and cultural backgrounds for displays and discussion with older children, or ideas for resources for younger ones.

Now think about whether any of the equipment, resources or experiences you give the children are counteracting stereotypical images. Do you include women and men in non-traditional gender roles in your stories and pictures? Do you have any men on your staff? Do you invite visitors from different walks of life to speak to the children - female fire fighters, male nurses, people from minority ethnic groups and people with disabilities in positive and successful roles? Do you visit local places of interest, including places of worship or community buildings of the different ethnic groups? If you are in an all-white area, have you made links with a nursery or school with a high proportion of children from different ethnic groups? Have you made links with the local school for children with disabilities, or taken positive action to include these children in your setting?

Think about your own language and attitudes - do you separate boys and girls unnecessarily, or do you make sure that you encourage both sexes to do the whole range of activities? It's not always enough to say that they all have access to all the equipment. It's a useful exercise to observe over a period of time how long boys and girls spend on each kind of activity. You may find that you hardly ever have boys sitting at the writing table or in the book corner, or girls using the wheeled toys or the construction materials. How can you make these areas more attractive to the boys, or to the girls? Do you give praise where it is due, and encouragement where it is necessary? Do you give children the opportunity to talk to the others about their achievements or efforts? Do you have special sharing times to allow children to do this? Do you always look for something good to say about each child, rather than constantly bringing up the negatives?

Which evidence?

Read through the performance criteria, range and notes on the element to familiarise yourself with the requirements. The notes offer some helpful suggestions for activities and experiences which will enable you to help girls and boys from a range of cultures, family groupings and those with special needs to develop a positive self-image and identity. If there are any aspects that you don't understand, discuss them with your assessor.

Your assessor needs to **observe** one aspect of each range category and half of the PCs in this element. She may have observed some of these over time, during other activities. If not, prepare an **activity plan**, perhaps using the following activity. Get the children to look at themselves using a mirror, and to describe themselves. Ask them to describe their friends and what they like about them. Then they can paint or draw themselves and their friends and make a display of things they like about each other. Think of a special thing to say about each child, and write a caption to go with their picture. Have a range of skin and hair colours available for the children to use, or help them to mix their own.

Your assessor may also wish to **inspect the setting** to check on how your setting promotes positive images. She may ask you **oral questions** to check your understanding. You could use **diary** entries, a **reflective account** or **child observation** to identify where you have helped children to develop a positive self-image. Think about examples of children who have had a low self-image, how it affected them, and how you helped them to overcome it.

The related *knowledge evidence* statements for this element are 10, 11, 12, 20, 21, 25, 33, 34, 35, 36. This is an important area which you need to be sure that you understand. You may need additional training, reading and research to fulfil the requirements for the knowledge.

to keep her informed about when will be a good time to do this.

The related *knowledge evidence* statements for this element are 2, 13, 22, 26, 36. Try to cover these in your other evidence. The article on 'Getting ready for "big" school' (see page 161) will give you some helpful information.

Element C5.6 Prepare children to move on to new settings

Key issues
Some children will be anxious about moving into school, so you need to make the transition as painless as possible. It's important that you don't make any negative comments, and that you make it something that the children will look forward to as far as possible. If you have the opportunity, reinforce this message with the parents as well. It's fairly easy to prepare children for school if most of the children move into the local school, but often children attend nursery from a wide geographical area, so it's not easy to arrange visits.

You need to know what the procedure of your setting is for preparing children to move on, and include a copy, or describe the procedure. If the setting doesn't have a written procedure, you may like to make suggestions for one. It will depend on your position in the setting whether you will be allowed to try it out. It's important that you agree with colleagues and parents what procedure you will follow. The notes on the element have some suggestions such as role play, stories about starting school, or moving house, talking about what it will be like, and visits to the new setting.

Which evidence?
Read through the PCs, range and notes on the element, so that you know what the requirements are. Think about how different children in your setting may react to having to move on, and how you can help them. Those who are more confident will perhaps not need as much support as those who find it difficult to relate to new adults and situations.

You will probably need to do this element in the term before the children start school. If you have individuals leaving for other reasons, such as moving house, this will provide some suitable evidence to cover other areas of the range. Look for opportunities as they arise, and make a *diary* entry or write a *reflective account* of how you helped the child to prepare for the move. Your assessor is required to *observe* half of the PCs and one aspect of each range category, but you will need

Only when a young child feels secure, happy and confident can a sound basis for learning be established. Gay Wilkinson looks at the vital role of personal and social development

Personal, Social and Emotional Development

Beginning any new experience arouses a mixture of feelings - excitement, curiosity, anxiety - in adults as well as children. Adults can draw on other similar experiences to help them cope with these feelings but young children do not have such a reservoir to tap into. It is vital, therefore, that the pre-school environment, both inside and outdoors, is carefully planned and organised so that children can feel secure and recognise that they are an important person within it. Only when a young child is secure, happy and confident can a sound basis for learning be established.

A display which has photographs of each of the children will give powerful messages to each child of how the adults value them as special members of their community. You can also use these photographs as a basis for discussion, perhaps at story time, about the differences and the similarities between the children - size, gender, colour of hair, eyes, skin, language and any other elements that the children suggest - and how they feel and think about these.

The use of story books which celebrate children's achievements regardless of gender, race or other physical differences can be a useful extension to such a discussion as can displays of artefacts representing other cultures which children can look at, handle and speculate about. Play resources - jigsaws, home corner equipment - which show that differences are recognised; the celebration of a variety of festivals and special events; visits from parents with special interests, backgrounds or experiences; visits from people within the community who do particular work regardless of gender will all contribute to the development of tolerance, trust and respect for others within the pre-school environment. Sensitive adults can also use the planned environment to provide

experiences which will enable young children to feel a sense of wonder and awe in the world around them in their outside play, through the care of pets and through carefully displayed artefacts which will encourage reflection and quiet thought.

At home children know where many things are, especially their own toys, are able to choose and take responsibility for much of their own activity, decide how long they will take to do something, perhaps who they will do things with and have learned about many things through exploration, investigation and play. They see themselves and act as learners and this is often reinforced by their parents. This helps them to feel secure, happy and powerful and they are therefore confident and motivated to continue to carry on finding things out.

They may take part in the day-to-day activities in the home, such as preparing a meal, washing up and putting their toys away. These experiences help the child to feel that they belong in the family and motivate them to make the effort to abide by the family rules.

The pre-school environment can feel and look very different to the young child and uncertainty can make the child feel helpless. Such feelings can damage their sense of self-worth and self-esteem and lessen their motivation to carry on being learners. You should make every effort to ensure that the environment makes sense to the child and allows them to take responsibility both for themselves and the setting.

Resources and equipment should be grouped together by kind, be accessible and labelled so that children can find what they need. Since most young children have limited reading skills, consider how materials and equipment are to be stored and distinguished to support their self-help skills. Open crates of cardboard boxes, plastic sweet bottles or containers (local supermarkets and newsagents can provide a

'Successful personal, social and emotional development is critical for very young children in all aspects of their lives and gives them the best opportunity for success in all other areas of learning. It is crucial that settings provide the experiences and support to enable children to develop a positive sense of themselves.'

Curriculum Guidance for the Foundation Stage

useful and often free supply) all allow children to see what is inside. The use of pieces of equipment as labels is helpful, such as a jigsaw piece (save that old and incomplete jigsaw!) or a sticklebrick. Pictures can be cut from catalogues, or drawn, and fixed to the containers as well as onto the shelf where they are stored.

There should be plenty of opportunities for children to make choices about what they are going to do, who they are going to do it with and enough time to finish their activity to their satisfaction. Equally they should be encouraged to clear equipment away when they have finished using it so that it is ready for someone else to use. It is important that children see that this is a genuine role that is expected of them by all the adults working in the setting and that they are making a special contribution to the well-being and comfort of everybody. They might need support to undertake this successfully, but they should not see the adults doing it again after they have finished or have it done for them. They may interpret this as meaning that what they had been asked to do was not a serious request.

Since the way we feel influences everything we do it is important that adults should both plan specific activities for children's emotional development as well as respond positively to spontaneous events within the nursery. Puppets can be useful resources for focusing on feelings with a small group of children.

For example, introduce a sad teddy who tells the children what has made him sad. The puppet teddy can be passed around the group and each child invited to say what else has made the teddy sad that day. A range of puppets, each identified with a different feeling, can be collected and used on different occasions. If these are always

available then they can also be used by individual children when they are finding it hard to cope with difficult feelings. Structured role play with small groups can also be helpful.

The adult tells a simple story in which conflicting feelings are aroused - for example children refusing to share toys and fighting. The children are then invited to talk about the situation, the feelings of those involved and enact alternative ways of dealing with the situation. In this way they can be helped to develop alternative behavioural strategies and learn how to manage their feelings in an acceptable manner.

Children join a pre-school setting from a variety of home experiences and backgrounds. They have already learned a great deal about how people relate to each other through observing and imitating family members and people they know in their immediate community. They have begun to find ways for themselves of trying out aspects of relationships - their behaviours and their associated body and spoken language - in their imaginative play and with their family. In the new setting, with new adults, they will continue to observe and learn from others and will need opportunities to try out what they are learning both here and at home in their play.

They need to see the adults around them demonstrating positive relationships with each other, with parents and with themselves. They also need to be provided with a range of play situations which will allow them to try out how some of these social relationships work. Domestic play and other social play settings, such as the doctor's surgery, a shop, a cafe (there are many others) will allow them to experiment with relationships and different ways of behaving with others without worrying about getting it wrong. In the play they are always in control and can change or mediate the action if they feel that things are getting out of their control. This sort of play -

trying on different roles - provides them with an opportunity to see what it feels like to be someone else and this in turn allows them to develop a better understanding of how and why people behave as they sometimes do and develop greater tolerance and understanding.

As well as taking on other roles children sometimes also need to play out events within relationships without wanting to put themselves directly in the situation. Small world play such as playing with the dolls' house, small model people, cars or animals often gives children the chance to work through a particular social script that interests them, but at a distance, so that confusing and uncertain feelings can be managed.

There are a wide range of storybooks which provide children with opportunities to talk about their feelings and those of others and these can be used to support particular situations.

The ability to make friends is particularly important to young children and will play an important role in their later achievement in school, particularly as they become adolescents. Young children may need adults to help them to develop and use appropriate strategies, for making and sustaining friendships; adults may need to intervene when situations of disagreement or conflict occur and discuss possible solutions with the children. Positive social behaviour such as sharing, helping and caring for others should be recognised and praised publicly. In this way the children will begin to establish a set of values which will guide both their present and future lives.

Gay Wilkinson

You need to be absolutely clear about what your setting's policy is on settling in. Mary Townsend offers some advice on how to make it a positive experience for young children

Settling-in procedures

For young children starting in an early years setting, it may be the first time they have spent any length of time away from their parents. Children will come to the setting with very different experiences. Some may be used to seeing other children and adults because they are part of a close-knit family, and they have spent lots of time with grandparents, aunties and uncles and cousins. But this is often not the case nowadays, with families moving to different parts of the country for their work. They may have met other adults and children in a mother and toddler group, or they may have been at home without much contact with anyone outside the immediate family. Starting nursery may be quite a distressing time for some children, so it's important to try to make the transition as painless as possible.

It's important to consider the particular difficulties associated with the age at which the child starts to attend an early years setting. Young babies will generally settle without any difficulty as long as they are well cared for, and their routine is more or less the same as at home. They should as far as possible have a key worker who carries out most of their care.

From the age of about eight months, when babies begin to be wary of strangers, until about two and a half years, when children begin to enjoy being with other children and adults, is the most difficult time for a child to be separated from their parents, so it's crucial that extra care is taken to settle them in gradually. My most distressing memory during a visit to a nursery was a little girl of about 15 months old who was absolutely inconsolable. She had just started at the nursery, and had no understanding of what was happening to her. So how can this be avoided?

Full day care providers such as nurseries and childminders, who take children at any age,

need to emphasise to parents the need for a gradual introduction to the setting. Most do insist that parents at least have one pre-start visit with their child. Some pre-schools, nurseries and childminders have developed their own effective settling-in strategies to suit the circumstances of working parents. It's not always easy when parents are working, but with a little thought and care, you can usually arrange for the child and the parent to spend some time together in the setting before the child is left for long periods. Most parents are anxious about leaving their children and will be only too happy to make sure that they are happily settled.

Most local authority schools and nursery schools have a well planned settling-in procedure which may include some or all of the following:

❑ A visit to the child's home to talk to the parents and to the child. Sometimes it will be the teacher and the nursery nurse who will visit so that while the teacher is talking to the parents and filling in any relevant forms, the nursery nurse will

bring an activity to do with the child. They may leave a pack for the parents and child to do together, to prepare them for starting in the setting. Some parents may find a home visit a bit threatening, so it's important to explain beforehand what the purpose is, and to respect their wish if they don't want a visit.

❑ An initial meeting at the nursery or school to give parents information about the school's policies and aims, and to explain the curriculum. Often, the children will go into the classroom and do activities with the teachers and nursery nurses or classroom assistants while the parents have a meeting with the

headteacher, and fill in any relevant paperwork. The parents may then be encouraged to spend some time with their children in the classroom.

❑ The parents may be invited to bring their child in for several short sessions, staying with the child the first time, then leaving the child for short periods, before attending for full sessions at the nursery or school.

❑ On starting school or nursery, parents are encouraged to stay and play with the child until they are settled, then leave. Often, children only attend for half a day for the first few weeks. There may be a staggered intake, so that staff can give plenty of attention to each child.

Sharing information

It's important to gather as much information about the child from the parents as possible. Every setting must have records which include the child's dietary needs, medical background, relevant family details, contact addresses and telephone numbers and permission for emergency treatment. But there is other useful information which will help you to get to know the child better. Some settings have an 'All about me' book or something similar, which parents are asked to fill in about their children's development, and their likes and dislikes, fears and anxieties. Parents are their children's first carers and educators, they know their own child better than anyone, and you need to show them that you respect them as such. Too often, carers see themselves as the experts, and don't take enough account of what parents can tell them. You need to work in partnership with parents, so that you provide continuity of care and education for their children.

Many nurseries, especially those who care for babies and young children, have a diary in which both carers and parents write important events in the child's day - from how much feed they took, how many nappy changes and the amount of sleep they have had to milestones in the child's development and exciting activities the child has done. This is an important part of helping both children and parents feel secure and happy with the setting, and for ensuring continuity of care. Children need to see that their parents and their carers have a good relationship, too. It will make them feel more secure.

Most early years settings have a brochure which they give to parents. This will contain useful information about the nursery aims, policies and regulations, but they will often contain much more:

❑ how they ensure children's health, safety and wellbeing at all times

❑ how their equal opportunities policy is put into practice
❑ an explanation of the Foundation Stage and what it means
❑ detail about the educational value of activities, to show parents that children are not 'just playing'
❑ how they will support children with additional needs
❑ an explanation of how their behaviour policy works in practice
❑ how they will ensure quality of care and education
❑ how they value parental involvement, and suggestions about how parents can be involved

This may well be supported by parents' evenings and open days to give parents further insight into how they work.

Making new children and parents feel welcome

This is the most important aspect of helping children to settle in. If they are greeted by a happy, smiling member of staff, who takes the trouble to know their names, and has time to listen to them and their parents, they are far more likely to settle in easily. You need to be aware of the particular difficulties and anxieties of children and parents from different cultural backgrounds, whose home language may not be English. The notices and displays in your setting should reflect the different cultural groups in our society, so that children and parents don't feel that the setting is completely alien to them. Many people from minority ethnic backgrounds have grown up in this country, and won't have difficulty with English, but you do need to check this beforehand, so that you can have an interpreter present if you need to. You may be able to get support from your local intercultural support service to work with a child who doesn't speak English.

If the new child has additional learning needs or a disability, the parent will be able to tell you what the child's particular needs are. Find out if the child is supported by a specialist agency, and make contact with them. You may be able to get additional support in the setting for children with additional needs.

Show the parents and child around the setting, pointing out their coat peg with their own name or picture on it, their drawer or other space for their own possessions, and the toilets. Point out and explain things that may be unfamiliar and worrying for the child. Talk about the routine of the day, bearing in mind the age of the child and how much they are able to cope with. Make sure there are lots of interesting activities which will encourage the child to join in, and encourage their parents to play with them for as long as possible. With older children, it's nice to get a confident child to go and talk to the new child, or explain to the group that Jacob may be feeling a bit nervous as he's only just started nursery, so could they be particularly kind to him today and invite him to join in their play. The parents will perhaps be able to tell you what approach the child is most comfortable with. Some children like to just watch for a while until they feel confident to join in, others will prefer to sit with an adult. Some like a cuddle, others hate being touched. Some children will join in with no difficulty. Children may like to keep a comfort object with them - something from home which makes them feel more secure.

When the parents are ready to leave, insist that they say goodbye to their child. Some parents think it's better to sneak out once their child is absorbed in an activity, but that is the worst thing they can do. There may be tears when they go, but at least their child won't feel as if they've been abandoned. They should tell the child what they are going to do, and when they will be back, using an event the child can relate to, such as 'after lunch'. Then the carer can remind the child what the parents said, to reassure him. Once the parents have gone, give the child as much attention as you think he needs, and make sure that you explain the routine as new things happen, such as snack time, outside play and so on. For some children, being separated from their parents is always going to cause them distress, but if you follow these guidelines, you will know that you have done everything you can to minimise their anxiety.

Mary Townsend

Only by establishing relationships with familiar adults and children based on mutual care and respect will children be able to learn as they play together and interact with the adults within the group, says Caroline Jones

Forming relationships

Forming relationships is about communication, about children feeling they belong and recognising their lives are connected with other people. A child who is able to establish effective relationships will grow up to be a secure, sensitive and caring adult.

You can promote children's ability to form effective relationships with adults and other children by spending time communicating with and getting to know them and by constantly offering children choices as to what to do and who to be with.

Encouraging children to establish effective relationships with other children and with adults and to show sensitivity to others, including those of other cultures and beliefs, is an important part of the programme for personal, social and emotional development. However, it is not possible to isolate personal, social and emotional development from the rest of the pre-school curriculum. The programme must be given high priority, as it crosses all six areas of learning. Some opportunities will occur naturally in the daily routine as patterns of activities for each day provide opportunities for learning in which children work, talk and play alongside each other in small and large groups.

Equally, positive relationships can be fostered through a range of well-planned activities, resources and routines.

Planned activities

Planned activities which encourage collaboration, interaction and co-operation are vital. Some common examples include: table games, floor games, music and movement - partner work, songs which involve turn taking or holding hands, cooking, parachute play, throwing and catching, mini-football.

Role play

Relationships can also be fostered through carefully planned opportunities for role play. One approach is to have a theme or topic such as 'People who help us'. Imaginative play themes allow children to play out the roles and relationships they observe, to try out what it is like to be someone else. Through their role play children learn to relate to adults and other children, using both verbal and non-verbal communication. As they play together and share resources, they learn about being co-operative and caring.

Most pre-school workers are familiar with the endless 'cups of tea' children bring out from the home corner! Role-play themes which encourage co-operative play include: Indian/Chinese restaurant or English cafe, shoe shop, post office, fruit shop, bakers, garden centre, hospital, dentist, hairdressers, travel agents, bus/boat/train.

The stories children are told, their imaginative play and the discussions they have with adults should further their understanding of the wider world and their part in it. Stories, objects and pictures can be used in circle time to promote positive images of children and adults with disabilities and from other cultures. Providing resources, listening to music, celebrating festivals and sampling food from other cultures also helps children develop sensitivity towards others.

Community links

Help children begin to learn about membership of groups, within and beyond their family and to be aware of the local community and their place in it. Reinforce this with local walks, for example, to the shops, park, railway station or simply walking and exploring the locality. These experiences offer an opportunity for children to observe and ask questions about their community.

Visitors coming into your group also give children the chance to relate to other groups to which familiar adults and children belong. Some of these may be regular, for example the librarian, others may be special visitors. They could include: policeman/woman, fire fighter, dentist, nurse, chef, children from the local school, a parent or grandparent.

Caroline Jones

Politeness is a social convention that we all abide by. It is one of the accepted norms that sticks society together but it does not always come naturally! Judith Harries explains how you can help to develop good manners

Learning to say
please **and** thank-you

Babies have no concept of manners and politeness. If a baby is hungry, he or she cries and mum or dad responds. A toddler just learning to talk, points at an apple and carefully forms the word 'a-pul'. Mum and dad are delighted and full of praise for their youngster's first attempts to ask.

It's not long before this is punctuated by constant demands, so the child is encouraged to say please and thank-you with every request.

Role models

Encouraging a child to be polite is part of helping children learn to respect themselves and others. The *Curriculum Guidance* for Personal, Social and Emotional Development says 'If the practitioner says 'please' when making a request and allows children time to finish what they are saying before responding, children will learn to be courteous and attentive.' Clearly, it is important that we set a good example to the children in our setting by using please and thank-you when we talk to them. When giving instructions to the children, don't forget to say please: 'Put the cars away now, please, and then come and wash your hands ready for snack'. Always remember to say thank-you to the children for something each day. For example: 'Thank-you for helping me to tidy the home corner', or 'Thank-you for looking after Peter when he fell over'.

It is also important to encourage the children to use please and thank-you when talking to each other as well as adults. It can really make a difference!

'Lucy won't let me have a go on the bike', said Oliver, as he stood looking intently at the girl whizzing around the hall on the red tricycle.

'Have you asked her?' said the teacher.
'Yes!'
'Did you say please?'
'No.'
'Well, try again.'
'Lucy, please can I have a turn?'
Lucy stops pedalling and climbs off ready for Oliver to clamber on.
'Oliver, don't forget to say thank-you!'

Routines

There should be opportunities during the routines of a nursery session to practise using please and thank-you. The most obvious one is at snack time. As I work at a Christian nursery, we begin our snack time by saying a simple thank-you prayer - 'Thank-you, God, for our food and drink'.

Try playing this game with the children as they choose their snack or select a coloured cup. Pretend that your arm is a crane-like machine that only works when it hears 'please'. The snack or cup is then picked up and presented to the child but not released until the machine hears a 'thank-you'. By accompanying the machine movements with suitable noises, the children soon join in the fun!

You could use this response rhyme at the end of snack time:
'Put your cup/plate on the tray,
And what do you say?
Thank you for my snack.'
At the end of each session, we say a thank-you prayer - 'Thank-you God for our morning/afternoon at nursery, for all the fun we've had and all the friends we've made'. Alternatively, you can have a circle

Role play
'Children learn many skills and attitudes in well-planned role play' (Early Learning Goals). If you set up the role-play corner as a shop or cafe, there will be lots of occasions to use please and thank you. You can model this for them by taking on the role of shopkeeper, waiter or customer and being particularly polite or not!

Special days
Organise a 'Be Polite Day' for the nursery when all the children and staff make extra special efforts to be polite to each other. You will need to explain what 'polite' means. The children could take home badges saying 'I was polite at nursery today' or 'Don't forget to say please!'. Create a 'Thank-you' notice board and invite the children to stick thank-you drawings and messages on it.

Say please
Try playing this simple movement game - an adaptation of 'Simon says'. Ask all the children to find a space to stand in and listen for the instructions. When you say 'Please, tap your knees', they must follow the actions, but when the please is missing, that is, 'touch your toes', they must stand still. When they have got the hang of this, you could ask for volunteers to lead.

time together and ask the children to think of something they have particularly enjoyed that day. This can lead to them thanking a friend for the game they have played or thanking a teacher for helping them.

When children forget to say please and thank-you, what should our response be? We probably all say 'What's the magic word?' or 'Ask nicely!' and children do need to be reminded frequently. It is also effective through role play to show them how it feels when people forget their manners. Try being a very rude customer in the cafe demanding lots of extras and, of course, forgetting to say thank-you. Next time one of the children is giving out their birthday sweets, you can remind them of how it felt not to be thanked and hopefully saying thank you will have more significance.

Judith Harries

Many pre-school setttings have their own variations on circle time. What works best? Sara Stocks shares some approaches that she has found useful and some techniques for managing different situations

Organising **circle time**

Circle time should be a relaxed session where everyone can join in and you can get to know the children in your care a little better. Your aim is to allow them the opportunity to get used to speaking out in a group and also to having their comments listened to with respect. You may use circle time as an opportunity to introduce new ideas or to go over old issues - either way it should be a reassuring time of calm and quiet.

Set the space up somewhere where you are unlikely to be disturbed. A carpeted area is ideal. Some groups have a formal circle with children and adults cross-legged around the perimeter. Others form a group, sitting on knees or cuddled in a corner. If you have a larger group with more than six or so children then the informal cuddle corner may become hard to manage but with fewer children it can be cosy and comforting. A group of more than 12 pre-school children is hard to manage effectively at circle time and you should consider breaking the group up into smaller key worker groups for this special time of the day.

Children under the age of three are unlikely to benefit from circle time and will probably disrupt the group. New or shy children will probably want to sit on the leader's lap, which is fine for a while, but integrating them into the group and making sure that everyone gets their fair share of cuddles is important, too.

Children of this age love routine. They like to know what is going to happen next and this applies as much to circle time as it does

to any other session. You may find that starting with a story will put the children at ease and encourage them to contribute later on in the session. Try not to go over the 'magic' 20 minutes, as the children's attention span will not stretch further.

When you start your circle time you will be aware of the themes and topics that the group is currently covering. Picking rhymes and games which support new learning is a good idea although being too rigid could lead to a stilted session. There are always some children who want the same rhyme no matter what the theme. Accommodate them without boring everyone else by having that rhyme sometimes!

The introduction of new vocabulary is an important part of early years work and giving the children confidence to try new words is an appropriate and useful activity for circle time. Choose appropriate words that link with your theme and have a simple definition prepared beforehand. Try not to use new words in the definition or you will quickly confuse the children!

Show pictures that may encourage comment or conversation and ask simply what the children think is happening or how the people in the picture feel (Sunday magazines are a good source of these type of photos but filter them carefully.)

You may feel that the rules of your group are clearly understood - the children may well understand them perfectly but, nonetheless, they will get broken! Minor problems can usually be solved in a non-confrontational way if you gently remind the whole group that throwing sand or spitting or whatever the sin is that has been committed is not allowed and explain again why. Circle time is often used in schools to underline the rules and sanctions of the class. Your children are too young for you to dwell too heavily on this aspect of circle time but it is useful to raise points now and again. You can use this time for praising too, in fact, if you have had a minor moan then praising ought to follow pretty quickly!

There are plenty of games and rhymes that encourage the children to engage in question and answer sessions. Setting the scene for conversation this way will lead gently in to a more general discussion time. If the child has heard their own voice as part of a game then speaking out with an individual comment is slightly less frightening!

Rhymes to get attention or to signal the start of a session are useful in circle time as they are throughout the day. Start singing the first line and let it be a signal that the children should join in and at the end they should be sitting quietly.

My hands upon my head I'll place
Upon my shoulders, on my face,
At my waist and by my side,
And then behind me they will hide.
Then I'll raise them way up high,
And let my fingers fly, fly, fly.
Then clap, clap, clap, and one, two, three,
Just see how quiet we can be.

Finger rhymes and games, even old favourites, can be given a new lease of life by changing the names used and including the names of the children instead. 'Peter Pointer, Peter Pointer, Where are you?' can easily become 'Emma Smith, Emma Smith, Where are you?' And will encourage Emma to reply: 'Here I am, Here I am, How do you do?' Try choosing the quieter children; it will give them the opportunity to speak out in a safe and structured environment.

Humour, such as the ever popular 'Tiny Tim', breaks the ice and prepares the ground for many questions.

I had a little turtle,
His name was Tiny Tim,
I put him in the bath tub,
To see if he could swim.
He drank up all the water
And ate all the soap
He woke up in the morning
With bubbles in his throat!

Follow up with questions such as: Who has tasted soap? Was it good? Could you drink a whole bath of water? What is a turtle? Do you know anyone called Tim? Who goes

swimming? Is it fun? Who do you go with? Do you play games in the water? Who can put their head under?

Using hands, fingers and movement is a great confidence booster and manipulation skill practice as well as good fun. Try this rhyme from the USA and see which movements work best - be creative!

My little puppy's name is Rags
He eats so much that his tummy sags
His ears flip flop and his tail wig wags
And when he walks he goes zig zag

My little puppy likes to play
He rolls himself in the grass all day
And when I whistle wwwwww
He always runs the other way!

Flip flop, wig wag, zig zag,
Flip flop, wig wag, zig zag,
Flip flop, wig wag, zig zag,
Flip flop, wig wag, zig zag,

If you have had fun as a group you will then find it much easier to sit down for a quiet time and a proper chat. You will have

expended some energy, raised a smile and practised some new words and sounds before even asking any child to contribute to a discussion.

A question and answer rhyme is an obvious prelude to open discussion. Start with all the children answering you (you may need an adult to cue them in) and build up to children leading or groups working together.

Did you feed my cow? Yes ma'am, Yes ma'am,
Could you tell me how? Yes ma'am, Yes ma'am,
What did you feed her? Corn and hay
What did you feed her? Corn and hay

Did you milk her good? Yes ma'am, Yes ma'am
Did you milk her like you should? Yes ma'am, Yes ma'am,
How did you milk her? Squish squish squish
How did you milk her? Squish squish squish

Young children are not yet shy of the sound of their own singing voice and you should be able to make something of this when you are working with a small group of pre-schoolers. Singing is a therapeutic activity for staff and children alike and you should try not to miss the opportunity!

Try this to the tune of 'Mary had a little lamb' and encourage the children to sing out their answers:

What does (name) like to do, like to do, like to do?
What does (name) like to do? When it's time to play?

I like playing with my (dolls), with my (dolls), with my (dolls)
I like playing with my (dolls), when it's time to play.

Finally, remember that story telling and holding a group's attention are skills that need training and practice. Although some early years training courses tend to omit this essential teaching skill there are ways of brushing up if you do not feel as confident as you would like. Speak to whoever is responsible for your professional development.

Sara Stocks

What to do **if** . . .

The children don't settle

Make sure that you are doing it at the right time of day, the children should not be too tired. Don't keep them waiting on the mat while you prepare yourself. Start with something more interesting!

An older child walks away

Have a spare adult sit with the child to encourage him or her to stay. Observe the child throughout the day and make sure that he or she is generally able to concentrate and join in. Failure to do so may indicate a problem.

A young child walks away

Let them go. There will be other adults who are around and who can occupy the child who is obviously not ready for this yet.

More than one child regularly disrupts the group

Make the time more interesting!
Evaluate your own skills.

A child disrupts the group by fidgeting and bothering the children around him

Have a spare adult sit with that child. Work towards him being able to sit on his own.

A child discloses a serious problem such as abuse

Don't over react.
Make sure that the child has finished talking and then thank him or her for contributing.

Don't ask probing questions. Finish the session.

Find an excuse for someone to play one to one with the child while urgent expert advice is sought from the duty social worker.

A child gives you the same news each day

This is very common! Praise the contribution and move on. After several sessions of repetition you might like to help the child to say something else. Prompt them with a question: 'Didn't I see you going home for tea with Sam yesterday? What did you play with at Sam's house?' or whatever.

A child never contributes

Prompt the child with a question and then praise any contribution at all. Monitor the child throughout the day to make sure that they are communicating adequately in other situations.
Rehearse a question and answer before the group starts.

A child hogs the limelight

This is quite a tricky one. Confident he may seem but limelight hogging may be a sign of nervousness. Being on your knee during the session may well help to keep him or her quiet while the others have a turn. Make sure he or she gets the opportunity to say their piece though and then encourage the child to listen to the others' comments.

A child expresses anti-social opinions

Even if the comment itself is offensive, remember that it is highly likely to be a 'picked up' opinion. You are quite within your rights to express an opinion that contradicts the child's comment, but do so gently: 'Actually Matthew I don't agree with you that all women are stupid. I know some very clever people and many of them are women.' Make a note of the opinions the children express and evaluate your equal opportunities policies in the light of them.

The word 'benevolent' is defined as meaning 'wishing to do good, actively friendly and helpful, charitable, well wishing'. How can we encourage children to foster these attitudes? Lesley Button has some ideas

Thinking of **others**

It is important that the nursery setting is a warm and caring environment and that every child feels they have a part to play in maintaining this 'feel good' factor.

New children need to be made to feel welcome and secure. We use circle rhymes using names not only to introduce new children but to help them learn other children's names. It also encourages the group to be aware of the need to welcome and involve: 'Hello Sarah (x3) how are you today?' This can be followed by a personal question - How is the new baby? Is mummy feeling better? This not only helps to personalise the relationship but encourages the child to share information and others to listen until it is their turn.

Another introductory rhyme is: 'Sarah, Sarah, it's a lovely day. Sarah, Sarah are you coming out to play? Go and get your jacket on, tell your mummy/daddy you won't be long, We'll be waiting on the corner.' The child then leaves a seated position to join a dancing ring.

We use games to encourage sharing and taking turns, and role play and meal times to develop these attitudes. If you wish to focus attention more specifically perhaps it's the time to extend a caring project, such as 'People who help us'. If you are talking about ways in which adults give help throughout their lives perhaps it could develop into how children can also help.

Friends and family

Talk about who the children care for amongst friends and family. Make a list of who and why. Perhaps the children could make a display/book of pictures with their own captions - 'I like Peter, he plays with me.' 'I love granny. She cuddles me.' Then try to take this one stage further. These are the things they do for you - what do you do for them?

Ask children what makes them feel nicest inside, someone being friendly, smiling and talking to you or being shouted at or ignored. Encourage children to ask others to join in games so that an adult doesn't need to engineer the participation of the new or quiet child.

At circle or group time, single out especially kind or thoughtful actions. 'James gave India a big hug when she fell over. Wasn't that kind?' 'Mary shared her crayons with Lindsey' (especially good if they are not renowned for this!). Praise helps to build self-confidence and makes a child feel special. Concentrate on the positive rather than negative aspects of behaviour to encourage the attitudes you wish to foster.

During the winter, many of you probably put out food for birds or even make bird tables. This is a caring project for animals who need our help. Extend this into thinking about people who need extra support - old people, less fortunate children, either locally or worldwide. It can be the ideal opportunity to discuss why people need extra help and care and a time to involve not only the children but their families, too.

Helping your community

This will need you to do some finding out first. Who within your community would welcome contact or gifts? The Salvation Army, amongst others, collects tins of food at Christmas to be distributed to those alone and elderly. Perhaps the whole nursery could become involved. Invite one of the organisers to visit you and talk to the children. The contacts you make in this way could be maintained throughout the year.

It is valuable for children to appreciate what they have and to begin to extend their thoughts to those who have so much less. This thinking can be brought closer to home. Do they know someone who lives

alone? Could they make a special card or picture for them? Does granny have a tape recorder? Could they record some of the nursery songs/voices to send with a special message?

Do bear in mind that if you are encouraging children to think (and do) for others not within their immediate family then you may be relying upon parental involvement. Not all parents may wish to take part. Avoid this leading to a 'They don't care, why should I?' attitude. Your setting needs to provide an alternative - 'Some of you are sending/taking special presents and some of us are going to make a very special card.'

Lesley Button

Useful books

Lucy's Picture by Nicola Moon (Orchard Books)- caring for grandparents.

Nini at the Carnival by Errol Lloyd (Puffin) - friendship.

A Baby Just Like Me by Susan Winter (Dorling Kindersley).

Through my Window by Tony Bradman/ Eileen Brown (Little Mammoth).

The Trouble with Babies by Angie and Chris Sage (Puffin).

Rosie Runs Away by Maryann MacDonald (Little Mammoth).

Families by Nicola Baxter (Watts) - ideas!

Sharing does not come naturally - children need to be taught to behave in a way that is socially acceptable. Carol Boylin and Linda Henderson suggest some activities to reinforce the right messages

Taking turns and sharing

Taking turns and sharing is a vital part of personal and social education and children who do not master this advanced skill may find life increasingly difficult as they progress through school.

The Early Learning Goals state that children should: 'have a developing awareness of their own needs, views and feelings and be sensitive to the needs, views and feelings of others' and 'work as part of a group or class, taking turns and sharing fairly . . .' To ensure this development, you should facilitate children's play and ensure that they are given encouragement to use the apparatus on offer whilst recognising and respecting the needs of other children.

Children need to learn how to share - it does not come automatically. It is a concept which should be taught and reinforced. They need to recognise that:
❑ some things belong to them and some to other children;
❑ apparatus in group settings is available for all children to use but is not owned by any individual;
❑ some apparatus in group settings can be played with by more than one child simultaneously and some can only be used by one child at a time.

What do we mean by sharing?
It is useful to qualify exactly what it is we are expecting from children when asking them to share as we could be expecting one of three things!
❑ When children are sharing their own toys with other children or siblings we are, in effect, asking them to be part of a lending/borrowing system.
❑ In pre-school settings, when using apparatus designed for individual use, we are expecting children to take turns in their use of the apparatus.

❑ When asking children to share their sweets, we are really asking them to give some away!

Children have varying degrees of sharing experiences, depending upon family size and opportunities they may have had to play with larger groups of children. Children under two and a half will not yet have an understanding of sharing, so don't expect too much of them. When entering pre-school settings, children will be expected to learn the social skill of sharing with not only a very much larger group of children, but also with a greater range of apparatus than they have previously experienced. Resources should be varied and of sufficient amount to encourage children to use them co-operatively without too much restriction on time. Children must have enough time to experience the apparatus of their choice without worrying that it will be put away before they have 'had their turn'.

Adult intervention
Observation of children at play is important as children will never learn how to take turns if all they experience is that a particular piece of apparatus is never on offer to them because of the refusal of stronger willed children to relinquish control. Adults may have to intervene to help children negotiate with each other over the sharing of equipment. Interaction in children's play, with the adult calmly showing by example how to take turns and share in a small group situation, is far more productive than removing the child who finds it difficult to share as this may lead to more aggressive behaviour. Dealing with children with little skill in this area demands a firm and consistent approach from all team members coupled with a manner which is non-judgmental of the child but which offers them alternatives to their behaviour. This early intervention and help will give

Suggested activities
Pairs of children using one toy
Ball/hoop: rolling it back and forwards between each other.
Car: taking it in turns to roll it down a slope, one child being the roller, the other the catcher, then changing roles.
Large apparatus (something which requires two children to make it go): one child sits in whilst the other child pushes/pulls the apparatus - the story 'Lazy Bear' could be used before this activity.

Small groups of children - one toy
Slide: waiting their turn to go down the slide.
Frame: waiting their turn to climb up and jump down - perhaps giving the children a number 1-3 might help.
Ball: passing a ball in a three-way group.
Bike: perhaps use a timer if a particular bike or ride-on toy is a favourite so that children know when their time is up.
Table-top games: snap, lotto, dice games, anything which involves the child waiting for the others to take a turn, pass the dice, and so on.
Group games - ie Pass the parcel.
Snack/milk time: children pass the plate/straws around to each other.
Role play: role play situations are an ideal way for children to take turns and share apparatus and again the interaction of an adult within the play helps to encourage children to interact positively with each other.

children a framework upon which to build a sharing relationship with others.

Carol Boylin and Linda Henderson

Teaching young children to take turns is an important part of their personal, social and emotional development. However, it cannot be taught in isolation; it takes practice and some children will learn more quickly, whilst others will need sensitive adult support and encouragement

Learning to
take turns

When children start pre-school it is often their first experience of a large group. It may be in the pre-school that a child begins to realise he cannot have every toy exactly when he wants it. This can lead to tears, temper tantrums and squabbles. How often have you seen two children holding on tightly to the same toy which they both declare they had first!

The role of the adult and the language they use is crucial. Fairness and consistency are paramount. There are many ways adults could respond to this scenario:

❏ The adult takes the toy away completely and says something like - 'Well, if you're going to argue about it, neither of you will have it'.

❏ The adult finds another similar toy and suggests that 'You have this one and let Jonathan have that'.

❏ The adult takes one of the children away from the situation and says 'Come and help me do this puzzle'.

❏ The children are left to sort it out for themselves.

Whilst all these responses may be appropriate at certain times with certain children, and may even stop the fight and the tears, they do not necessarily help the children understand the idea of turn taking or incorporate the language of 'turns'. Instead, the adult could spend a few minutes with the children and make the most of the opportunity. If it were a toy car, for example, the adult could say:

'Oh yes - you both like the car do you? It's a lovely car.' *(Acknowledges the children's feelings and gains attention)*

'Let's all have a turn with it. First it's my turn, then David's and then Sophie's. Well done!' *(Allows the children to know they will*

actually get to play with the car and introduces the idea of 'turns'.)

'Yes, you're taking turns now, well done!' *(Gives positive reinforcement when the turn taking takes place, rather than negative for squabbling.)*

Many activities lend themselves naturally to encouraging turn taking. Begin with only two children taking turns, for example, pushing a car to each other, then build up to a small group situation and finally to the wider context of a large group.

Activities include:

❏ table games such as picture matching, lotto, Kim's game, games involving dice

❏ baking - each child takes a turn to stir the cake mixture or add ingredients

❏ feely bags or smelly jars - passing it around, taking turns to have a 'feel'

❏ taking a turn to give out the cups and biscuits

❏ taking turns to help feed the fish, water the plants, get the bikes out of the shed, hold the book or turn the pages in story time

❏ taking turns to pick his or her name card from a table and hang it on the name board

❏ taking turns to be the leader of the line

At the painting easel or sand and water tray, children need to learn that numbers are restricted perhaps to two, three or four at a time. Adults need to explain this and make sure children understand that if it's not their turn, they will eventually have a turn. Sometimes you can put out less resources than the number in the group, deliberately creating a situation where the children have to take turns, for example, three rolling pins between four at the dough table. The adult role would then be one of observing and intervening when necessary. Adults are so

important here in using the right language - 'It's not your turn yet, but it will be in a minute' or 'Whose turn is it to give out the biscuits today? Yes, it's your turn, Suley. Jennie had a turn yesterday.'

Singing time

Many popular nursery songs and rhymes lend themselves to taking turns. For example, number rhymes where children can take turns to be the five little speckled frogs. In circle games children take it in turns to choose each other. Games based on pass the parcel or hide the teddy also encourage turn taking.

Outdoor play

With the ride-on toys you could set up a system for turn-taking - there might be a station or bus stop and children could be allowed to ride up and down to and from certain points, then get out for the next child to have a turn. They soon learn to accept the rules and routine. It is important to observe the quieter children and make sure they have a turn on the popular toys, too. Again adult intervention and language will reinforce the message - 'One at a time'; 'Take it in turns, Katie first, then William, then Arminder'; 'Don't worry, you'll all have a turn!'

When the children are playing independently and you hear them saying to each other 'No, it's his turn now' then you know you've achieved your aim. However, remember, even teenagers will argue about whose turn it is to sit in the front of the car!

Caroline Jones

Children may talk as they play, but you also need to provide opportunities for them to think about the language they use. Describing similarities and differences between themselves and others is a good starting point, says Lisa Bessinger

Talking all about me

All of these activities are best done with small groups of children. They are designed to encourage each child to observe carefully, to listen to what is being said and, most importantly, to join in and extend their vocabulary. You can also use them to reinforce work on colours and naming parts of the body.

You will need to adapt the activities to suit the age group or level of development and the individual needs of all the children in your care. To stimulate discussion, always try to ask children open questions - ones that don't just call for a 'yes' or 'no' reply.

Observation skills

Ask parents to bring in a recent close-up photograph of their child - or take some yourself with a Polaroid camera. Mount them on card and fix to a display board. These make an excellent starting point for talking about how we look and the similarities and differences in our appearances and for promoting positive attitudes to children from different minority ethnic groups, and children with disabilities. If you don't have these in your group, use some of the excellent books and stories now available.

Talk about the size and shape of eyes, faces, colour and type of hair, and so on. Make a set of name labels and ask each child to place their label underneath their own photo. Later, you could turn some of the labels upside down - or even swap them round - to see if any of the children spot the deliberate mistake!

You could also extend this activity by bringing in some unbreakable mirrors so that the children can study themselves.

Guess who?

The children take it in turns to describe another child's hair, eye colour, skin colouring, clothes, and so on. The others in the group see if they can guess who is being described. This is an excellent activity for increasing vocabulary. Emphasise positive descriptions! Encourage observation skills by asking the children to find someone with the same colour eyes as themselves and then to find someone whose are different.

I spy . . .

Play 'I spy' with the children saying, 'I spy someone wearing a red dress . . . green shoes', and so on. The children must guess the name of the child you are describing. Encourage everyone to take turns. You can extend this further by saying things such as 'I spy some children with black hair *and* blue eyes'. These children should stand together so that the others can see how they are similar. This links in well with any mathematical activities on sets and sorting.

Same and different

Pick a group of about 12 children and sit them in a semi-circle. Choose four children from this group to stand in front of the others. Be sensitive about this - some children may be reluctant to stand up in front of their peers; you may need to stand with them for reassurance. Ask the seated children to study the ones who are standing in front of them. Talk about what each of them are wearing and point out similarities and differences in appearance. Introduce the language of comparison such as 'smaller than', 'taller than', her hair is 'longer than'. You could also talk about opposites - short/ long, straight/curly hair, same/different.

Try to involve each child in the discussion and encourage them all to use each others names. When you've finished talking, ask the children to close their eyes while you give a hat, scarf and gloves to one of the children in the group standing. It might be fun for them to swap items of clothing, such as jumpers or shoes, if they fit. Then ask the other children to open their eyes and tell you which child has changed and why. Encourage the use of full sentences.

The postman game

Ask one child to be the postman, delivering a letter. Hand out an envelope and say 'Knock, knock, here comes the postman with a letter for someone wearing . . . a red dress'. Each time specify a particular item on a child - colour of hair, eyes, clothes - and see if the children can guess to whom you are referring. All the children can join in and help the postman deliver the envelope to the right child, who then has a turn at being the postman. By gradually choosing smaller items which may be difficult to notice you can encourage the children to be more observant.

Lisa Bessinger

Once children have mastered dressing themselves, their self-esteem rises and they gain a sense of independence and confidence. This is particularly helpful when children go to school and find themselves in a class with 29 other children, all waiting for the one teacher to do up their coats or help them dress after PE

Getting dressed

Fastenings

Resources - clothes with a variety of fastenings for children to try (buttons, zips, Velcro, hooks and eyes). If possible, keep these as standard items in the dressing-up box.

Children need the opportunity to practise fastenings in a calm, non-hurried situation. Most of the time children are under pressure when getting dressed - in a rush to do up a coat to go outside or being told to hurry up and get ready. If children are not able to do their own fastenings it leaves the adult

> Give plenty of praise to children who can dress themselves independently! Award stars or have a chart on the wall which they can add their name to when, for example, they can do up the buttons on their coat or put their socks on without help.

frustrated and the child anxious and feeling a failure. Children need time to master difficult and unusual fine motor skills. After all, no other action is like that of a jacket zip.

Choice of clothes

Resources - mail order catalogue pictures and clothes for teddy

Give children the chance to express their own ideas by talking about their own clothes - what they like and what they don't like. They may not be used to giving their own opinion or having a free choice. They may need to be reassured that their opinion is valid and that there is no right or wrong answer. Cut out a variety of clothes from a mail order catalogue and let them make a collage of their favourite outfit. Alternatively a variety of clothes for teddy can be used as a starting point for a discussion about their favourite outfit for teddy.

Caring for clothes

Resources - a variety of clothes in the home corner to sort, washing line, pegs, toy washing machine/tumble drier.

Caring for clothes can be part of the teaching about care of objects within our environment. Talk about why we need to care for our clothes. So often children hear 'Be careful not to get paint on those trousers' or 'Don't play on the grass in those new shoes', without any explanation why. Can they think of some of the possible reasons? Talk about their sense of responsibility for things that belong to them. Discuss how people care for clothes. You could extend this by looking at the historical perspective and the importance of labour saving devices - washing machines and tumble driers.

Care for ourselves and others

Resources - clothes for a baby doll, full-length mirror.

Children should be encouraged to take pride in their own appearance. Using a full-length mirror, let them see for themselves that even if we have no choice over what we wear we look different, for example, depending on whether we tuck our shirt out or in, stand up straight or slouch.

Children need to develop sensitivity to the feelings of others. Most young children reach a stage when they become acutely embarrassed if they need changing during the nursery session. The whole group needs to develop understanding and encourage a sense of dignity.

Encourage sensitivity as well towards those in the wider community who can't get dressed by themselves, for example, babies, some of the elderly and some people with disabilities. If possible, invite a parent or carer in with a

> Dressing up is not just for girls, boys enjoy it too and they need to be encouraged to join in if they are not to miss out in this important aspect of social play. Make sure there are men's jackets and hats as well as dresses and encourage them to try non-traditional clothes - boys as nurses, girls as doctors.

baby to bath and dress with the children. The same exercise may be done using a doll, talking with the children about how capable they are and how much they have developed since they were a baby. Help them to realise that they have gone from being helpless to a stage where they can now be helpful to others.

Naomi Compton

One way we can help children to express their feelings is to give them something concrete to relate to. Sue Hedley shares a strategy she has found useful in her setting - the idea of a Golden Centre

Developing children's self-esteem

Children are often in our care for long periods of time - anything from two to ten hours a day. How we communicate with these children, our attitudes and our values can have a profound effect on them. Even our gestures and facial expressions can communicate messages about self-worth.

For the first three to four years, a child's self-esteem is formed exclusively by their family. After the child starts nursery or school, other influences come into play. Outside forces tend to reinforce the feelings of worth or worthlessness the child learned at home. The confident child can weather many failures, but the child with low self-esteem can experience many successes yet still feel a gnawing doubt about his or her own value. So, how do you begin to develop children's feelings of high self-esteem? First and foremost, children must be allowed to express their feelings. Secondly, those feelings must be acknowledged in a positive way.

Encouraging children's efforts and remembering what we do want rather than what we don't is much more likely to get a positive result. One recent observation at circle time went like this. Andrew was preoccupied and very excited about making a puppet in the following small group time. He kept jumping up and asking when it was small group time. Not wanting to dampen his enthusiasm I acknowledged how he was feeling by smiling at him and saying, 'I can see that you are really excited about making your puppet and that you want to get started, but we need to finish circle time first then it will be small group time and you can make your puppet.' Andrew moved close to me, went to seek my hand and smiled up at me and said, 'OK Mrs Hedley' and finished singing with me. The outcome was positive,

the feeling between us was positive. I acknowledged his feelings and he went to make his puppet focused and enthusiastic.

The Golden Centre
Encouraging children to express their feelings with each other as well as with adults is equally important to develop a child's self-worth. One strategy that we have found successful in our setting is the concept of the Golden Centre. The Golden Centre is something that each and every one of us has. It belongs in our hearts and shines when we are happy and feel good about ourselves. When we are feeling low and unhappy it doesn't shine. Using this concept gives young children something concrete to relate their feelings to, helping them to express exactly how they feel.

One little girl came in one day and told me: 'My Golden Centre's not shining today because my daddy has gone back to work on the ship for a long time'. Sharing these feelings in a group encourages sensitivity to the needs and feeling of others. First, you have to acknowledge the child's feelings then share that feeling with the other children, creating a supportive, caring climate. Ask the child and the rest of the children how you can help. One child in the same position suggested drawing a picture to send to the dad and put lots of kisses in!

Introducing the idea
We introduced this idea of the Golden Centre at circle time.
We needed:
• One large candle/matches
• Two large pieces of paper
• Felt tips, red/yellow
The children sat in a circle with the adults.
We put the paper and pens in the middle.

The adult began:

Teacher: 'For circle time today we are going to talk about something very special - our feelings, our feelings inside of us. Does anyone know what our feelings are?'

Steven: 'Sometimes you feel sad.'

Sean: 'Sometimes you feel angry when you don't want to show.'

Stephanie: 'You can feel happy.'

Teacher: 'What makes you feel happy Stephanie?'

Stephanie: 'When my mam cuddles me and when she makes banana sandwiches.'

Teacher: 'Sometimes our feelings make us feel happy, sad and angry. What other things make us happy?'

Danielle: 'When people are kind.'

Teacher: 'Yes Danielle, I feel happy when people are kind to me, too. How can we be kind?'

Ryan: 'Help somebody finish their jigsaw.'

Teacher: 'That would be very helpful.'

Sonia: 'Help them with their model.'

Jack: 'Yes - hold the masking tape.'

Teacher: Gives examples of how children help at tidy-up time.

Teacher: 'Today for circle time I am going to tell you a story about a little boy who had sad feelings.'

(Draws pin figure on a big piece of paper.)

Teacher: 'This little boy was called Luke. He went to nursery but was sad because . . .

Stephanie: 'He didn't have any friends.'

Teacher: 'Is that why he was sad?'

Children: 'Yes.'

Teacher: 'Luke had something very special inside him. Something that everybody has.'

Rachel: 'A heart!'

Teacher: 'Yes, a heart. Inside our heart is where our feelings live, in our Golden Centre.'

Teacher: (Draws heart shape inside the figure and colours it in yellow.) 'But Luke's Golden Centre wasn't shining because he was sad.'

Stephanie: 'Because he didn't have any friends.'

Teacher: 'What could we do? How could we make his Golden Centre shine?'

Ryan: 'Somebody could play with him.'

Teacher: 'I really think he would like that idea Ryan.'

Teacher starts to draw second figure.

'The next day Luke and Ryan came to nursery. Ryan's Golden Centre was shining.'

Draws Golden Centre inside heart shining (add lines/rays of light around heart shape), because Ryan had a good idea.

'Ryan sat next to Luke and asked him, "Would you like to work in the transport area with me?"'

'Do you know what happened next? Something very, very special.'

Teacher lights large candle to show how it is shining.

'Luke's Golden Centre began to shine! He had such happy feelings inside his heart.'

Teacher makes Luke's Golden Centre shine and joins the hands of the two drawings together. Children begin to clap!

David: 'Look how he's smiling. I'm smiling. I'm happy!'

Jordan: 'My Golden Centre's shining!'

Teacher: 'What sorts of things make your Golden Centre shine?'

Children were very focused.

Luke: 'When I come to nursery.'

Philip: 'When I play in nursery.'

Lauren: 'When I get sweets.'

Stephanie: 'When I play with my friends Sabina, Lauren and Elisabeth.'

Matthew: 'When I'm at home playing with my Batmobile.'

Jack: 'When I play with dinosaurs.'

The children have adapted this strategy and use it many times throughout their nursery day to express their thoughts and feelings: 'My Golden Centre's shining because I'm going to Kamaljit's party!' 'My Golden Centre is not shining because I was sick in my bed last night.'

This strategy has also filtered into the home environment. (I have done a workshop to explain the concept because parents were so interested in it.)

We followed up this circle time by asking the children to draw about what makes them happy, what makes their Golden Centre shine.

No matter how old we are or what part of the world we come from we all need to feel accepted, to be loved unconditionally, to have feelings of self-worth. If we nurture this from an early age and encourage children to express themselves, to communicate their needs, listen to another person's point of view, and celebrate rather than fear differences among people, as adults, these children will help to create a more peaceful and just society.

Sue Hedley

Our children need positive messages about:

• **Being**
Their right to be here, the fact that they are loveable and worthwhile just because they exist.

• **Doing**
Their ability to contribute, the fact that they are capable and can do well.

• **Thinking**
Their ability to work things out for themselves, to feel confident enough to express their view and feelings in the knowledge that they will be listened to and their opinions considered.

Children can look noticeable for many reasons. Birthmarks, cleft lips, burns and scars are just some conditions that can affect appearance. Jane Frances offers advice on coping with concerns, managing staring, comments and building a child's self-esteem

Supporting a child who has a **disfigurement**

'For the child who looks unusual, the problem is not their appearance but other people's reactions'

One in 500 children has a blemish, mark or scar which significantly affects their ability to lead an ordinary life. One in 100 has a noticeable facial or other feature. Sheer inexperience can make it hard to know what to say or where to look when we first meet someone whose face is damaged or in some way different.

Children can have a facial disfigurement or an unusual appearance for many reasons. They may have been born with a condition, for example cleft lip, Apert's, port wine stain, Moebius syndrome. They may have had a traumatic injury such as a burn or dog bite or they may have developed a condition, for example eczema or vitiligo. Some conditions are permanent and relatively stable, for example loss of an eye, facial paralysis. Others change over time.

Medical treatment includes major cranio-facial surgery, laser treatment and ongoing management. Plastic surgery can often make conditions less conspicuous but complete transformations are rare and for many disfiguring conditions no effective treatment is available.

For the child who looks unusual, the problem is not their appearance but other people's reactions. As they grow up, they will need to learn how to deal effectively with other people's curiosity, concern, and also staring and rude comments, so that they can get on with their life.

Just a few well thought-out actions on your part can help a great deal.

❑ getting a bit of background on how we are affected by disfigurement;
❑ checking out your own attitudes to appearance and disfigurement;
❑ developing a good professional relationship with the parents;
❑ obtaining appropriate information about how this child is affected by their disfiguring condition or injury;
❑ ensuring that all staff and helpers are fully briefed;
❑ encouraging good social skills and promoting self-esteem;
❑ looking for opportunities to share and enjoy difference and diversity.

Some background

Parents can usually give you at least some basic information about the injury or condition affecting their child's appearance - the cause, treatment which the child has had or is planned, ongoing management and, in some cases, other ways in which the child is affected. However, the child's condition may not yet or only recently have been diagnosed and the parents themselves may know little about it.

Surprisingly, the apparent severity of a person's disfigurement is no guide to how it will affect them. A child may be seriously affected by their unusual, changed or changing appearance, even though it does not look so bad to others (perhaps because people's reactions to a minor disfigurement are less consistent).

Checking out your own feelings and beliefs ...

Whenever we see someone new who is facially disfigured we experience a range of reactions. Find time to notice these. You may feel uncomfortable or touched with pity, or shocked, upset, even repulsed by a child's unusual appearance. Recognising and understanding your reactions and beliefs about appearance and disfigurement will help you to support the child better.

... about appearance

How important is appearance for you? What does a person's outward appearance say about them? How are you affected by different people's appearance?

Increase your awareness of the things you notice and like about people other than how they look - character, attitude, energy, sensitivity, imagination and humour.

... about disfigurement

Throughout history and across cultures, beauty often goes with goodness and happy endings, ugliness with badness. What do you think? What are your hopes and fears for this child?

Developing a supportive professional relationship with the parents

The parents of a child with a disfiguring injury or condition will have experienced comments and questions, stares and furtive glances, whenever they've gone out. Some parents find it so hard to cope with other people's reactions that they avoid taking their infant anywhere.

Although it may seem that it is their child's appearance which 'causes' these difficulties, it is other people's reactions to disfigurement which are the problem.

There may be issues of blame and guilt, as well as grief for the child's lost or dreamed-of good looks. Families often also experience disruption and isolation and relatives and friends may be affected, too. There may have been many hospital visits with high hopes turning into disappointment. The family's other children may have had to stay with relatives or neighbours.

Your ability to accept the family's situation as you find it, and to act with informed and sensitive understanding, will help them to feel good about their child meeting other children, playing and learning.

Preparing playworkers for action

Because other people often do not react in the best way when they first see or meet a child who looks unusual, it is important for staff to be calm and self-assured. Background information can help staff achieve this.

Ensure that the child rather than their disfiguring condition or injury is the focus of the information:

❑ Who is this child? What has happened to her?
❑ How does this affect her? (Speech? Breathing? Swallowing? Hearing? Sight? Sensitivity to heat or cold?) How does she manage?
❑ Is her condition stable or will it/could it alter? Gradually or suddenly?
❑ Does she have any special needs related to this disfigurement?
❑ Is she having/going to have any treatment? If this will mean time away from your setting, how can staff, parents and health professionals work together to ensure her continued sense of belonging in the group?
❑ How is she likely to be affected longer term?

Getting everyone on board - having something to say

The parents of the child who looks unusual will probably already have discovered that trying to get other people to ignore it doesn't seem to work. The fact is that people can't help being curious - it's a very human reaction to 'zoom in' on anything unusual about someone else's appearance.

Small children are not generally troubled by variations in appearance, especially if

whatever curiosity they express brings an appropriate informative response. But if adults are uncertain and anxious about what to do or say, children pick this up.

Because of this, it is better not to gloss over a child's disfigurement as if 'she or he is just like everyone else'. It is more effective to acknowledge and accept that some surprise, curiosity and concern will be unavoidable, and to have prepared a response. A little information and reassurance is usually all that's needed, followed by changing the subject in an appropriate way. 'That's just Jo's birthmark. Don't let it worry you. Come and look at the dragon he's been painting.' This helps people to see beyond the disfigurement and attend to the child properly, as a person.

Ensure that all staff and helpers are prepared for curiosity and know what kind of response they should be aiming to give. 'Kylie's got eczema. It's a bit sore but you can't catch it. Who was it you wanted to see?' The tone needs to be calm and self-assured, and the natural change of subject afterwards is important. 'Paul's had an operation but he's fine now. Are you Jamie's Mum? - Jamie's certainly been on form this morning!'

When another child is staring or asks a question, it can help to divert their attention back to themselves. 'That's Amin's birthmark. Most people have a birthmark. Mine's on my elbow. Have you got a birthmark somewhere?' Managing curiosity in this way takes preparation and practice but it is effective. If you can model this effective response to curiosity, you will be helping prepare the child to try it for themselves one day when they are ready.

Don't be tempted to set a good example by, in a sense, pretending not to notice or pretending that there is nothing to notice.

Building good social skills and self-esteem

Making and keeping friends is a particularly important social skill for a child whose appearance is disfigured. It may be harder for a child who looks unusual to pick up good social skills because of the curious and

awkward reactions their appearance draws from the adults and older children they meet.

If adults can model key basic social skills, they help a child to start learning ways to minimise and overcome the social challenges they may face as they get older.

❑ Greeting people by name with eye contact and a smile;
❑ Using people's names more;
❑ Starting a conversation or changing the subject by asking a question: 'Have you got any pets?' 'How's your new sister who was born last month?'
❑ Asking to join in a game or have a go at something which others are already doing;
❑ Dolls or toy animals can be used to play at talking, making a new friend, or joining in a new game;
❑ Sharing and enjoying difference and diversity.

With a small group of children, draw their attention to themselves and the other people around. Name an ordinary feature of your own appearance (for example straight or curly hair). Or start with a child who you know to be confident of their appearance and happy to be in the limelight. 'Ella has such brown eyes.' Encourage the children to notice the ways in which they are not like each other:
red/fair/brown/black/straight/curly hair, eye colour, freckles, relative tallness/ smallness, scars on knees ...

If you have a child with a noticeable feature or disfigurement, include this in the sequence of differences but not first or last. Similarly, if there are identical twins in your class, include the feature (perhaps just one freckle!) which physically distinguishes them from each other.

Jane Frances

For further information and practical advice when a child looks unusual or noticeable, please contact: Changing Faces, 1 and 2 Junction Mews, London W2 1PN.
Tel: 020 7706 4232
email: info@changingfaces.com
website: www.changingfaces.co.uk

Do you spend enough time telling the children in your care how much you appreciate them? Sara Stocks suggests that each child has a day on which everyone concentrates, just for a short time, on the skills and gifts that they bring to the group

Special days

Self-esteem comes from a huge range of experiences, both good and bad and predominantly family based. Healthy self-esteem starts with the way a new-born baby is handled and responded to and carries on through toddler tantrums, early educational experiences and throughout the growing- up years. No nursery or pre-school activity is ever going to change a life single-handedly, of course, but you can begin by raising awareness of the importance of self-esteem for your group and their families.

There is something quintessentially British about playing down any skill for fear of 'spoiling' the child. Modern psychology challenges this belief. It feels good to be praised and this 'feel-good factor' encourages more good behaviour. The knock-on effect is recognisable, even to the sceptical. Simple really - tell a child that they are good at something and they will want to do it more, to hear the praise again!

Nurture self-confidence

Children under eight are still forming their characters and personalities and these early years experiences are crucial. A child who believes that they are 'no good' will soon stop trying and the prophesy is soon sadly self-fulfilling.

Do we spend enough time telling the children in our care how much we appreciate them? Especially those who are in extended care situations? In a family a child is likely to be hugged and kissed and praised for little successes through that astonishing gift we are handed along with the new-born - parental love! Even seemingly unlovable little monsters are the apples of their parents' eyes, and that is how it should be. As carers of very young

children it is often too easy to forget to nurture the child's budding self-confidence, especially if this is in reality an intellectual exercise and not one which comes with hormonal help!

The best way to nurture children is to do it all the time, in all of your dealings with them and in all of your conversations. Your activities should be planned with all of their needs in mind, including the requirement that their environment should foster self-confidence and self-esteem. This is the only way to support young children successfully away from parents.

Being seen to be doing what you say you are doing is always another matter! It cannot hurt to make a point of praising the children in your care - providing that making the point does not replace the constant consideration of the effect of your activities and environment on the fragile self-confidence of each child.

Planned praise

One easy way to implement this idea is the 'special day'. Each child has a day on which the group concentrates, just for a short time, on the skills and gifts that child brings to the group. During a circle time, the leader could inform the group that 'Today is Jake's special day'. The leader starts the ball rolling by saying why she enjoys Jake's company. The children should be encouraged to join in and describe their positive feelings for Jake. Some special work, a picture or a model that Jake has made can go on the 'special day tray' along with the 'special day certificate' (see page 146) that confirms how kind, funny, considerate or imaginative Jake is and maybe a note from Jake's family giving their support.

Be prepared

This process should not take longer than a few minutes and is not intended to make poor Jake curl up with embarrassment, so handle it sensitively and make quite sure that you are prepared with valid comments. Children will see through false compliments and they become worse than useless. If you really can't find a good point then you have a problem that you should have identified before now! Delay that child's special day for a while and spend some time urgently observing and assessing what is going wrong.

Be careful what you praise. Praise enthusiasm, exuberance, exploration, humour, questioning and challenging as well as the easier good, quiet and nice behaviour! Don't fall into the trap of praising girls for quiet, good behaviour and boys for assertive exploratory behaviour - it is surprisingly easy to do. Don't be afraid to praise children for being clever, there is nothing wrong with it, just keep a balance and praise a child who is not clever for his skills too, with the same enthusiasm.

Sara Stocks

Use something like this certificate and letter to involve parents and make sure that you send all special day paperwork home - parents need praise too!

Celebrating **special days**

The certificate has been left blank for you to copy and fill in. The wording might say something like:

'This special day certificate has been awarded to Jane Smith on the 1st July 2000. Jane's friends and teachers like her so much because she is kind to other children. She can make them laugh with her funny stories and she can ask interesting questions.

Well done Jane!

Example letter for parents

Dear Parents,

Once during each term we have a special day for each child. On this day we celebrate that child's strengths and let them know how important they are to us all!

The special day tray will have the child's name, some work that they have chosen to go on the tray and a certificate that records what was said at 'special day time' about that child during our group conversation. Your child will bring the certificate home.

Your child's special day is on _____

Please could you complete the sentence below to add to the value of this important day for your child. We will read it out at group time.

(child's name) is loved by us because

_____

Special Day Certificate

....

....

....

....

....

....

Children like to explore new ways to play and learn and puppets are a remarkable tool which can encourage them to experience all areas of learning, especially personal and social development, says Elizabeth Coller

Puppets and emotional development

Puppets are fun and easy to make. Once you have given your puppet a definite look, character and most importantly a name, they come to life. They are a great aid when telling stories and make good visual props. A child is captivated when puppets are performing and can be encouraged to communicate with the puppet and even instruct it what to do. Their imagination will be stimulated and you will be encouraging their language development.

Storytellers

In the past, puppets were used to retell stories about everyday events that happened around the country. Travellers would earn their keep by relating what was happening in neighbouring towns and villages. Not only was this a good way of hearing the news but it was entertaining and was a means of escaping into the wonderful world of imagination.

Puppets come in all shapes and sizes and in various forms - finger, hand, glove, string, shadow and rod. Most can be made out of junk materials - card, fabric, socks, gloves, tubes, tissue, pipe cleaners and plastic containers and boxes, the list is endless. It is

a good idea to start a bitbox for small items such as buttons, eyes, ribbons, lace, wool, felt bits, and so on, and a scrapbox for larger pieces of card, boxes, tubes and fabric. Here are some simple ideas.

Finger puppets

Hand/finger puppets were the most popular form of puppetry in this country. The simplest of finger puppets is Thumbelina, made by placing a small oblong of material over the thumb, fastening it with an elastic band or piece of ribbon/thread and then drawing a face onto the fabric. You can retell the Hans Christian Andersen story and create some more visual aids.

Faces are not difficult to draw, the simpler the better. (Some basic looks are given here.) Children can express their emotions by using puppets with different features. They can use skills of communication, planning, memory recall, language and concentration when they create their own puppet and stories.

Another form of finger puppet is a walking one, where your finger

becomes the legs or nose of the puppet. These can be made out of card or felt and can be a great aid when singing nursery rhymes. Make a spider to use for 'Incy Wincy' or 'Little Miss Muffet'.

Pinocchio

Use your finger to make a nose grow or make up a story about a bad mannered person whose nose grew when he got angry!

Hand puppets

Hand puppets can be made as simple or as elaborate as you want. The two main methods are sewing or gluing, the latter is easier for small children. When making a hand puppet template do make sure that your hand fits it!

Children can be encouraged to sew using plastic bodkins and brightly coloured wool. They will be using skills of planning, cutting, threading, joining, manipulation, design, handling tools and various materials.

The value of puppets

Children will work independently to make a puppet, choosing the materials, solving any problems that arise and asking for help when they need it. They will also develop their concentration skills

When performing with a puppet children work as part of a group, taking turns and sharing. They gain in confidence and are able to express their feelings by using the puppets. A shy or sensitive child can be comforted by an adult manipulating a friendly puppet. Puppets can be used to encourage a withdrawn child to communicate. Role play with puppets can highlight ways to behave, how to use good manners and children will experience joy and achievement when given the opportunity to use their creation.

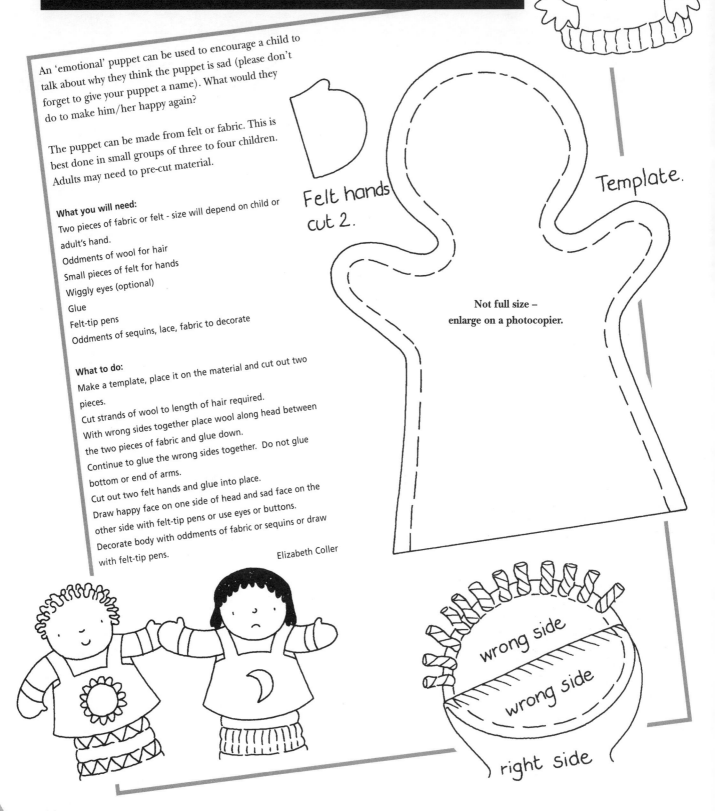

Socks can be turned into wonderful puppets. Create a mole by using a dark or grey sock, add buttons for eyes and nose, some pink felt pieces shaped like feet and a pink tongue.

Take a shoe box and make a hole in one corner big enough for your hand and arm and then paint the box an earthy colour. Place some small twigs, leaves, acorns and stones in and push your mole puppet through the big hole. Cut some smaller holes for your fingers and use them as worms.

For a more realistic mole, use black fur or velvet, make into a tube and then attach decorations.

An 'emotional' puppet can be used to encourage a child to talk about why they think the puppet is sad (please don't forget to give your puppet a name). What would they do to make him/her happy again?

The puppet can be made from felt or fabric. This is best done in small groups of three to four children. Adults may need to pre-cut material.

What you will need:
Two pieces of fabric or felt - size will depend on child or adult's hand.
Oddments of wool for hair
Small pieces of felt for hands
Wiggly eyes (optional)
Glue
Felt-tip pens
Oddments of sequins, lace, fabric to decorate

What to do:
Make a template, place it on the material and cut out two pieces.
Cut strands of wool to length of hair required.
With wrong sides together place wool along head between the two pieces of fabric and glue down.
Continue to glue the wrong sides together. Do not glue bottom or end of arms.
Cut out two felt hands and glue into place.
Draw happy face on one side of head and sad face on the other side with felt-tip pens or use eyes or buttons.
Decorate body with oddments of fabric or sequins or draw with felt-tip pens.

Elizabeth Coller

Felt hands cut 2.

Template.

Not full size – enlarge on a photocopier.

wrong side

wrong side

right side

Emotions affect all of us in each part of our lives, whether we're at work or play. Children deserve to be given the opportunity to discuss their emotions and time to reflect on appropriate ways of expressing their feelings, says Naomi Compton

Expressing feelings and emotions

Young children experience a wide range of emotions and they need to learn to express them appropriately. Many children will learn this almost instinctively, but others will need reassurance and encouragement to express themselves appropriately or they may simply explode with joy, sorrow or anger in a confusing or disturbing manner.

One of the most effective ways of doing this is by introducing a topic such as 'Happy and sad' which gives children the opportunity to talk about their own feelings and gives staff an insight. We may be able to discover what makes children happy or sad and why.

Wonder

As adults we rarely use the word 'wonder' and sometimes forget that first thrill of a new experience because we are seeing with eyes that have seen before and are rationalising with experienced or understanding minds. The sense of exhilaration and wonder that children feel needs to be fostered and valued so that their experiences become meaningful. We must ensure that we give proper attention to times of wonder and reflection.

Sorrow

Children's sorrow often arises from situations that they cannot understand and may find confusing. Young children don't have an understanding of the life-cycle and are quite likely to show sorrow when flowers that have grown from seeds die when the season ends. Perhaps one of the things that saddens children most is experiencing relationships that they find confusing such as bullying, the new baby who now has all the attention, the death of a pet or the distress of a close adult. Children need an opportunity to discuss these feelings in a safe and secure environment with adults whom they trust.

Joy

This is another word that adults do not use often. Joy is a deeper emotion than happiness. It implies a singing from the soul. For young children we hope that joy is an emotion they experience often:
- the joy of realisation, when they understand something for the first time
- the joy of independence, perhaps when riding a two-wheeler bike for the first time without stabilisers
- the joy of close relationships
- the joy of bathing a baby brother or sister and seeing them smile 'just at me!'

Children need to have these feelings of joy valued and confirmed or they learn not to share or even not to value them.

Suggested activities

Play a variety of taped music. Ask:
- How does it make them feel?
- Why? (talk about fast/slow, instrumental/vocal)
- Extend into appropriate gestures, movements or dance to express the feelings evoked by the music

Look at different paintings, drawings or other expressive artefacts.
- How does it make them feel?
- Does it make their friends feel the same way?
- Why? (talk about colours, subject matter and so on.)
- Can they paint their own picture to evoke the same feelings?

Grow plants from seed.
- Give opportunities for the expression of wonder as the first shoots appear, joy when they flower and sorrow when they die.

Use a candle as a focus for reflection. Ask the children:
- To think about what makes them happy.
- What could they do to make someone else happy?

Discuss happy times such as different cultural and religious celebrations - birthdays, weddings, births, Easter, Eid.
- Plan your own celebration, think of a reason to celebrate.
- Organise invitation cards, fancy hats or costumes, food, candles, music, and so on.

Use music as a focus for reflection. Ask the children:
- To think about what makes them sad.
- What makes other people sad?
- What makes them feel better?

Visit places in the community:
- Places of worship
- Homes for senior citizens
- Baby clinics

Talk about welcoming and rejecting people.
- Discuss feelings caused by having a new baby in the family. How can we help to welcome the baby? (set up a 'baby clinic' or bath a doll with care.)
- Discuss the feelings of new children joining the group. How can we welcome them and show them the activities we enjoy and ask them if they would like to join in?

Naomi Compton

Most young children co-operate because they want to please you. Developing this further, so that the child realises that his or her own actions or intentions affect others, is quite complex and needs our help. Vicky Hislop shares some ideas

Teaching **right** from **wrong**

Children come to your setting from different cultures, traditions and religions and bring with them differing moral values. What is right for one may be wrong for another and it is important that we recognise this when developing moral codes.

The children will already have learned a great deal at home, particularly about role expectations, so it is important to recognise this and provide opportunities for these values to be explored. It may be acceptable at home for the first child not to share their toys or to eat lunch with their fingers, but in a group situation like pre-school, these actions will have an impact on the group.

We have developed a set of moral codes linked specifically to conduct and attitudes within the nursery. Parents smile when they first hear their children say 'We don't do it that way, we do it this way in nursery', but this way we tackle difficulties such as sharing and good manners without undermining the values present at home.

Role play

Role play can be a great way to explore the impact of our own actions. You might like to try playing a board game using two adult helpers as actors. One adult can be domineering, not allowing the other to take his or her turn, challenging where the counters are placed, telling the other what

number they have thrown, moving their pieces for them, and so on, and eventually pushing the board away.

❑ Use your helpers as actors, set the scene and ask them to 'act it out'.

❑ Ask the children to watch and think about what is happening.

❑ Don't make the scene too long or complicated.

❑ Discuss the outcome.
Was that the way to behave?
(Wait for a response.)
No? Why not? What did they do wrong?
(Again, wait for responses.)
What would you do?
Encourage the children to give you explanations.

❑ Replay the scene with the children.

❑ Make it fun. Even though these issues are serious, for children to learn and take on board the messages, they must enjoy what they are doing.

You can continue this throughout the session when situations arise. Rather than 'telling the children off' or just saying 'well done', try asking them to think and talk about what was good or bad and why.

The theory

Morality is what you perceive as being right or wrong within your own environment, an agreement of a group of people as to the acceptability of a type of behaviour. Many theorists see morality as a set of developmental stages, which need to be learned. One such theorist is Lawrence Kohlberg. His theory is based on the idea that the stages build on each other in order of importance and significance to the person. He also found that 'moral growth' begins early on in children and that by the time they begin pre-school education, most of them will have reached the stage of wanting to co-operate as it reaps a reward which they find pleasurable. Developing this further for the child to realise that his or her own actions or intentions affect others is quite complex and needs our help.

Story time

During story time introduce books such as *Look What I've Got* by Anthony Browne. (Jeremy has difficulty sharing and shows off about all the new things he has. Each time he loses the chance to have a friend to play with by being self-centred and rude.)

Aesop's Fables, published by Ladybird Books, has tales told in simple language with an outcome to discuss at the end. These can be used to illustrate everyday occurrences that the children will understand. I am asked daily to tell the tale of 'The dog and his reflection' which highlights the effects of greed.

These activities enable the children to 'feel' what it is like to be someone else, to explore emotions and to understand rules and fairness. By making children aware of their actions, we can build on those experiences and encourage development to the next stage of understanding, awareness and empathy for others.

Vicky Hislop

Not every setting will experience the tragic loss of a child or member of staff but many children will have to deal with the death of a grandparent, an elderly relative or even a much loved family pet. Do you feel prepared to help them cope?

Coping with **loss** and **bereavement**

When a child starts pre-school she experiences and responds to a form of loss as she transfers from the support of her parent or carer and forms a relationship with the new adults in her world. You will all be aware of the different reactions displayed as a child adjusts to their new environment - some are confident and excited, others appear withdrawn and unsure of themselves and need support and reassurance.

Almost all early years workers - whether childminder, playgroup leader, teacher or nursery nurse - have developed their own repertoire of appropriate responses. Many will have excellent strategies to support the individual needs of the child. Many nurseries have carefully planned programmes of pre-school visits, induction programmes and close contact with the family to support a child through a phase that may be their initial experience of loss and separation. This phase is often handled with confidence and a sense of direction by the adults involved.

You might want to take this a step further and think about appropriate strategies when working with children and families who are coping with other forms of loss, particularly the irreversible forms of loss through the death of a family member, pet, school friend or someone close. The pain and distress of loss cannot be avoided. However, there is a great deal that a well prepared and caring staff can do to help support the child and family through their grief.

It is helpful to recognise some of the stages of grief that many of us pass through when experiencing a bereavement.

Stages of grief

A bereavement can trigger a wide range of emotions which result in various forms of behaviour in adults and children. The following stages and emotions may be experienced from time to time and may last for many months.

Anticipatory stage

The bereavement may have been anticipated and follows a period of anxiety, preparation and turmoil within the family. A sick member of the family, whether in hospital or nursed at home, often creates stress within normal family life and changes in routines for the young child. When the death finally comes there is often a resurgence of grief.

A sudden death, as in an accident or suicide, creates an element of shock as an additional emotion. This can present as a form of physical pain. The person may become withdrawn or show apathy when coping with initial practical tasks.

Loss

There is a feeling of emptiness. There is a space which was once filled by that person. Their departure will have created a gap in the existence and routine of others. This loss can be experienced through a bereavement, a separation, divorce, child leaving home, a trusted colleague moving in the wider field. A loss may be experienced through redundancy, retirement, loss of status, youth, illness, financial hardship, confidence, respect and many more. Each person reacts to their own loss uniquely.

Numbness

Often, during the very early days of a bereavement, you see a bereaved person coping with life and routine as if nothing had happened. This is a primitive response as a basic protective mechanism.

Anger

A bereaved person may look for someone to blame for the pain of their loss. Their anger may be directed towards other family members, members of the medical profession following a death through illness, or as a child, aggression and physical retaliation towards other children after the loss of a family member, favourite toy or even a close member of staff.

Guilt

The stage of anger is often a defence mechanism against the possibility that the person themselves may be partly responsible. During the stage of guilt, they may reproach themselves and say things like, 'If only . . .'

Searching

The bereaved person often continues to live their life as if the missing person was present. They set their place at the table or imagine they can see them in a crowd of people.

State of denial

Having experienced a loss, one often tries to deny that the object that is lost will not be found again. This is common in divorce, or separation from a parent. There is a disbelief that the loss may be permanent and sometimes a resistance to let go and move on.

Acceptance

As the other stages are gone through and dealt with, a stage of acceptance is reached.

Letting go

Following acceptance that person can start to 'let go' of the loss and become less pre-occupied with the emotion surrounding their grief. They move towards adapting to their new situation and moving forward to the final stage of regrowth. Many people who have been through a particularly difficult bereavement say that their new life is very different and totally replaces their old way of life.

Your relationship with parents/carers

The parents/carers of the child may often be the first member of the family to inform the nursery of any situation that may cause a child distress. The adult may see the secure environment of the pre-school setting as a place where they wish to communicate their own feelings on the bereavement. The opportunity to talk to a member of staff in a quiet area of the nursery over a cup of coffee can give the message that we empathise with their loss. It acknowledges that there may be implications for the child that can be supported within the nursery. In our nursery we are fortunate in having the flexibility to adjust and extend children's placements on a temporary basis to cope with their needs. Extending a placement to full-time, perhaps around the time of the funeral, can often help a family, particularly where there is difficulty with additional child care.

Parents often appreciate the opportunity to talk and to have someone listen who they know is not going to advise or make judgements. Sharing with someone a little removed from their own situation can be helpful particularly when passing through the sometimes unnerving stages following a death. The parents' room can often offer a source of support from other parents and members of the community. A display of leaflets and helpline numbers for parents who feel that they may benefit from additional support can also be available in the parents' room.

Working together to **support** the child

Recognising reactions to bereavement

Each child is unique with their own set of life experiences. A child's understanding of death will depend very much on:

1 Past experiences of loss
❏ Separations
❏ Losing a favourite toy
❏ Hide and seek
❏ Separation from parents/carers by joining a nursery or attending childminders.

2 Past experiences of death
❏ Dead flowers
❏ Dead birds
❏ Dead animals
❏ Death portrayed through books, videos and television
❏ Death of a pet
❏ Death of a known person
❏ Funerals, graves and coffins

When developing ideas about death it is useful to consider:

1 The age and understanding of the child
2 The past experiences of loss, bereavement and death
3 The level of comprehension and language development

The idea of death is often disturbing and complex to adults. Often the time when children require the support of close family members is the time when parents are involved in their own grief and do not have the time or energy to respond to their children's emerging needs.

In order to support the development of a child's understanding it is helpful to respond to the loss as it arises, taking into account the age of the child.

Babies

Babies can be affected by their parents well-being and may respond by displaying sleeping and eating difficulties and in more severe cases failure to thrive. They may be generally unsettled for a time.

Toddlers

A very young child often finds difficulty in understanding the permanence of death and often believes that the lost person will return.

Nursery/infant stage (age three to seven)

It is often not until around the age of seven that a child fully grasps the idea that death means that the person is not living and cannot be reversed. It is common for a child to experience confusion between death and the absent person who will eventually return. They may believe that their thoughts or actions were responsible for the death and the preoccupation of the adult with the loss can also support this belief. The child may become interested and curious but also sensitive towards the reactions of others around. They often ask repeated questions and engage in a searching stage as they attempt to seek the person and make sense of the explanations. The child may have periods of sadness and become listless and withdrawn. Children of this age may experience many of the emotions that are common to adults, such as anger, guilt and a lack of acceptance. Questions indicate their confusion and lack of understanding.

The child might re-enact the death or express ongoing emotions through imaginative play situations. This can be helpful in coming to terms with their emotions and making sense of the experiences. Some children become fearful that they may die themselves or they will lose others around them. They often wish to remain close to a familiar adult or parent.

Junior stage (seven to 12)

Children of this age respond to accurate accounts presented sensitively. They gradually accept that death is permanent and irreversible and come to the realisation that they themselves will die one day.

Adolescence

This is the stage where the young adult comprehends the death as other adults and accepts the finality.

Sometimes the young person may feel uninvolved and unacknowledged in a loss situation that can be as equally distressing as to an adult. One of our parents shared her experiences of the loss of her husband five years ago telling us that Nathan, the second of her five children, had taken the situation particularly badly. She felt he was displaying aggressive behaviour and becoming involved in solvent abuse. During a quiet period over the summer holidays when our nursery was open, Nathan came in and discussed his feelings. He had been protected from the details of the tragic accident believing that his father may have been murdered. He was not involved in the funeral and had little understanding of the events that were taking place at the time. Through talking about his feelings he gained the courage to approach a bereavement agency and has also developed

an awareness of his own feelings and reactions and those of his family. He now feels more settled at home.

A young child's reaction to death

Adults usually react by mourning after the loss of close friends or relatives. The reaction of the young child to death and separation may be many and varied.

❏ The child may regress and revert to behaviour more appropriate to a younger child, often seeking reassurance from others.

❏ Separation from familiar adults can prove to be stressful and the child may become anxious and unwilling to be far away from home or attend school or nursery.

❏ The child may experience sleep related problems, finding difficulty in sleeping, with fear of the bedroom, possibly related dreams and nightmares and a fear of the dark.

❏ There may be a tendency to suffer from minor illnesses and the child may adopt a more pale complexion, withdrawn appearance and may be prone to feeling cold.

❏ The child may become more selective about their food or may find difficulty in coping with full meals.

Caring for a child who is experiencing a bereavement

If possible, keep the child in touch with familiar people, places and routines.
The child may seek comfort or want to ask questions regarding the bereavement.
A sensitive adult can be available to 'tune in' to the child's feelings and offer support as required.

Honest, age appropriate explanations can help a child to begin to make sense of the situation and avoid confusion later on. Young children may confuse death with sleeping, hence the importance of refraining from confusing language, for example 'a long sleep'.

The child may have the opportunity to experience part of the ritual according to the wishes of the family. Some quite young children join in seeing the dead person, attending the funeral and visiting the grave. Children may wish to hold their own ceremony and become involved in the burial of a deceased pet.

Videos, albums and photographs can be a source of comfort and also provide an opportunity to recall some of the positive past events. Favourite foods and comfort foods can be reassuring. The young child may regress to a bottle, dummy or require a favourite toy or blanket for a time. A soft furry hot-water bottle, familiar stories and a night light may provide comfort at bedtime. It may be necessary to adjust routines to meet children's differing needs and emotions during the initial period of bereavement.

By helping a child to work through their grief we are enabling them to cope successfully with one of life's many experiences.

Books to read

Adults

Bereavement - Colin Murray Parkes (Pelican)

Helping Children Cope with Grief - Rosemary Wells (Sheldon Press, 1985)

When a Child in your School is Bereaved - The Society of Compassionate Friends, 6 Denmark Street, Bristol BS1 5DQ

Good Grief - Barbara Wood (19 Bowtree Road, Uxbridge, Middlesex UB8 1PT)

The Pre-School Child - Open University publication

On the Death of a Child - Celia Hindmarch (Radcliffe Medical press)

Children

Where has Daddy Gone? - Osman and Carey (Heineman, 1990)

Emma Says Goodbye - E Nystrom (Lion, 1990)

Come Back Grandma - Sue Limb (Redfax 1995)

When People Die - Sarah Levette (Watts, 1997)

Scrumpy - E Dale, F Joos (Anderson Press, 1996)

Badger's Parting Gifts - Varley (Picture Lions, 1992)

What's Happening - Death - K Bryant Mole (Wayland, 1992)

Sudden/tragic bereavements

The death of a child

A few years ago we all experienced the sudden death through tragic circumstances of the sibling of a child attending our nursery. The whole of our supportive tight-knit community surrounding the nursery was affected including many of our staff who had known and worked with the deceased child.

A few simple guidelines can help to ensure that the children experience as little disruption as possible and that family members and staff are supported.

1 Whilst keeping the nursery routine in place, try to ensure that children from the bereaved family are protected from other parents and visitors who may wish to point out or offer untimely comfort. We found that small group work in a quiet area of the nursery enabled staff to control remarks and explanations offered by other children.

2 Liaise promptly with family members and professionals involved to support the explanations offered to the child.

3 Encourage staff to listen and empathise by sharing feelings with the members of the community.

4 Recognise that staff require time to de-brief and allow time to support one another.

Our staff invited a community liaison officer from the local police force to a staff meeting. We were prepared for anticipated reactions from the local community and offered support and guidance. As a staff we valued the time to acknowledge our own feelings and reactions.

The death of parents

From time to time we have worked with children in the nursery who have been bereaved of one or both of their parents.

Where a death has been anticipated there have been opportunities to plan ahead and form a network of support with other professionals to help the family.

As a headteacher I applied to become a registered driver with Social Services. This simple yet practical step enabled me to offer transport to a family of four children when their mother died in hospital and they needed the comfort of each other.

Following the sudden and unexpected deaths of both parents of children in the nursery we were able to work closely with family members to offer immediate and practical information on the children. This ranged from the sleep patterns of a 17-month-old child to appropriate explanations to a four-year-old. In the months that followed the family saw the nursery as a source of support and guidance, often feeling comfortable to share their feelings or approach staff before moving on to other agencies. This can be a time when others are feeling vulnerable and in need of appropriate care and guidance.

Support was offered by the nursery to make special cards and accompany a grandmother and the children on the first visit to their parents' graves.

The suggestions I've given (see below) can be used as a resource for staff or in some cases may be useful as a handout when working with adults.

Jill Sansom

Suggestions for surviving a bereavement

- ❑ Know you can survive. You may not think so, but you can.
- ❑ Struggle with 'why' it happened until you no longer need to know why or until you are satisfied with partial answers.
- ❑ Know you may feel overwhelmed by the intensity of your feelings but all your feelings are normal.
- ❑ Anger, guilt, confusion, forgetfulness are all common responses. You are not crazy; you are in mourning.
- ❑ Be aware you may feel appropriate anger at the person, at the world, at God, at yourself. It's OK to express it.
- ❑ Having suicidal thoughts is common. It does not mean that you will act on these thoughts.
- ❑ Remember to take one moment or one day at a time.
- ❑ Find a good listener with whom to share. Call someone if you need to talk.
- ❑ Don't be afraid to cry. Tears are healing.
- ❑ Give yourself time to heal.
- ❑ Expect setbacks. If emotions return like a tidal wave, you may only be experiencing a remnant of grief, an unfinished piece.
- ❑ Try to put off major decisions.
- ❑ Give yourself permission to get professional help.
- ❑ Be aware of the pain of your family and friends.
- ❑ Be patient with yourself and with others who may not understand.
- ❑ Set your own limits and learn to say no.
- ❑ Steer clear of people who want to tell you 'what' or 'how' to feel.
- ❑ Know that there are support groups that can be helpful such as Samaritans, Compassionate Friends.
- ❑ Call on your personal faith to help you through.
- ❑ It is common to experience physical reactions to your grief, such as headaches, loss of appetite, inability to sleep.
- ❑ The willingness to laugh with others and at yourself is healing.
- ❑ Wear out your questions, anger, guilt, or other feelings until you can let them go. Letting go doesn't mean forgetting.
- ❑ Remember that children need to grieve in their own way and at their own pace.
- ❑ Unless absolutely necessary this is not the time to move house, or make major changes. Don't add to your stress.
- ❑ Know that you will never be the same again, but you can survive and even go just beyond surviving.

With many marriages ending in separation or divorce the pre-school setting inevitably has a role to play in a young child's life as they face the upheaval

Coping with **divorce** and **family breakdown**

Divorce and separation are inevitably about loss and change. About one in three marriages now ends in divorce and as most divorces occur in the first ten years of marriage, many involve children under five.

Separation can mean changes in a child's life on a number of levels.

On a practical level:
- moving house;
- changing nursery or school;
- changes in routine;
- different standards of living and less money;
- losing touch with family and friends and a familiar community;
- getting used to a parent who used to be at home being out at work more;
- changes in responsibilities - having to help in the home.

On an emotional level:
- experiencing a range of strong and difficult feelings such as sadness, anger and guilt;
- missing a departed parent;
- wanting to blame someone;
- establishing a new relationship with someone who no longer lives with them;
- coping with parental emotions and changed behaviour;
- anxiety about the departed parent;
- fear of being left by the remaining parent;
- divided loyalties.

Early years practitioners need to be aware how all of these changes can affect a child's demeanour and behaviour at pre-school. In the midst of all these experiences, a child's nursery or pre-school situation may well be the only area of stability they have for a while, and the teacher is often the one constant presence in some children's lives.

Legal duties and responsibilities

Supervisors and nursery heads or managers, in particular, should be aware of the legal requirements and responsibilities which are laid down in the Children and Family Law Act 1996.

When a couple begin divorce proceedings, they have to make decisions about the welfare of the children and submit a detailed Statement of Arrangements for Children.

The Court will want to know:
- where they are to live and who with;
- whether the other parent will see them and how often;
- about their day-to-day care;
- about their health;
- where they will go to school;
- what financial support they will receive;
- any special arrangements to help or protect them that have been made.

The Act also requires that parties are encouraged to consider the wishes and feelings of each child and that children should be given the opportunity to express them. It is also considered desirable that age-appropriate information booklets and/or videos should be made available to children involved in family breakdown.

The final decree absolute of divorce cannot be obtained until the Court considers that the arrangements made for the children are satisfactory. When couples have disputes over children which they cannot sort out, the Court will issue orders. The most common types are orders for financial support and Section 8 orders, which are:

- **Residence Orders** which say who the children should live with;
- **Contact Orders** which tell the person the children live with who to allow them to

see or receive letters or telephone calls from;
- **Prohibited Steps Orders** which prevent a child's parents, or any other named person, from taking certain steps such as taking a child abroad without first getting the Court's permission;
- **Specific Issues Orders** which set out precisely how a particular matter about the children should be handled, such as their schooling.

The Court can also make orders such as Care Orders or Emergency Protection Orders where the children are being abused or at risk of harm.

It could be that a supervisor or manager is required to be a named person in reference to some of the above orders. The court service issues helpful leaflets about these legal responsibilities and the National Children's Bureau also has leaflets (*Childfacts*) about the implementation of the Children and Family Law Act.

How conflict affects children

Studies have shown that how adults deal with the conflict before they separate has an impact on their children and may be a source of some behavioural problems at this time of stress. They can become angry, upset or sad when their parents are unhappy or arguing.

If children see their parents being aggressive, shouting, hitting or throwing things or being withdrawn or depressed, they may copy that behaviour.

Children may suffer from lack of time and attention from parents who are preoccupied with their own problems and parents may also be slack or inconsistent over discipline or domestic routines. Parents may be unable to offer reassurance or comfort to children who are distressed and they may miss out on cuddles and hugs and may even seem neglected.

When parents stop talking to each other or shout all the time, a child may divert attention onto himself by developing a problem such as bedwetting, not eating, overeating, stealing or not going to school.

Some children have adapted to their parents' behaviour to the point of denying that there is a serious problem, so much so that they are taken by surprise when one parent leaves.

Every child reacts to parental separation in his or her own way. Even within the same family each child's experience will be different because of differences in their ages, sex, personality, experience and relationship with each parent. For almost every child, however, this will be an acutely unhappy time.

During the first 12-18 months of parental separation/divorce, children's predominant reactions are governed by their age.

How children manage distress

Children often experience distress in bursts. One minute they can be upset and the next they can be playing as though nothing has happened.

- ❑ Don't assume that because they are playing the pain has gone away.
- ❑ Accept that children can be very different in different places. They may be fine at school and awful at home or vice versa. All these different selves are valid.
- ❑ Allow them to tell or show you that they may still be upset, confused or angry. They do not have to be brave for their parents.

Children's needs

Children can be helped to cope by reassuring them, unconditionally loving them and maintaining their security as far as possible.

Age related reactions

Pre-three years

Infants and very young children will become frightened and insecure and very clingy to the remaining parent or carer. They are less able to cope with long separations and disruption of routines such as feeding or bed-time. They may want to be fed, revert to wanting a bottle, wet themselves or suck their thumbs and become generally anxious and distressed at playgroup or nursery. It is difficult for them to understand what is happening or to express their feelings.

Pre-school (three to five years)

This is a vulnerable age because the capacity to verbalise is limited. The child has a different sense of time and theirs is concrete, omnipotent and magical. If thinking something can make it happen, and if they are the centre of the world, then what happens is also their fault.
Common behavioural responses at this age:
- ❑ regression to earlier stages of development
- ❑ clinging possessiveness to people and objects
- ❑ sleeplessness
- ❑ help-seeking or aggressive attention-seeking
Main emotional reactions:
- ❑ blaming self - it is their fault or responsibility
- ❑ intense fear of abandonment by both parents
- ❑ fear of being sent away/replaced

Five to eight years

The child is preoccupied with feelings of loss, rejection, guilt and loyalty conflicts. There is intense grief and concern over the parent who has left home and intense longings that he/she will come back. It is particularly difficult for boys of five to eight as they are often frightened to be left in their mother's care at a time when they are identifying more closely with their fathers and developing their own masculine identity.
Five- to seven-year-olds may regress into thinking/feeling like pre-school children, using fantasy and magical thinking to distance themselves.
Eight-year-olds are often particularly vulnerable. They cannot regress like younger children but do not have adolescent coping mechanisms either. They may appear sensible, coping and composed but this may mask confusion and depression.
Other different behaviours in children may also be signs of stress such as:

- ❑ being withdrawn at home or school
- ❑ staying in their own room more *or* needing to be with siblings more or fight with them.
- ❑ trying to reconcile, reassure or comfort
- ❑ trying to be extra good at home or school
- ❑ trying to take the place of the missing parent

Smaller children notice much more than we like to believe. It is a mistake to assume that because a child is very young they will not notice what is happening and feel pain as a result.

They especially need:
- ❑ someone to talk to them;
- ❑ reassurance that it is not their fault and that both parents still love them;
- ❑ to be able to voice their fear/anxieties/anger/sorrow;
- ❑ not to be ignored;
- ❑ comfort and attention;
- ❑ somewhere stable where nothing is changing, for example nursery, school, grandparents', or friend's house;
- ❑ gentle and simple honesty.

It is important for parents to:
- ❑ keep the conflict as far away from the children as they can;
- ❑ try not to encourage children to take sides;
- ❑ encourage extended family and friends to concentrate on the children rather than

the parental dispute;
- ❑ get some support for themselves from other adults or from the community;
- ❑ resist the temptation to derive their main support from the children. They cannot deal with this emotional burden;
- ❑ fight the urge to detail the other parent's failures and wrongdoings;
- ❑ allow the children to talk about the parent who has gone and to make visits as easy as possible;
- ❑ try to respond to children's questions as honestly as possible with only as much detail as is appropriate;
- ❑ accept that children will be angry and difficult at times as they try to manage a painful situation;
- ❑ vent their own distress in private.

How you can help

School can be a secure and stable place for children during a family breakdown, but the role it plays in supporting children is ill-defined. Not all parents want people outside the family to be involved in what they regard as a private matter and there may be a fine line between helpfulness and intrusion. But parents' needs for privacy may have to be balanced with their children's need for support and reassurance at a time of acute stress. It is important for you to maintain confidentiality but also to be clear which members of staff need to be aware of changes in a child's life.

If your school or centre has an initial welcoming procedure or booklet, it should be straightforward to mention that you be kept informed of any changes at home that might upset a child, such as the birth of a new baby, death of a grandparent or divorce or separation. Teachers may well find anyway that parents turn to them for advice in such situations about what the children should be told. Within the limits of their role and relationship with parents, they can try to ensure that someone helps the child at home in some of the ways previously mentioned - especially to give explanations, opportunities to talk and express feelings and to provide continuity and consistency.

On a whole-school level it is important to raise staff awareness of this issue and how it affects the school, because you are required to keep a current record of all people with parental responsibility for your children, including parents who no longer live together. Procedures could be clarified as to what information needs to be known and recorded in the event of parental separation. (A simple form of record is given on page 160 as an example.)

Teachers should have certain skills, in other words good listening and counselling skills and legal knowledge relating to parental separation so that they feel confident in acting as a source of information to parents and to be an advocate for the child. School can respond flexibly in a child-centred way allowing children to express their needs to a

Books

Books and lesson materials often refer to the stereotyped family which does not correspond to the experience of a large number of children. The inclusion of books with one-parent families and opportunities to discuss different family structures are important.

For adults

Helping Children Cope with Divorce Rosemary Wells (Sheldon)

Helping Children Cope with Separation and Loss Claudia Jewett (Batsford)

Chain Reaction: Children and Divorce Ofra Ayalon and Adina Flasher (Jessica Kingsley)

Divorce and the School - Kathleen M Cox and Martin Desforges (Methuen)

The Relate Guide to Divorce Rodwell (Vermilion)

Divorce: the Child's Point of View Yvette Walczak and Sheila Burns (Harper and Rowe)

Children of Divorce - Helping Your Child to Cope Dr Brynna Kroll (BBC Education)

For children

Where Has Daddy Gone? Trudy Osman and Joanna Carey (Mammoth)

Are We Nearly There? Baum (Bodley Head)

We Have Two Houses (a book of photographs to talk about) Amor and Newnham

Children Don't Divorce - Rosemary Stones (Dinosaur)

Dinosaurs Divorce Laurie Krasny Brown and Marc Brown (Collins)

I have Two Homes, My New Family Althea Braithwaite (Dinosaur)

Divorce - Let's talk about series Angela Grunsell (Aladdin)

Goodbye, Daddy Brigitte Weininger (North South Books)

When a Parent Marries Again - Coping with Family Change Marge Heegard (Woodland)

I Feel Sad Brian Moses (Wayland)

The Soul Bird (about feelings) Michal Snunit (Robinson)

familiar teacher as and when they want to. It also needs to be responsive to creating flexible times to see both parents and send separate copies of letters and other information. School is the one place where parents can co-operate for the benefit of the child, make involvement easier and give a good message to children.

There are a number of ways in which teachers can help. They can:

❑ provide continuity and consistency of approach in school;

❑ provide pleasant creative activities as diversionary tactics in the form of art, drama, story-telling and story-making and use of water, sand and clay;

❑ help children to identify, share and accept a wide range of feelings including sadness, anger or guilt;

❑ reinforce a child's self-concept and self-esteem in encouraging the belief that they 'can do';

❑ teach assertiveness and self-control;

❑ reduce 'magical thinking' by talking and explaining in real terms and rehearsing situations a child may experience;

❑ raise awareness of what change is and the acceptance of unavoidable changes;

❑ reinforce social support through support friendships with peers;

❑ give support and encouragement and help them understand the parental situation;

❑ give the child extra attention, reassurance and comfort;

❑ provide satisfying new activities;

❑ create a life-story through either a life-book, self-collage, family photo album or a simple time-line;

❑ have a good range of books on various aspects of the situation - loss, feelings, fiction and non-fiction - and be prepared to lend them to parents and have lists available.

June Smith, bereavement counsellor and trainer

Further help

If, over a period of time, a child's behaviour gives cause for concern, you need to be aware of how to seek help or to suggest helping agencies to parents. Children who are in difficulties seem to respond primarily in two ways:

❑ They do not express feelings of sadness/anger in situations where most children of their age would or become very withdrawn.

❑ They express much more sadness or anger more frequently or display extreme regressional or aggressive behaviour.

The educational psychological service can be an initial contact to seek advice or help or seeing the family GP with a view to refer a child for family therapy. Organisations that can help locally are Citizens Advice Bureau; child and family guidance clinic; family mediation or conciliation services; Relate; Gingerbread (for single parents), court welfare officers, social services. To get in touch with these organisations, contact the local CAB or look for numbers in a telephone directory.

Helpful national organisations offering newsletters, books, leaflets and helplines include:

National Family Mediation, 9 Tavistock Place, London WC1H 9SN Tel: 020 7383 5993

Gingerbread (Association of One-Parent Families), 1st Floor, 7 Sovereign Close, Sovereign Court, London E1W 3HW. Tel: 0207 488 9300

Families need Fathers (support network for fathers) 134 Curtain Road, London EC2 3AR Tel: 020 7613 5060

The National Children's Bureau, 8 Wakely Street, London EC1V 7QE Tel: 0207 843 6000

Parentline Plus Helpline 0808 800 2222 Gives support to parents and stepfamilies on divorce and related issues.

National Family and Parenting Institute Tel: 0207 424 3460 Gives advice on parent-child relationships.

African-Caribbean Family Mediation Service Tel: 0207 737 2366 Provides family mediation to black couples who are separating.

Information regarding children of divorce

CHILD'S NAME: Date of birth:

PARENT OR GUARDIAN LOOKING AFTER THE CHILD:

Name:

Address:

Child's address if different:

THE OTHER PARENT:

Name:

Address:

IS CUSTODY SHARED?

DATE OF SEPARATION:

DATE OF DIVORCE:

WHEN WAS SCHOOL INFORMED OF THE SEPARATION?

By whom?

What instructions have been given the school regarding its contact with (or inclusion or exclusion of) both parents?

(a) Mother

(b) Father

Which household circumstances have changed significantly? eg move, finances, step-parent, step-siblings, parent working, etc.

Are separate letters, reports, etc required by both parents ?

Preparing young children for school is extremely important for all concerned. The challenge for pre-schools *and* schools is to plan well for a smooth transfer. We look at some of the issues you need to consider whether you're a reception class teacher, a nursery head or a pre-school supervisor

Getting ready for 'big' school

'Are you going to school soon?' is a question young children are often asked. To a four-year-old, with little or no experience of what school is, the effect can be disturbing and quite different to what was intended by the kindly adult asking a casual question.

The challenge for pre-schools and schools is to plan well for a smooth transfer. There are three groups to consider before any practical planning can be addressed:

❏ the setting (school and pre-school)

❏ the parents

❏ the children

Schools can be intimidating. The scale of everything is likely to be larger than anything the children will have experienced, and therefore daunting. The classrooms may be big and the playground, too - playtime can be difficult if all the children are out at one time. The layout will be new (where are the toilets?), and the structure of the day will be different. There will be a lower ratio of adults to children than in pre-schools and nurseries, so the children will also have fewer adults to ask when they are unsure.

It is also a difficult time for parents. Many will still remember the anxieties they felt when starting school and will be especially anxious to prepare their children to cope with their new environment. Schools are often in the news, and discussion of standards and curriculum abound which also raise questions and add to the pressure on parents as to whether they are doing the best for their children.

For the children it is probably a question of uncertainty and fear of the unknown. For some the change from pre-school to school may be exciting, for others it may be traumatic. Some children may be able to express their concerns, but many won't and they will express their anxieties through differences in behaviour. Children with no older brothers or sisters may have limited understanding of what school is, or they may have picked up comments from older children. Last year a child in our group was told by an older sister that school was 'horrible', and children are often told they will have to work hard. They may see a rather imposing building through railings, or watch crowds of large children running in a playground and feel extremely unsure. Some will become withdrawn and fearful, perhaps with disturbed sleep. Others will become boisterous and loud and be more difficult at home or in their groups.

The pre-school and school

The key to a smooth transition from pre-school to school depends on the relationship between the two settings. Some pre-schools have strong links with first schools, some may use the same premises and share equipment.

Others, like ours, are in a city centre and feed children into different schools. There is much talk of partnership, but this needs to be a reality.

Obviously it will be harder to achieve in some situations than in others. Below are some thoughts and suggestions which might help, although it is good to remember that these relationships may well take a long time to develop:

- If pre-schools and schools share a site they could have a formal agreement on issues of importance to them both. This could cover, among other things, intake policies, sharing resources, working together to plan the curriculum and keeping continuity in children's records.

- For those settings not sharing a site, it will obviously be harder. Perhaps staff from each setting could visit each other.

- There could be joint 'partnership' meetings to discuss particular issues, especially those involved in the transfer to school and sharing what the children have done, and will be expected to do.

- Anything which shows that the school values the work of the pre-school is very encouraging. This could involve schools asking parents to see the records pre-school staff have kept, and school staff visiting children in their groups before starting school.

- Try holding a fund-raising event together.

Working and planning together, and opportunities for the school staff to make frequent visits is obviously an ideal, although there are constraints which make this difficult to achieve. Pre-school staff, especially those who are working in the voluntary sector, can sometimes feel intimidated by schools. School staff have pressures on their time, and may be unable to find supply cover for visits to pre-schools. Schools and pre-schools may feel a sense of competition for keeping four-year-olds because of external pressures to maintain numbers.

However, even an initial, brief meeting can help to alleviate some of these difficulties and provide a beginning to increasing trust and co-operation between groups. It may take courage to make the initial phone call, but the rewards for the children will be great.

The parents

Parents need to know about local schools,

intake policies, and then have specific information about what will help their child to settle in to a particular school. They also need opportunities to discuss any questions or anxieties they may have. Try any of the following:

- Put up a large notice on which parents can write down anonymous questions to gain an understanding of the sort of information they would like to have. Common questions concern when a child can start school, what are the pros and cons for going later, and whether children need to attend for a whole day when they first start.

- Remember that parents of children with special needs, or children from families where English is not the first language, may have specific anxieties or questions. Be prepared to seek advice and ask the school for specific information.

- Ask a local teacher to come to a meeting to talk about preparing children for school.

- Invite parents in to the pre-school when teachers visit the children.

- Provide as much information as possible about the transfer to school, either through a newsletter or on an information board. Hopefully the local schools will be arranging opportunities for children to visit with their parents.

The children

Children come to pre-schools to learn through play. Preparation for school is of great importance, but it should be part of the overall planning of the group, not an 'add-on'. All activities relating to the Early Learning Goals will be of value to children's learning when they start school, although the two areas of Personal, Social and Emotional Development and Communication, Language and Literacy have aspects which are especially relevant to this transfer time between pre-school and school.

Personal and social development

Independence and confidence are of prime importance. When children enter a Reception class they may have just two adults to thirty children and will need to feel confident enough to manage by themselves. Areas where this is especially important are being able to use the toilet and wash their hands without help, and being able to dress themselves for PE or to go outside. Independence is also extremely important in the classroom. Choosing appropriate materials for an activity, fetching the pens and collecting an apron all require confidence.

Adults in pre-schools need to be aware that we should allow children time to do things themselves. It is often tempting to help with buttons or turning on taps through kindness and the pressure of time.

- There are play dolls which have different fasteners, or the group could keep a box of fasteners as an activity.

- Changing the home corner to a shoe shop and providing dressing-up clothes with different types of fasteners is helpful. Provide dressing-up clothes which are possible for even very young children to put on unaided. Simple tabards are a good start.

- Try allowing the children to be as independent as possible at snack time by having a choice of food, and helping children to pour their own drinks, and encourage them to look after one another.

- Try putting craft materials on a separate table to the one where the activity is taking place to encourage children to get up and choose what they want.

- Encourage the children to value their own work, and that of others too, by displaying it to the other children and by talking about what they have achieved.

- At the end of the session encourage children to put their work in the correct place to dry, and to help tidy materials and activities away.

Language and literacy

Children start school at many different stages of ability. It will do great harm if we pressure children to try to go beyond what they are ready for. However, everything we do at pre-schools to encourage children to be able to express themselves will be of value, as will a love of stories and books, and the confidence to make marks with pens and crayons.

The ability to listen and the ability to recognise their own name are particularly relevant to children when starting school.

❑ Play games which involve listening, such as sound lotto.

❑ Encourage listening in music sessions - perhaps play a tape of a new song, or ask a parent to bring in a musical instrument.

❑ Help the children to listen to one another, perhaps showing the group something they have brought from home.

❑ Talk together about the activities the children have done during session.

❑ Take every chance possible to display the children's names, perhaps with a picture on their peg, or with their photograph on a board.

❑ Try playing a game which involves doing something when they see their name on a card. It is easy to nod at the little ones who don't yet recognise their names.

❑ Ask children if they would rather write their own name on their work, even if it is illegible!

Obviously it is possible in all the areas of learning to think of activities and play which will help the children find the transition to school easier. Some groups, including our own, have a special session for older children. This is great as it is possible to do more adventurous activities, to allow the children more independence than might be feasible in a mixed group with two-and-a-half-year-olds, and activities which involve discussion and listening to one another are easier. A danger is that it is easy to attempt to do what the schools will be doing in Reception classes and to forget that learning

through play should remain the most important aspect of pre-school groups. Again, working with local schools and sharing information about each other's curriculum and expectations of the children should help here.

Finally, when the time comes for the transfer, the most important way of relieving anxiety is for the children to see where they are going and who they are going to be with. This needs to be a two-way process with the school staff getting to know the children in

the safety of their pre-school setting, and the school inviting the children and their parents into the school.

For schools on the same site this may have been long-term, continual working together. Other schools, where the distances are greater, can use many methods such as home visits, teddy bears' picnics at the school, encouraging children to come into school for an afternoon before starting, and invitations to fun events, such as fairs and barbecues.

Obviously the more times the children can visit the school, the more confident they will become. Yet again this is not always easy. City schools take children from many different playgroups and nurseries, supply teachers may have to be brought in to release teachers from their own classes. There is nothing, however, as reassuring for children, or their parents, than going to the school and seeing for themselves what it is going to be like.

Jessica Glauert

Building a Portfolio Book 2 • • •

Chapter 6

Unit C7: Provide a framework for the management of behaviour

About this unit

Unit C7 deals with aspects of the management of children's behaviour. The unit emphasises the importance of positive reinforcement of acceptable behaviour, and of setting boundaries for children, as well as acceptable strategies for managing unwanted behaviour. You need to understand the different stages of children's development so that you can set appropriate boundaries and expectations. It's no use trying to make a child of two share toys, because at that stage of development he does not understand the concept of sharing. Likewise, you would accept a temper tantrum in a two-year-old as quite normal, but not in a seven-year-old.

It's imperative

that your setting has a policy for managing behaviour which all staff adhere to, so that you all work within the same boundaries and provide consistency of care for the children. If you're not aware of your setting's policy, find out about it.

As with C5, this unit is best left until later in your programme, so that you can gather evidence over a period. You may have covered aspects of this unit in C10 and C11, while carrying out activities with children. C5 and C7 are closely linked because behaviour is very much part of social and emotional development. You have already looked at ways of helping children to relate to each other, deal with their feelings, be self-reliant and confident and have a good self-esteem. If you have helped children to achieve all these things, you will be less likely to have difficult behaviour to deal with, and will probably already have strategies in place to deal with it when it does happen.

Values

As with all the other units, the values statements emphasise the welfare of the child, learning and development and the importance of being a reflective practitioner across all elements, and safety is emphasised across most elements. In addition, there is a particular emphasis on the importance of working in partnership with parents, so that you can achieve continuity between what is acceptable at home and in the care setting as far as possible. If you're developing a strategy for managing unwanted behaviour in a particular child, it's important that you involve the parents in the discussion about how best to work with the child. The values also emphasise the need to liaise with outside agencies such as a child psychologist, paediatrician or specialist therapist should the need arise. You may need to ask for help from one of these agencies if the behaviour persists.

We would recommend that you attend specialist training on managing behaviour, because it's crucial that you know how to deal effectively with children who are having difficulties. Some methods of dealing with unwanted behaviour do more harm than good, and physical punishment such as smacking or rough handling must never be used under any circumstances. It may be necessary to physically restrain a child for his own safety in some circumstances, but you need to be very clear about what is acceptable and what is unacceptable.

never

use physical punishment on a child in your care.

Getting started

In this unit you are going to show how you can:

◆ Negotiate and set boundaries for behaviour

◆ Promote positive aspects of behaviour

◆ Respond to unwanted behaviour

Have a look through the whole unit, and use the personal skills check-list to identify areas you are confident about and areas where you feel you need more training or experience. Find out what training is available, either through your assessment centre or from your local Early Years Development and Childcare Partnership.

If you feel ready to start being assessed, plan the whole unit with your assessor. Don't forget to check which bits you have already covered in other units. Your setting will probably have policies and procedures for managing behaviour. Make sure you know what they are, and think about whether they are appropriate and effective. Find out whether the parents had any involvement in preparing the behaviour policy. If you have the opportunity, discuss the effectiveness of the policy and procedures with colleagues and parents, and make suggestions for improvement if you're in a position to do so.

Element C7.1 Negotiate and set goals and boundaries for behaviour

Key issues

It's essential that your setting has a policy on behaviour which all staff adhere to, so that the children know what is expected of them, and there is consistency in the way staff promote acceptable behaviour and deal with any behaviour problems. When agreeing rules for the setting, try to put them in positive rather than negative terms as far as possible - for instance, instead of saying 'no running indoors' say 'always walk indoors' or instead of 'no hitting other children' say ' be kind to each other' and so on. If the children are old enough to understand, get them to help make the rules. Also explain the reason for the rules in a way that they understand. If you do this, they are more likely to act responsibly and regulate their own behaviour.

It's also important that parents are aware of the boundaries set for their children and that they have been consulted as far as possible. Parents should be informed about your setting's policy for behaviour management and other important policies including equal opportunities before their child starts in the setting. Most settings will have this information in a brochure, and many will have a meeting to discuss important issues. Check that the boundaries you have set fit in with parental expectations and cultural differences as far as possible. There may be occasions when you are not able to do this - for instance, if a parent tells their child not to play with black children, or where a parent has told a child to hit back if someone hits him. This would be totally unacceptable within the setting, and you would need to explain this to the parent.

Which evidence?

Read through the PCs, range and notes for this element, to check what you need to cover.

Your assessor will need to **observe** you carrying out all but two of the PCs and at least one aspect of the range, preferably over a period of time so that she can see that you are consistent in your goal and boundary setting. You will notice that there is only one range category in this unit. It's likely that your assessor will be able to observe more than one aspect, because they are quite closely linked. Plan with your assessor what she will need to observe, and what she has already observed in other units, and agree on what other evidence you will need.

You will find it useful to carry out some **child observation** to

check whether your policies and procedures are being effective and that goals and boundaries are realistic. It's also a good way of trying to find out why a child is displaying unwanted behaviour. Observe the child over a period of time, and see if there is a pattern of behaviour. Take into account other factors, such as information you have received from parents or colleagues.

> **Remember,**
> if you need help with how to carry out child observations, you will find some guidelines in C16 in Chapter 4 in Book 1.

Include the **policy and procedures of the setting**, with a note to say how you use it, whether the parents were involved in preparing it and what involvement you had. You may wish to write a reflective account about how you have implemented it with groups or individuals, how you have explained the goals and boundaries to the children, and evaluate its effectiveness.

The related **knowledge evidence** statements for this element are 1, 3, 4, 14, 15, 16, 17. Try to cover as much as you can in your other evidence. Fill the gaps if necessary by a short assignment, but always try to include examples from your own work practice. You will find the articles later in the chapter useful.

Element C7.2 Promote positive aspects of behaviour

Key issues

Children are more likely to behave positively if they have access to a range of interesting activities at the right level for their stage of development. If you have a group of children doing an activity which requires them to be watching or waiting for more time than they are actively doing things, the activity is not appropriate, or the group is too big. If you are doing most of the work for them, the activity is at the wrong level. You will lose the children's interest and they will start behaving badly.

Be enthusiastic, encourage the children constantly and use praise appropriately. Remember that the effort the child makes is the important thing, not the finished product. Look out for times when children are being kind and helpful to each other, and make a point of commenting on it. When the parents come in to collect the children, always try to say something positive about what each child has done that day. This is so much better than always picking on the negative things children are doing.

Be specific about why the behaviour is positive - for instance, say 'Thank-you for giving Sandeep a piece of your playdough, that was very kind', rather than 'good boy!' so that the children learn what the behaviour is that you are pleased with. Equally, if you are dealing with unacceptable behaviour, say why the behaviour was unacceptable: 'It wasn't kind to snatch the bike from Daniel because he had it first. He will let you have a turn soon.' Never say things like 'You are naughty, I don't like you when you do that.'

Make it clear
that it's the behaviour you don't like, not the child.

Try not to over-praise because then it becomes meaningless. For instance, if an older child tells you she has finished a piece of writing and you think she could have achieved more, rather than saying 'That's really lovely, well done!' you could say 'That's good but perhaps you could add...' so that you are encouraging them but not accepting something less than you know they are capable of. You must know the child well enough to be able to make a judgement because what is not enough for one child might be a brilliant piece of work for another.

Which evidence?
You will notice when you read through the PCs, range and notes on this element that it very much builds on the first element. That was about setting the goals and boundaries, and this is about how you apply those goals and boundaries consistently. Your assessor will need to *observe* all but one of the PCs and one aspect of the range, which again has only the one category covering social, physical, verbal and emotional behaviour. She has probably already observed you promoting positive behaviour while you have been carrying out other activities with the children, so this may not need a separate observation.

If your setting uses incentives for good behaviour such as star charts or badges, include a copy or a photograph in your portfolio, explaining how it works. If you have a 'good behaviour' assembly or special time when you celebrate good things that children have done, write about it or describe it to your assessor. Write a *reflective account* of times you have encouraged positive behaviour or a *child observation* to show how children are responding to the goals and boundaries set. You can use the same reflective accounts and child observations for Element 1 and 2, as long as you cover the relevant points, or you may find that you already have suitable evidence from C5 or other units.

The related *knowledge evidence* statements for this element are 5, 11, 18, 19. Try to cover them in your other evidence. The articles 'Thinking of others' and 'Special days' in Chapter 5, as well as the articles at the end of this chapter, will help you.

Element C7.3 Respond to unwanted behaviour

Key issues
It's really important that you have a good understanding of appropriate strategies for handling unwanted behaviour, and we would strongly recommend that you attend training, if you haven't already done so.

The important thing to remember is to remain calm, and try to avoid a confrontation. Often, small incidents of unwanted behaviour can be ignored, or defused simply by distracting the child into another activity, or by sitting them next to you to help you, or by involving them in the story you are telling. You will be able to think of other little strategies you have. If the behaviour is causing hurt, either physical or emotional, to another child, or serious disruption to the group, or damage to the setting or to the child himself, you will need to remove the child from the group and explain why the behaviour is unacceptable. If your setting already has a set of boundaries which have been explained to the children, this will help. Remember what we said in Element 2, to be clear that it is the behaviour which is unacceptable, not the child.

If you find that a child is persistently behaving in an unacceptable way, you need to look at the reasons behind it. Observe the child over a period, and talk to the parents about your concerns if that is within your job role. If not, ask your supervisor to have a word. It may be that something has happened in the family which has upset the child, or there may be certain foods or drinks which cause hyperactivity. There may be more serious problems in the family.

You will need to agree a strategy within the team and with the parents, to help the child overcome the difficulties. Make sure that you are not 'picking on' the child all the time for his or her unacceptable behaviour. It's sometimes better to ignore negative behaviour and, instead, look out for times when he or she is behaving positively, and give lots of praise. A star chart may help. *Never* use physical punishment. *Don't* use a 'naughty chair', and *never* shut a child alone in another room.

You may need to call in specialists such as a child psychologist if the behaviour does not improve. Your setting should have information about how to contact the appropriate people. If not, your local authority social services or education department, or health visitor, will be able to advise you.

Richard Woolfson, a child psychologist, described the ABC of behaviour, and an action plan for changing behaviour (NNEB Training Day 1994) in a helpful way:

Antecedents of behaviour:
◆ family factors (eg family values and attitudes, family stress)

◆ nursery factors (eg nursery ethos and rules, previous response to this behaviour)

◆ child factors (eg child's personality, general health, social skills)

◆ situational factors (eg children had been arguing, only one jigsaw of this type)

Behaviour itself - your description should be:
◆ factual not emotional (eg 'He hits David when they play together' not 'It drives me bonkers when he starts to fight with David')

◆ precise about frequency, not vague (eg 'He has done this three times this week' not 'It happens a lot')

◆ specific not general (eg 'He spat on Jenny during break' not 'He was horrible to some children'

◆ situational not general (eg 'It happened during story time' not 'He did it yesterday'

Consequences include the effects of the child's behaviour on:
◆ the child himself (eg satisfaction, attention, guilt)

◆ the other children (eg fear, pleasure, sadness)

◆ nursery staff (eg frustration, anger)

◆ the child's parents (eg upsets them)

His action plan for changing the behaviour is:
◆ Accurately and precisely describe the behaviour you want to change.

◆ Consider the antecedents that may be significant in causing the behaviour.

◆ Look closely at the situation in which the behaviour occurs, to identify relevant features.

◆ List all the consequences that may be positive from the child's perspective.

◆ Set clear targets for change, and aim to achieve these targets in small stages.

◆ Specify who will be responsible for implementing and monitoring the change (including parents - *our words*).

◆ Tell the child about the targets, and explain to him why you are aiming for change.

◆ Pick a time to start the strategy for change, and a time to evaluate its impact.

◆ Implement the change consistently during this period.

◆ After the implementation phase, review its success, and modify as required.

Which evidence?

Your assessor is only required to **observe** two of the PCs in this element, but if she has the opportunity, it would be ideal to observe more. She may have already observed incidents, so ask her, and check the cross-referencing sheet for C7. Your supervisor or colleagues may be able to write a **witness testimony** if they have observed you dealing with incidents.

If your setting has **policies and procedures** for dealing with unacceptable behaviour, include them as evidence, explaining how you have used them. Include any case studies or child **observations** you have carried out, as long as you have asked permission, and removed any means of identifying the child. Check your **diary** for examples of how you dealt with unacceptable behaviour, or write a **reflective account.** If you don't have any serious behaviour problems in your setting, you may need to describe how you would deal with particular scenarios such as self-damaging or disruptive behaviour, verbal abuse and so on, in a short **assignment.** Check the knowledge statements for this element and make sure you cover those.

The **knowledge evidence** statements related to this element are 2, 6, 7, 8, 9, 10, 11, 12, 13, 20. There are some important issues here that you must show that you understand. The articles in the following pages will help, but you may need to do further reading. Richard Woolfson, the child psychologist quoted earlier, has written a number of books on child psychology, including one called *Understanding Children - A Guide for Parents and Carers*, which you will find helpful reading.

> **Remember**
> that you should be keeping a record of where you can cross reference evidence, on your cross-referencing sheet for each unit.

One of the most important roles of the early years setting is to make sure that children learn to behave in an acceptable way in a group setting. It is important to establish a policy so that all the adults in your setting work towards common standards and goals. Caroline Jones explains how this can be done

Managing children's behaviour

One thing is certain, no child is an angel. He or she has to learn, often through trial and error, what is good, desirable and acceptable. However, 'good' behaviour cannot be 'taught' in isolation from the rest of the pre-school activities but pervades everything going on in the group. It is important not to see behaviour as a separate issue, but within the wider context of the group, as an integral part of the learning taking place and the overall organisation of the sessions.

Children's behaviour is also influenced by wider social, emotional and cultural factors. How children behave will depend on how the group is organised, the planning of the daily routine, the quality of the activities available, the choices on offer and the quality of the interaction between the adults and children and between the children themselves. Children's behaviour is closely related to relationships. Other factors such as partnership with parents and carers will also have an impact on the children's behaviour in the group.

As the way children behave is such an important factor in their learning, each pre-school setting should have a written behaviour policy, which is often referred to as a discipline policy. However, managing children's behaviour is not simply about 'discipline', or 'getting them ready for school'. Discipline in the pre-school situation is about having order within the group. It is not about orders to be mindlessly followed, but about helping the children understand right from wrong and helping them learn to behave in appropriate, socially acceptable ways for the rest of their lives.

What is a policy?

A policy is a working document which clearly explains the group's philosophy, procedures and approaches to managing the children's behaviour on a daily basis. The main reason for having a written policy is to share this information with all those involved in the group to promote consistency. If adults are clear, consistent and fair the children will benefit.

It is important that those involved in carrying it through in practice have 'ownership' of the policy. In other words, the policy should be something to which staff, parents and even children should have an input, not something written by or imposed from above, or some sort of standard list produced by an organisation or copied from another setting.

A staff meeting is a useful time to brainstorm ideas. A draft could be sent to parents for comments. Each policy will be individual to each group and the content should be developed and discussed by all staff, in response to the group's needs and circumstances. The length of the policy will vary from group to group. The main point is that it should be clear, practical and easy to understand. The whole idea is for unwanted behaviour to happen as little as possible.

'Now think hard, children. Was leaving Mrs Conway buried overnight in our sand area right or wrong?'

Who is a policy for?

The policy is for the benefit of anyone involved in the running of the group. This includes the staff, parents, volunteers, students, any management committee and, ultimately, the children in the group. A policy provides clear guidance for the adults in the group on procedures for encouraging wanted behaviour and dealing with unwanted behaviour. Whilst children are often accused of being very good at 'playing adults off' one against the other, they are actually testing out the consistency of boundaries that are being set and can feel confused by inconsistent responses. To give a simple example, if only two children are allowed at the sand tray and one day someone allows three children to play, they become confused, especially if another adult then appears and tells them off! It is important for children to have a minimum number of clear rules which are consistently applied. These could be attached to or included in the policy. Some simple rules can be displayed in pictorial form using matchstick people. Typically, these might include points of routine organisation such as 'four in the sand tray'.

If parents are given a chance to read the

policy, they will be clear before their children start attending the group, about the procedures which will be followed and any support available in the case of a child with a particular difficulty. The parent may then choose to adopt similar procedures in the home to support the work of the group.

A policy is also a valuable tool for allowing outside agencies, such as Social Services or Ofsted, to see that the group is professionally managed and has given careful thought to this element of learning.

Last, but most important, the children themselves will benefit from the policy. Through its implementation, they will learn the difference between acceptable and unacceptable behaviour and they will learn to take responsibility for the consequences of their actions. They will be helped to develop self-control, respect for the needs of others and respect for property.

What should the policy contain?

Although there is no such thing as a model policy, there are some points which can be applied to most pre-school groups. As a guide, the policy should contain clear statements on the following points:

❑ an overview of your group's approach, aims, philosophy

❑ procedures for encouraging acceptable behaviour

❑ procedures for dealing with unwanted behaviour

❑ procedures which are unacceptable for managing behaviour

❑ any agreed rules

❑ name of person to contact in case of concerns

❑ date produced or reviewed

Remember to make sure that new staff are aware of the policy. Staff could be asked to sign to say they have read and agree to implement the policy. It is also important to reflect on how it is working in practice, to review and if necessary update the policy from time to time. Once the policy is in place it needs to be translated into practical situations in the day-to-day organisation of the group.

Sample policy - Happyland Pre-school Group
Overview

Happyland sets high expectations of behaviour through encouraging and praising good behaviour. At Happylands we encourage children to respect themselves, each other, adults and property. We apply simple rules fairly and consistently. We aim to provide a happy, caring environment with challenging activities. Under no circumstances do we use any form of corporal punishment. In the case of a particular incident or persistent unacceptable behaviour we always discuss ways forward with parents.

Our agreed rules are clearly explained to the children and are on the parents' noticeboard. They are based on the following principle:

❑ Unwanted behaviour is behaviour likely to hurt, injure or upset another child, himself or an adult. Unwanted behaviour shows a lack of respect for others, disrupts their play and learning or damages their property. Below are our procedures for managing the children's behaviour.

Positive procedures for encouraging good behaviour

❑ prevention – anticipation and removal of potential problems (stop the fight before it happens!)

❑ interaction – plenty of adult attention (so that there's no need to misbehave to attract attention!)

❑ praise or reward – all adults should offer explicit praise for good behaviour, for example turn taking, co-operation, sharing, listening . . . drawing attention to the good rather than the bad

❑ provision – provide physically challenging and emotionally satisfying activities for children to 'let off steam'

❑ clear expectations applied in a positive way – 'No pushing in the line' becomes 'Stand nicely'

❑ leading by positive examples from adults.

In certain circumstances, such as racist language, physical abuse or dangerous behaviour an instant adult response is required.

Procedures for dealing with unwanted behaviour

❑ redirection – distract to another activity or join in with activity

❑ a firm 'No' and a clear explanation of why the behaviour is unacceptable

❑ speak calmly, clearly and firmly to gain control

❑ give a warning of the consequence if the behaviour does not stop

❑ use the consequence, for example, removal from the situation, or removal of the toy

❑ a fresh start afterwards

Unacceptable procedures in managing behaviour

These should never be used and, if seen, would and should be reported immediately to the person in charge. Such conduct could result in staff dismissal.

❑ shouting, criticism and comparison. Shouting conveys a loss of control.

❑ labelling the child, rather than the behaviour, as 'naughty' or undesirable

❑ use of any form of corporal punishment, including smacking, pinching, poking or rough handling

❑ use of any other humiliating and frightening punishment, including shouting, offensive language, name calling or isolation.

Named person - If you are concerned about any child's behaviour or our responses or have any other comment on this policy please contact: Lesley Smith

Date: ....

As adults we appreciate the differences between right and wrong, but how does our understanding develop? Keeva Austin suggests some general ways in which to support children's understanding and gives an example of a planned activity based around a suitable story

Establishing **codes** of **behaviour**

Children reach conclusions about right and wrong not so much from what staff say, but from the examples they set and the atmosphere within the setting or school. Codes of behaviour and positive attitudes should be implicit in the learning environment. For example, the choice of books, toys and equipment should show the children that it is right for all people to be equally valued and respected.

Your attitude to sharing and turn-taking should be obvious in the way you choose children to help you with daily tasks, for example, giving out drinks, taking the register. Do you have a rota so each child gets a turn or is it pot luck? You also need to be explicit in explaining your values. Racist or sexist remarks or bad behaviour should be challenged immediately by giving the child an explanation as to why they are wrong. Good behaviour should be reinforced through praise.

Use spontaneous interactions as a means of reinforcing right and wrong. For example, a small group of children are playing in the water tray. One child says, 'Don't keep dropping that big bucket in the water, I'm getting splashed and my dress is all wet'. Take this opportunity to discuss with the children why the child is dropping the bucket into the water. Why is it wrong to splash another child? When and where would it be acceptable? Why doesn't the child want a wet dress?

Drawing up rules

Consider any rules you may have. Rules help children with the concept of right/wrong but must be based on good reasons. Children need to discuss these reasons so that they come to understand the principle upon which these decisions

have been made. Encourage the children to draw up the rules for themselves. For example, decisions on sand tray rules may depend on the answers to the following questions:

❑ How many children should be at the sand tray at any one time and why?
❑ How can the sand tray equipment be shared fairly?
❑ Should we throw sand? If not, why not?
❑ What do we do about spilt sand?
❑ How should we respect the creations others make?

Once you and the children have reached some conclusions, clearly label the rules near to the sand tray. Do this for each activity area within your setting.

Using stories

Understanding right and wrong will also help the children be sensitive to the needs, views and feelings of themselves and others. They learn that it is right to form good relationships, take turns and understand the need for agreed values and codes of behaviour. In addition they are encouraged to consider the consequences of their words and actions.

Alongside these general points you need to plan activities specifically to promote an understanding of right and wrong. Take the story of *Bad Mood Bear.**

Other stories which could be used in a similar way:

A Duck so Small by A H Benjamin (Magi Publications). Duck is teased and made fun of because of his size. This book gives adults the opportunity to discuss the importance of treating everyone with respect and understanding. *Peaches and Plum in Trouble* by Caroline Repucick (Paragon Book Service). Peaches and Plum play a trick, which results in someone else taking the blame. This book encourages children to consider the consequences of their words and actions on others.

The story is about Bear. Bear can't sleep. The next day he is very tired and in a bad mood. He throws his porridge on the floor, screams and pokes his tongue out at his mum, is rude to his friends and kicks his grandad, causing him to fall over. His dad sends him to his room where he screams but eventually falls asleep. When he wakes up he thinks about all the wrong things he's done and goes downstairs to apologise. Young children often find it hard to look at themselves critically. Stories help them to discuss issues in a non-threatening way. Use this story initially for discussion:

❑ Why was Bear in a bad mood?
❑ What did he do wrong?
❑ How would his friends and parents have felt about his behaviour?
❑ Is it right to use a bad mood as an excuse to do wrong?

Once they are able to recognise Bear's wrongdoing encourage them to think about themselves. When have they ever done wrong at pre-school? Do they know why? What did the adult do? Extend the discussion and explore feelings and emotions. How do we feel if we have done wrong? Do we feel better if we are doing right? Perhaps make happy/sad bear faces to express their feelings. Encourage the children to draw things that are wrong, then ask them to draw the right things they should have done instead.

* *Bad Mood Bear* by John Richardson (Random Century 1991).

Keeva Austin

Children with 'challenging behaviour' can create heartache in the early years setting as they cause themselves to be isolated from their playmates at an early age. Caroline Jones puts forward some strategies for getting rid of bad behaviour before it becomes normal

Establishing **better** behaviour

If a child is misbehaving the first thing adults need to consider is whether the child is misbehaving deliberately or might there be another reason for his actions. Sometimes adults need to step back and consider the cause of the unwanted behaviour, particularly if a child's behaviour changes from being normally co-operative to difficult. Other reasons for so-called 'naughtiness' may include:

Expectations or language not matched to stage of development

Interaction with children must take account of their stage of development. Young children can only cope with a limited amount of instructions at any one time and may not be being deliberately disobedient but genuinely not understand what is expected. For example, a child who has limited comprehension or auditory memory will not understand a complex series of instructions such as 'When you've finished, hang up your apron, wash your hands, go to the toilet and then go into the other room' and may end up looking blank when he or she is then told off for not going into the other room. The same child would have responded appropriately to one or two instructions at a time.

A child who is tearful or clingy or having a tantrum is not necessarily being naughty.

Sometimes they are being asked to do a task which is not matched to their level of understanding. In other words the task is too hard or too easy and they become frustrated, perhaps resulting in a tantrum or a squabble. They may not have heard the instruction the first time and need it repeating. Sometimes,

they do not have the language to understand the instruction in the first place. It is easy for an adult to become frustrated or cross when a child appears not to be doing as he or she was told. For example, the instruction 'Find a space' often results in children wandering around all over the place. Is the adult sure the child knows what a space is? Is the child walking around looking for it? Often a child can be labelled naughty for something which is merely developmental, for example, wetting pants, not sitting still for long, lack of attention, when maybe he or she is just not ready or able to do what is being expected.

Sheer physical exuberance

If there is not enough outlet for a child's energy he or she may run around, start crawling under the tables, or climb on the furniture. It is important to ensure that if the children cannot go outside, perhaps due to the weather, some alternative form of energetic activity is provided indoors.

If a child tells a parent 'Mrs Jones got cross with me today', the parent may phone up wanting to know what's happened. It is professional to take the parent quietly to one side and explain the incident.

Insecurity

Children become confused if adults are inconsistent. They feel insecure if expectations are not made clear or something which is acceptable one day is not accepted the next day. They become confused if the routine changes for any reason or staff changes are taking place. Offering children an open choice may also result in confusion. 'Who wants to go first in the line?' will lead to chaos, whereas with 'It's John's turn to be first today and Joanne's tomorrow' everyone knows what they have to do.

Illness

Often a change in behaviour can be a sign of developing illness. The child does not feel right but does not know how to express the feelings. He or she becomes miserable and unco-operative, even cheeky. The next day the child develops an ear infection or breaks out in spots!

Anxiety

Factors outside the setting's control may have triggered the unwanted behaviour. Those working with young children are all too familiar with changes in behaviour when something is amiss at home which has upset the child in some way. It may be a way of releasing anxieties – the death of a grandparent, arrival of a new baby, a parent leaving the family home, fear of starting school. Children should be happy and develop relationships with adults and with each other which minimise negative behaviour. If they are encouraged to express anxieties and ask questions the need for anti-social behaviour as a response to anxiety is reduced. Any sudden change in behaviour should always be shared with the parents and monitored carefully by a named adult.

Anger

A child who is tearful or clingy or having a tantrum is not necessarily being naughty. Tantrums, for example, are very common among toddlers. The child has not yet acquired a sufficient grasp of language to express himself in words. The need to assert independence spills over into a tantrum. A tantrum is a very powerful feeling of anger and frustration and often the child needs comfort combined with restraint. A tantrum is a child's (and some adults'!) way of expressing very strong emotions. Inability to cope with people, things or situations is often the cause. Those working closely with children will recognise a tantrum from a child who is using a loud noise to attract attention and trying to control the adult or getting his or her own way. Responses may vary and will depend on the circumstances. Try to find out what is making the child angry. Often a child's anger can be redirected through playing with dough, role play, hammering pegs, banging a drum, or going out in the garden. Withdrawal to a quiet place or a little cuddle will help him or her regain control. The important thing is for the adult to remain calm and once the tantrum has subsided, to make a fresh start.

Testing the boundaries

Prevention is better than cure and many things can be avoided if the circumstances which trigger the unwanted behaviour are avoided in the first place. Of course, children will still explore and experiment to find out where the boundaries lie between acceptable and unacceptable behaviour. Where the situation or the adult is unfamiliar they will experiment with different kinds of behaviour until it becomes clear where the line is drawn. Often children look straight at the adult before actually doing the 'crime'! The absence of consistent boundaries leaves children insecure, dashing about waiting for someone to control them. Often they are labelled hyperactive, when really they are seeking boundaries to control their behaviour. Once the children have discovered what is allowed and what isn't allowed and the same rules apply all the time, they will be satisfied and direct their energies elsewhere. Of course, there are cases of children whose hyperactivity is triggered by additives particularly in drinks, so you may need to explore this as a possibility.

Positive strategies

Unacceptable behaviour is usually defined as action which interrupts the child's own learning or the learning of others or harms another person, themselves or property. Within a context of positive preventative strategies unwanted behaviour can be dealt with through light control methods, although in some cases stronger measures may be called for. Light control is appropriate in a situation which requires minimum intervention.

One example of light control is where attention is focused on the rest of the group, sometimes known as positively ignoring. This will often succeed in reminding the 'target children' who a few moments later can also be praised for behaving as they should. This will work in everyday situations such as the following:

**Example -
A child pushing in a line**

A negative response would be to say 'Jack, for goodness sake, stop pushing!'

A positive response would be to say 'Robert, Sarah and Emma are standing very still in the line. Well done!' Then, if Jack stops pushing. 'Well done, Jack! You're standing beautifully as well, good boy!'

Example - All the children are listening to a story, a few start to fidget

When a child is fidgeting instead of listening attentively, again praise for those who are listening is far more effective than constantly drawing attention to those who are not listening. The idea is to explicitly draw attention to the majority of children who are conforming to the acceptable norm.

Example - At drinks time

'Look how quietly these two groups are sitting' is much more likely to produce wanted behaviour from the third table, than 'Group three, you're the worst group in the room.'

In addition, it is important that the adult makes the desired behaviour clear. Telling children clearly what you want them to do is far more effective than telling them to stop doing something. 'John, stand still' is much clearer than 'John, stop running'. Children need to be told in language which they understand and are not confused by.

Distraction is also likely to produce the desired behaviour. If a child is picking her nose, for example, instead of saying 'Don't pick your nose!' say 'Wiggle your fingers'! As I'm sure you know, if children are told not to pick their noses, the automatic response appears to be to start picking again a moment later!

Rewards

Where there is a specific behaviour which a child is struggling to achieve, rewards may be effective in the short term. However, it is important not to over-rely on rewards. The adult has to remain in control and be the decision maker. For example, when a child has really made an effort and listened extremely well to the story (for him) he can be offered a reward. However, it is important that the adult is not bribed by the child, or does not put the child in control of the reward. For example, if the adult says, 'If you sit still you can have a star' then the child is in control. However, the adult could say, 'I may decide to give someone a star if someone sits beautifully.' Alternatively, the adult may say nothing and observe the child

closely. On spotting 'good behaviour' the adult will then reward the child and explain why. 'I saw you sharing that puzzle, well done, you can have a sticker'. Below are some types of rewards which are used:

❑ Social rewards - pleasant interactions such as a smile, praise, clapping, hugs.

❑ Activity rewards - having a go on the computer, choosing a song, choosing a story, playing a particular game.

❑ Token rewards - stars, stickers

❑ Material rewards - edible or usable items - such as a biscuit.

Discipline should be about positive re-enforcement of acceptable behaviour and positive role models. If a child is shouting and an adult responds by shouting at the child then the child will not understand that shouting is unacceptable.

Stronger action

Major incidents are fairly unusual. The most likely are bullying, either verbally or physically, name calling, or possible racist or sexist language. At pre-school level a child may hurt another child, for example, by

biting, pinching, hitting, pulling hair or throwing sand or throwing a toy. In these situations stronger action is needed.

❑ Deal immediately with it - do not leave it until later.

❑ Avoid getting into battle with the child or a confrontational situation.

❑ Use the child's name but beware of giving the child a label.

❑ Forgive and forget.

The child who has been attacked must be comforted and the child who is at fault helped to see reason for adult intervention, without feeling attacked or undermined himself. In all circumstances children need to know the consequences of their misbehaviour. Use of consequences is an objective approach - if you spill the paint, you will wipe it up, if you drop your coat on the floor, you will pick it up. The adult's tone of voice can have a major impact on children's behaviour. There is a major difference between shouting and speaking firmly. 'Oh darling, please, you mustn't bite', in a kind and gentle tone of voice will not give the message that biting is unacceptable.

The adult's words and manner must be firm and leave the child in no doubt as to what will follow. Be fair, be clear, be consistent.

1 Gain attention

2 Say what the unwanted behaviour is

3 Say why the behaviour is unacceptable

4 State the action warranted by the behaviour

5 Give the instruction which implements the sanction

Example 1

1 Jack

2 Throwing things

3 Can hurt people and

4 You will sit on the chair for a minute

5 And think about what you should have been doing.

In case of persistent misbehaviour adults can employ a warning procedure. Firstly, give a reminder of the rule: 'We do not throw sand'. Then a brief warning of the consequence: 'You will not play in the sand'. Then, if the behaviour persists, follow example 2.

Example 2

1 Jessica

2 Throwing sand

3 Can hurt people

4 You will not play in the sand

5 Come and have a think about it.

If a major incident does occur which requires strong words or action, which may even make the child cry, it should be recorded in a book and reported to the parent. If a child tells a parent 'Mrs Jones got cross with me today', the parent may phone up wanting to know what's happened. It is professional to take the parent quietly to one side and explain the incident.

After an incident, if the child has the language, the adult should ask the child to tell him or her what caused the incident and ask 'What would be a better thing to do?' If the child then is spotted doing the right thing, this can be acknowledged with a comment such as 'Jack, I'm pleased to see you're taking turns. That's good - your mum will be pleased. Do you think you can keep it up? I think so.' Other strategies include:

❏ Checking the physical setting - are they squabbling because there is not enough? Have they learned to share? Where is the adult?

❏ Changing the context - is it time to change the activity? Has the child been on the activity too long? Is it time to tidy away and get something different out?

❏ Providing help - for example, with a jigsaw puzzle thrown on the floor. Pick it up with the child and do it together.

❏ Changing the organisation - if the cars on the table are causing a problem, moving them onto the floor can diffuse the situation.

Whilst to say 'Come and sit on this chair and have a little think' may just help calm a situation, the use of a 'naughty' chair as a sanction is usually ineffective. Some children actually think the chair is 'naughty', and I know of one child who was sitting on it so often, he used to thump someone and go and sit on the chair without even being told to!

Discipline should be about positive re-enforcement of acceptable behaviour and positive role models.

Physical handling

The physical handling of children is a sensitive area. On rare occasions staff in groups can be accused of physical assault. The existence of a behaviour policy should clearly stipulate no use of corporal punishment or any other action which will frighten or humiliate a child. This would also include not only smacking but pinching, squeezing, hair pulling, isolation, putting a child in a cupboard or anything likely to cause emotional upset to the child. The adult must show that only 'reasonable physical restraint' was used to calm the situation and in particular to prevent the child from harming him or herself. For example, if a child was running towards a road or climbing over a fence and likely to fall, the adult would have no choice but to physically handle the child. Early years workers are probably in a less vulnerable position than teachers as there is usually another adult around to witness the incident. If staff have attended relevant training courses and a comprehensive policy is in place, there are unlikely to be any problems.

A small minority of children do have emotional or behavioural difficulties which cause higher levels of concern. The parent should be consulted and perhaps seek advice from the health visitor, who in turn may recommend the support of an educational psychologist. Strategies available include the drawing up of detailed individual programmes, personal counselling, therapy or focused support.

In summary, then, children's behaviour is complex but there are certain things that are known to encourage good behaviour. These are:

❏ clear rules

❏ praise

❏ showing correct behaviour

❏ consistency

❏ consequences

❏ preventing

❏ reinforcing good behaviour

Acknowledgements

Some of the material for this section has been drawn from Solity J and Bull S (1987) *Classroom Management Principles to Practice* published by Croom Helm and Finch G *Handling Children's Behaviour* NCH Action For Children.

Caroline Jones